THE TATAS

THE TATAS

How a Family Built a
Business and a Nation

GIRISH KUBER

Translated from the Marathi by
Vikrant Pande

HARPER
BUSINESS

An Imprint of HarperCollins *Publishers*

First published in Marathi as
Tatayan: Ek Poladi Udyamgatha
by Rajhans Prakashan in 2015

This English edition first published in hardback in India in 2019 by
Harper Business
An imprint of HarperCollins *Publishers*
A-75, Sector 57, Noida, Uttar Pradesh 201301, India
www.harpercollins.co.in

2 4 6 8 10 9 7 5 3 1

P-ISBN: 978-93-5277-937-6
E-ISBN: 978-93-5277-938-3

The views and opinions expressed in this book are
the author's own and the facts are as reported by him,
and the publishers are not in any way liable for the same.

Girish Kuber asserts the moral right
to be identified as the author of this work.

Typeset in 11.25/15 Aldine401 BT at
Manipal Digital Systems, Manipal

Printed and bound at
Thomson Press (India) Ltd

MIX
Paper
FSC FSC® C010615

This book is produced from independently certified FSC® paper to ensure
responsible forest management.

J.R.D. Tata used to say, 'Live life a little dangerously.'

This book is dedicated to all those who live by this perilous principle and have immersed themselves in wealth creation for the greater good of society against all odds.

Contents

Author's Note

The narrative of *The Tatas* spans almost 200 years. In condensing it to a 250-odd-page story with a popular appeal for the lay reader, I have re-imagined and reconstructed some scenes and conversations. This is also a work of translation from Marathi to English. As such, the words written may not be exactly the ones spoken, yet they are true to the meaning of the conversations drawn from the sources listed at the end of the book. While the translator, the editor and I have made every effort to ensure that the translation is as faithful to the original sources as possible, some inadvertent discrepancies may have nevertheless survived to the final draft. Any errors are deeply regretted.

Preface

Why have I written a book on the Tatas and why now? The answer is simple.

The Tata conglomerate is intricately intertwined in so many of India's successes and firsts, and most of these, incredibly, have remained uncovered. Not many know that it was the Tatas who brought silk to Mysore or that they were the ones who got strawberries to Mahabaleshwar, a popular hill station in Maharashtra now synonymous with the fruit. Not many are aware, either, that the world's earliest worker welfare policies were drafted in a Tata venture or that the Tatas were global pioneers in conceiving a hydroelectric project.

Though much has been written about the Tatas, it has been mostly from a corporate or industry-specific perspective, such as on Tata Steel or Tata Consultancy Services (TCS). My effort here is to tell the human side of this business story, from the common man's point of view, without resorting to jargon and mind-boggling numbers.

And there is a need to tell this story as there is a growing trend all over the world of measuring success purely on the basis of balance sheets. Profits do matter, no doubt, but that's not the only factor. Against this backdrop, it is fascinating to delve into this story that starts with a common Indian middle-class man who aimed high and, while achieving what he set his sights on, thought of what he could do for the country and cared for the environment. Whatever the Tatas did, it wasn't solely with profitability in mind. The Tatas did not just build companies, they also lent a huge hand in building the nation.

There are few stories of homegrown Indian business houses that have a global appeal. The story of the Tatas is one of them.

I wrote this book in Marathi as *Tatayan* about five years ago. The response to it was overwhelming. There have been a dozen reprints to date. From politicians of all hues to businessmen to readers from different walks of life, it touched every section of society. The most important reason behind the book's success, I feel, is the fascination Indians have for the Tatas. Incidentally, *Tatayan* is also the only book that chronicles the Tata story right from its inception about 200 years ago to now. That may be the other reason behind the book's sustained popularity. For *Tatayan*, I owe a big thank you to Mr Dilip Majgaonkar of Rajhans Prakashan, who took personal interest in producing it with élan.

I am equally thankful to Siddhesh Inamdar, Commissioning Editor at HarperCollins, for spotting the book, and to the HarperCollins team for deciding to take it to an English readership. *The Tatas* would not have been published without Siddhesh's active involvement.

I must also thank Vikrant Pande for the tremendous work he put in to translate the book into English, and Amit Malhotra for the cover design that perfectly captures the steely resolve associated with the Tatas.

I hope the book leaves readers feeling as inspired and invigorated as I felt writing it.

Girish Kuber

Mumbai
February 2019

1

Nusserwanji of Navsari

'This boy is going to rule the world. He will be rich enough to build a seven-storey bungalow,' prophesied the astrologer and quite predictably got a nice offering for himself.

'One expects to hear such things at a naming ceremony,' mumbled an elder, but the women, warding off the evil eye, waved their palms over the baby boy's face and cracked their knuckles. The boy was named Nusserwan, and no one bothered too much thereafter about what the astrologer had said. Nearly everybody in Navsari, including the ragged little urchins populating its dusty streets, had been foretold a glorious future.

Nusserwanji Tata, however, was to prove the astrologer right.

THE EARLY YEARS

Young Nusserwanji, born in 1822, was raised in a priestly household. His father would daily don prayer whites, pray and read from the Zend Avesta. His childhood was similar to that of his friends, which included being married off even before one learnt to walk properly.

Thereafter, the bridegrooms attended school, their brides having been sent home to grow up. The couples were reunited once they attained puberty, only to separate often when the wives went back to their parents for delivery.

Nusserwanji's story was no different. In the first decade of his life he was married off to a petite little girl with a name that bespoke a lifetime of experience: Jeevanbai. Mrs Nusserwanji was taken home promptly after marriage—in fact, the same evening—and stayed home for nearly ten years before rejoining her spouse. A year after she returned, her husband turned seventeen and she gave birth to their first child, Jamset, on 3 March 1839.

This child, Jamsetji Nusserwanji Tata, would become the grand old man, the 'Bhishma Pitamah', of Indian industry, laying the foundations of a global business empire. Though his star would take him high, Jamsetji Tata stayed true to his roots, following in the footsteps of his father.

Young Nusserwanji knew early on that he did not want to follow family tradition and become a priest. Driven by a deep passion to do something of his own, he knew his destiny lay beyond Navsari. No one else in the village had ever felt that way, not strongly enough to leave Navsari anyway. For its residents, the village was their world. Nusserwanji was the first member of his family to leave.

One cannot surmise today what led Nusserwanji to leave behind all that was familiar and head for Bombay, now Mumbai, to start a business. He had neither higher education nor knowledge of business matters, and no family tradition to lean on either. The only capital he possessed was a burning passion that lit up his path and helped him navigate an uncertain and difficult future; he had chosen to dream big, without fear of failure.

FIRST STEPS TO EMPIRE

Once in Bombay, Nusserwanji was drawn to cotton trading and set up his first venture with the help of a local banker and friend. Jeevanbai and Jamsetji joined him soon after the latter's Navjot ceremony, the ritual through which an individual is inducted into the Zoroastrian religion. The young family settled down to life and business in Bombay.

This also happened to be the period when the teaching of the English language in India—as propagated by Lord Macaulay in 1835, in his scathing (and now infamous) 'Minute on Education'—had begun apace. Impressed by the notion, the then Governor General, Lord William Bentinck, passed the English Education Act in 1835 itself. Bentinck was another ardent fan of 'civilizing' Indians and of teaching them English. So, by the 1840s and '50s, Indian citizens were getting their daily dose of the language.

The Parsis were among the first to realize the value of English education and produced stalwarts like Dadabhai Naoroji, Pherozeshah Mehta and many others. And Nusserwanji, seeing that his business was doing well, realized the importance of getting his son the best and highest level of education possible.

Getting an Education

Jamsetji Tata was a bright student and in 1856 he sought admission to the University of Bombay. He was accepted at a brand new college built the same year. It had been constructed at a cost of ₹2,29,000, collected by the residents of Bombay in honour of the Governor of Bombay (1819–27), Lord Elphinstone, revered for his enlightened approach.

It was as if the stars had aligned for Jamsetji. He was seventeen, had joined Elphinstone College, and now the English classes began. Those were early days when there were no graduate degrees such as BA or BCom. Jamsetji graduated with flying colours in 1858 as a 'Green Scholar'. His college years at Elphinstone also imparted a lasting love for the English language. Though he was to spend most of his life pursuing wealth and its accumulation, he retained a lifelong love for Charles Dickens, William Makepeace Thackeray, and the evergreen humorist Mark Twain, among others.

By the time Jamsetji had acquired a college education, he had also acquired a wife, twelve-year-old Hirabai Dabu. She had a large mole on her cheek, which was seen to signify beauty and wealth, and was an instant favourite among the Parsi community. Father-in-law Nusserwanji firmly believed that she would bring luck and that his business would expand rapidly. But before he could realize his dreams, he was gifted a grandchild by the young couple. Jamsetji was a father at the age of twenty and the newborn was named Dorab.

Jamsetji's First International Venture: The Far East

Jamsetji took up a job immediately after graduating, but Nusserwanji, wanting his son to gain international exposure, sent him to the British colony of Hong Kong, where he launched a company called Jamsetji and Ardeshir with three partners—Nusserwanji and two merchants, Kaliandas and Premchand Raichand. The Tatas, through this partnership, decided to deal in cotton and opium.

Nusserwanji's brother-in-law Dadabhoy Tata also traded in opium and had an office in Hong Kong. He had a son, Ratanji, who was seventeen years older than Jamsetji. When the local government in Hong Kong tried to ban the opium trade, Ratanji Dadabhoy Tata, RD for short, along with another businessman in the same trade, David Sassoon, petitioned the British government to intervene. In those days, trading in opium did not raise eyebrows the way it does in today's world. It had medicinal uses and had been used extensively in the Crimean War (1853–56). It was considered legitimate business everywhere but China, where it was considered a social evil.

The ruling Qing Emperor had banned the trade of opium in China, though poppy—the plant from which opium is extracted—had been grown in China since the seventh century. The habit of mixing opium with tobacco, spread by the Europeans, had led to large-scale addiction, hence the imperial ban on trading in opium.

British traders, not wanting to let go of their profits from opium, found a way out. They asked Chinese traders to sell them opium in Calcutta (the British victory in the Battle of Plassey in 1757 had given the East India Company control of the Bengal Province). On paper, the exchange could be shown as opium being received by British traders as payment for tea they sold to their Chinese counterparts. Once they received the opium, the British traders pushed it back into China through smuggling routes. The Industrial Revolution in Britain and the country's rapid growth thereafter were fuelled quite a bit by this opium trade.

RD later opened another business, dealing in pearls and perfumes. He was personally interested in both and would often go to France in this connection. It must have been these frequent visits that probably propelled him to learn the language too. Jamsetji hired a French teacher, a Monsieur Brière, for him. We are not sure how much French RD learnt, but he did manage to fall in love with Brière's daughter, Suzanne! RD was forty-five then and Suzanne was half his age. RD was also a widower, having been married in childhood to Banajibai, who had died soon after. But Suzanne and RD were in love and they got married.

Jamsetji's older son Dorabji was, however, mighty upset and wrote a long letter to his uncle RD: 'There are eight reasons why you should not marry that girl; there is nothing common between you two, you are much older to her in age, your cultures are very different, we Parsis do not marry outside our community,' and so on and so forth, Dorabji ranted. RD, now worried that his wife would not be accepted into the household and the Parsi community at large, requested her to convert to Zoroastrianism. She complied, taking on the name 'Sooni'. Meanwhile, Jamsetji pacified son Dorab. Peace was restored. This 'French Revolution' of his had created a social storm of sorts but RD was not about to be cowed down. The couple had five children, the second oldest being Jehangir, who would later be known the world over as JRD.

Eventually, RD would prove to be Dorabji's most able supporter and was of indispensable help to him in later life.

The Tatas were soon exporting cotton to Europe, opium to China, and importing cardamom, tea, gold and textiles. Business grew rapidly and they opened a second office in the Far East, this time in Shanghai, again headed by Jamsetji. However, it was a daunting task to establish a presence in China. The country was known for its weak leadership at the centre and was riddled with foreign imperialism; it was not an easy place to live in. Back home, India was in turmoil in the years that followed the events of the first battle of Independence in 1857, and it was against this backdrop that Jamsetji set out to establish the business in Shanghai.

Meanwhile, another opportunity loomed in the unfortunate form of the four-year-long Civil War (1861–65) in North America, which was at its peak—the southern states were against the abolition of slavery, decreed by President Abraham Lincoln. The cotton fields of the south, where slaves toiled day and night, supplied abundant raw material to the ever expanding textile industry in Lancashire, England. The expected disruption to cotton supplies now posed a threat not just to the mills in Lancashire but to the fortunes of the East India Company and to the Queen's dominion over a large part of the world. Textile exports from Britain played a significant role in building and maintaining the British Empire.

It was a window of opportunity the Tatas seized, demanding more than double the current rates. Jamsetji and his partners flourished to the extent that Raichand floated the Asiatic Banking Corporation and went public.

At this point, it almost seemed as though the Tatas had entered into cotton trading more by foresight than by luck! It is quite extraordinary that at a time when the North American continent was caught up in the Civil War, the Tatas were able to go public with a company they had floated in India. The success of their maiden venture opened up global horizons and they ventured out of Asia into Europe, opening their first branch in London.

First European Branch Opens

Jamsetji was the man asked once again to do the job. Air travel was still thirty-five years away and he set sail on a passenger ship. Sea travel was still quite rudimentary. It was well before the time of air-conditioned cabins. Pigs, goats and a very large number of chickens were carried along as fresh food; in fact, the number of chickens on board rendered the vessel more a seaborne coop than a passenger ship. A determined Jamsetji overlooked the stench, the seasickness and the long and arduous journey with single-minded focus: he must reach London to open his office in a country that ruled his motherland.

This was soon accomplished and, with a large number of orders in hand, Jamsetji assessed the situation. Matters would not remain rosy much longer, he realized. The American Civil War looked like it would end soon, possibly ending their budding cotton venture as well. He promptly warned partner Raichand, and his prediction did come true—by the time 1865 arrived, the beginning of the end of the Civil War was clearly visible, paving the way for American cotton to once again reach England.

The company lost all its orders, and investors started to hound partner Premchand Raichand for their money. Jamsetji assured investors he would return everyone's money and in return asked for time. The investors probably saw integrity in the man and agreed. In fact, they nominated him as the receiver at a monthly salary of £20. The owner of the company now worked for his own firm at a monthly salary! Jamsetji stayed on in London and he and his partners did all that they could to return the dues. Jamsetji also took this opportunity to gain a deeper understanding of the business of textiles.

In fact, the impact of the end of the American Civil War on the cotton trade was seen as far as Bombay, where some businessmen committed suicide due to insurmountable losses. Nusserwanji, who had proven the astrologer right by building a seven-storey building in Bombay, now sold it. Ironically, the very Civil War that had helped him grow his cotton business and build the house was now responsible for its sale. Eager to ensure that debts were paid off, Nusserwanji sent the money received from the sale of the house to his son. Perhaps, the trust associated with the Tata name began with this act.

Jamsetji, having stayed back in England, was meanwhile gaining a lot of exposure to manufacturing as he travelled across Liverpool and Lancashire. He realized he was merely a trader in cotton and, if he wanted to grow, he needed to get into manufacturing. In his spare time, he would meet intellectuals not biased towards any religion. He used every opportunity to discuss the views and philosophies of people like Thomas Carlyle, John Stuart Mill, Herbert Spencer and others. Stalwarts like Dadabhai Naoroji and Badruddin Tyabji would participate in these debates. What a period it was! In 1866, Dadabhai Naoroji formed the East India Association. Its members were men who did not discuss business, export-import, market dynamics and profits alone. Business for the sake of business was not their motto. They believed they needed to do something that would have an everlasting impact—something that would stay for hundreds of years, something beyond mere profit and loss. For such men, the closing of one door meant the opening of others. This was to happen for Jamsetji too.

It so happened that the King of Abyssinia (the Ethiopian Empire), for some strange reason, arrested the British ambassador and his staff. The two British officials sent to resolve the issue were also arrested and thrown into prison, forcing England to send in an armed force, which it did under the then Commander-in-Chief of the Bombay Army, Lieutenant General Sir Robert Napier. He left for Abyssinia with a force of 16,000 men.

An army of such size would require someone to manage food, blankets and other logistical matters. The man recommended for the job was Nusserwanji Tata. The opportunity was a godsend for Nusserwanji, who was still recovering from his losses in the cotton trade. It was the year 1868. As the British troops sailed across the Gulf of Aden towards the Gulf of Zula in Abyssinia, the King realized his folly and committed suicide. The imprisoned British officials were released and the entire operation cost the British government a colossal sum of £10 million. Well, Nusserwanji took home a hefty sum of ₹40 lakh*!

---

*   1 lakh = 100,000; 10 lakh = 1 million or 1,000,000

Expanding Business in India

Empress Mills

The money paved the way for father and son to rekindle their ambitions and, in 1869, Jamsetji bought a defunct oil mill in Bombay, which he converted into a cotton ginning mill. The mill, named Alexandria, ran successfully for two years before Jamsetji sold it at a profit. The mill and its subsequent sale were a prime example of Jamsetji's out-of-the-box thinking.

He also visited London and Lancashire again in 1873 to update what he had learnt during his previous visit, and returned with plans to start his own spinning and weaving mill. Not that the task was easy; it would take four months for the machinery to reach India from Europe, the railway network in India itself was still far from widespread and bullock carts were the most common mode of transport. Nevertheless, cotton supply from America was again available in abundance and the period witnessed a race in India to open textile mills, mostly around Bombay or Ahmedabad.

Nusserwanji and his son, however, decided to find a place closer to the cotton-producing areas and chose low-lying land in Nagpur, which had to be filled with large amounts of soil before work could begin. They found a contractor to do the job but the local moneylender refused to lend them funds, saying he would not pour money into an unviable project. Jamsetji soon managed the necessary capital and got the land ready. He was clear in his mind: the mill had to be technically superior and use the latest technology and machinery. He also found two capable men to run the mill—Bezanji Mehta, who worked in the railways, and James Brooksby, a technical expert. Next, he ordered the machinery from Brooks and Doxey, a specialist manufacturer in Manchester, on the advice of James Brooksby. The mill was christened Empress Mills on 1 January 1877 in honour of Queen Victoria, Empress of India.

However, Jamsetji was to face another challenge. The work culture in Nagpur was quite different from that of Bombay, where people believed in working even on holidays, if need be. On the contrary, Nagpur was more laid-back, and average attendance was always around 80 per cent. People took leave for the smallest of reasons and remained absent for weeks together. Instead of approaching the problem with a 'hire and fire' mindset and penalizing errant workers, the Tatas came up with an innovative solution.

They introduced a general provident fund scheme, which ensured that every worker would be able to manage a decent living after retirement. An insurance scheme helped to cover medical costs due to accidents at work. Family days and sports days were held regularly, the 1,000-odd families being rewarded with gold chains, wristwatches, cash awards and such. All these efforts led to a drastic reduction in absenteeism.

Indians can take pride in the fact that innovative schemes, including pensions, introduced by Jamsetji, were much ahead of their time. Some of these worker compensation schemes were not even part of the Factories Act of England, where most had not heard of such benefits for workers. Empress Mills is a fine example of his far-sighted approach to business and human relations. When praised heavily for his work, he simply said that the garden of success blooms if we keep in mind the welfare of the co-workers who contribute to it.

Empress Mills is considered one of Jamsetji Nusserwanji Tata's finest success stories. He nevertheless gave full credit to Bezanji Mehta and James Brooksby and refused to bask in borrowed glory. The journey to success can only be completed if you have travellers with you who are willing to travel the road even in difficult times. It was on their belief in this philosophy that the foundation of the Tata group was laid.

Incidentally, while on the way to locate land for Empress Mills, Jamsetji had been enamoured by the waterfalls in Jabalpur and had started dreaming of setting up a hydroelectric plant as well, but his father had reminded him of their mission and they had journeyed on. The Tatas did set up a hydroelectric power plant eventually, but that was to happen two decades later.

A century after the setting up of the Empress Mills, this founding pillar of the Tata group and of industrial India was merged with the

Maharashtra Textile Corporation in 1977. By then, it had been tottering for years and, after finally being declared defunct, was taken over by the state government in 1977.

The mill, standing for over a century, had been witness to the social, political and economic upheavals of Nagpur. Its chimneys finally ceased to emit smoke in September 2002. It is ironic that Empress Mills, a symbol of the Tatas' contribution to India's industrialization and the reason behind Jamsetji's fame as Indian industry's 'Bhishma Pitamah', shut down through a simple government order!

2

The Man Who Sowed Dreams

Even today, you cannot keep a good businessman out of Mumbai for long. More than a century ago, when Mumbai was still Bombay, it was the same for Jamsetji too. After staying for a couple of years in Nagpur, he itched to return to Bombay. He had plans for business and for new projects. In fact, his discussions with his friend Pherozeshah Mehta were always about what new project they could start. Mehta, who had started Ripon Club and the Parsi Gymkhana, now started Elphinstone Club with Jamsetji's help. The two would discuss world politics and Mehta was always eager to do things on the social front. He met a variety of people and kept busy creating awareness through various social initiatives.

Jamsetji's house in Bombay was home to his extended family, including his nephews and a widowed sister. After dinner, he would spend time in his library, his favourite place, which had a collection of nearly 2,000 books. He would read on diverse topics, whether gardening or construction. He took care of his family and had allotted shares of his company in the name of each individual.

His elder son Dorabji was now ready to join the business, having studied at Kent and then at Cambridge. He returned to India in 1879 at the behest of his grandfather Nusserwanji and joined his younger brother Ratan at St Xavier's College to complete his studies. It would have been easy for Jamsetji to place him in a senior position at Empress Mills, which was doing very well by then. But he sent him off to join the *Bombay Gazette* as a cub reporter, where Dorabji spent two years. He was then sent to Pondicherry, which was known for producing a fine cloth called French Ginny, and later sent to study the production and viability of producing the same in Nagpur. The idea was eventually scuttled by Jamsetji when he realized that the project did not seem viable.

SWADESHI MILLS

India was also waking up to the call of Independence and the Tatas realized that they needed to contribute to the cause. The 'Empress' was doing well and Jamsetji decided to contribute in his own way by building more Indian businesses. For instance, he bid a mere ₹12.5 lakh and bought Dharamsi Mills at Kurla in Bombay, which was being auctioned after the owner was unable to pay off a debt of nearly ₹55 lakh.

The mill covered 1.5 lakh square metres and had 1,300 looms with nearly a lakh spindles. It was a herculean task to turn the sick mill around. The machinery was worn out and had to be replaced. Jamsetji decided to buy second-hand machines for the mill. But following the cancellation of a large order from China, he was forced to raise capital to survive. The bankers refused to help him since the word had spread that the Tatas were in trouble. Jamsetji would not permit the Tata name to be besmirched and sold his personal shares to raise money. He got his best men from Empress Mills to work in Bombay at the new set-up.

Later, this mill came to be known as Swadeshi Mills and, until recently, held pride of place in the Tata empire. Jamsetji spent his entire time and energy in reviving Swadeshi.

FARMING IN PANCHGANI

Jamsetji had also bought land in the hill station of Panchgani to start a hospital for Parsis and, realizing that the place would develop into an important centre soon, decided to buy some more land. Any other businessman would have decided to build a hotel or thought of leasing such large parcels of land out. But Jamsetji had no such plans. He had travelled the world and realized that Panchgani's weather was suitable for the growth of Egyptian cotton. Thereafter, he devoted a lot of time and effort growing it, but met with only limited success. He decided to switch to strawberry or coffee, both of which suited the land as well. He travelled to Panchgani a lot, carrying saplings of those two.

It was not easy to reach the hill station in those days. The train to Poona would reach at 9 p.m. and one had to take another train to a place called Wathar, reaching there by midnight. Either one spent the night on the platform or looked for a local hotel and then left the next morning by tonga, which took five hours to negotiate the 28 km of mountainous tracts. The tonga also required a change of horses and two pairs took turns to pull the load.

Despite such logistical hurdles, Jamsetji's enthusiasm did not falter. He knew the place could turn into a popular destination in the future and eventually bought a car for the journey. This was the first motor car in Bombay. He built two houses in Panchgani and named them Dalkeith Home and Bel-Air. Today, the 43-acre property houses a hospital run by the Indian Red Cross Society.

The Tatas were always a few steps ahead of the others in charity. When, many years later, social reformist Vinoba Bhave called for the Bhoodan (donate land) movement, the Tatas donated their land in Panchgani that was lying vacant.

THE BIRTH OF MYSORE SILK

Meanwhile, always on the lookout to launch unique projects, Jamsetji, on a visit to France, found that the weather was similar to that of Bangalore and Mysore and brought back a few silkworms to try breeding them in India. Silkworm breeding was an old tradition he wanted to revive. At that time, silkworm breeding used to take place in Moradabad, but Jamsetji, dissatisfied with its quality and shine, wanted to create the best silk in Mysore province.

Buying large parcels of land in Bangalore and Mysore, he set up the Tata Silk Farm organization and encouraged farmers to try silkworm breeding. He also managed to bring down experts from Japan and took care of their hospitality so that they would stay on and provide training to the farmers. Not many people would know that the origin of the famous Bangalore-Mysore silk sarees lies in the silken touch provided by Jamsetji's efforts and passion.

MINI TOWNS TO DAIRY FARMING

The East India Company had given large parcels of land to Navroji Jamsetji Wadia in Juhu, which was then a fishing village. Jamsetji decided to buy land in Juhu, Parle, Madh Island and other areas and build a Venice-like city. The price was ₹3 per square foot, an expensive proposition in those times. In those days, Bombay extended up to Sion, but Jamsetji was looking beyond. His plans for the new town included not just Juhu, Bandra and Andheri, but land right up to Versova. He needed more than 1,200 acres of land to turn his dream into a reality. The British Resident of Thane supported Jamsetji but Wadia was unwilling to sell.

So, Jamsetji looked towards Mahim for his town project, but realized that the small dairies around the town would create a problem as it grew in the future. He realized, though, that the grass in western Bombay right up to Kurla, with its natural salt content, was ideal for grazing cows and would return a high milk yield. He therefore requested the government to allow him to develop 1,000 acres for cattle grazing. Even today, the large concentration of dairy farmers one sees in the Goregaon and Jogeshwari areas is testimony to Jamsetji's efforts.

FORAYING INTO IRON AND STEEL

While in London, Jamsetji had attended a lecture by Thomas Carlyle, who said a nation that understood the value of iron would reap its weight in gold. That point stayed with Jamsetji. Now in his forties, he came across a report by a German geologist talking of immense mineral deposits in Chanda district in central India. Chanda was close to Nagpur, and the discovery of coal in the Warora area near Nagpur had already been made public. Jamsetji wasted no time in sending mining samples from Warora and the surrounding areas to Germany for testing.

Unfortunately, the results suggested it was of an inferior quality with low calorific value. But Jamsetji's single-minded focus on manufacturing steel did not waver. For the next seventeen years, he went around India collecting samples and checking for iron ore. It would be 1899 before he met with success. The Viceroy, Lord Curzon, who had just taken over that year, had made the rules for mining easier, giving hope to Jamsetji. The same year, Major R.H. Mahon had published a report on the manufacture of iron and steel in India.

Jamsetji now sought an appointment with the Secretary of State Lord George Hamilton, who gave him a patient ear. Jamsetji told him about his dream, as a youth, of building an iron and steel manufacturing plant in India. Adding that he was now in his sixties and lucky to have been blessed with all that he had, he said he had just one wish: to build a steel plant in his country. Hamilton was impressed and urged Lord Curzon to provide whatever support Jamsetji needed.

Jamsetji then embarked for America, where he planned to see the big iron and steel plants and decide on the plant and machinery required for his venture. He visited Alabama, Petersburg and Cleveland. He met a famous geologist, Julian Kennedy, in Cleveland, who brushed off his idea, saying, 'You cannot afford me. The feasibility report itself would cost you a lot. I suggest you drop the idea.' However, seeing Jamsetji's determination to get the plant at any cost, even if it meant selling all his assets, Kennedy suggested the name of Charles Page Perin, a renowned geologist and metallurgist. Kennedy wanted his acquiescence before he began his study.

Walking straight into Perin's office without knocking, Jamsetji asked, 'You are Mr Perin, aren't you?' When the latter nodded, he said, 'I have found my man then. You must have received Kennedy's letter. I want to set up a steel plant in India and I need you as my chief advisor. Don't worry about the costs. I am prepared for it. I want you to be there with me. Will you come along?' Perin just stared. Here was an old man in his sixties, talking with a confidence that was impressive. He was tempted to refuse but the determination and zeal in Jamsetji's eyes kept him from saying no. Finally, he agreed, much to Jamsetji's relief.

Perin sent his geologist, C.M. Weld, to India. It was 1904 by then. Jamsetji's older son Dorabji, his nephew Shapurji Saklatwala and Weld got busy in their pursuit of mines in the wild jungles of Chanda district, where British officers enjoyed hunting tigers. But the three of them were keener on hunting things below the ground than above! It was a dangerous mission. Travelling in bullock carts and walking through the jungles, Weld collected samples meticulously for testing.

But their efforts were futile. While the land did show some promise of iron ore, it did not indicate enough quantities to mine. When Weld expressed a desire to quit, Jamsetji pleaded saying that he had arrived just a few months ago, why not stay for some more time? He suggested the team look in other places. Weld could not turn down Jamsetji's request and stayed on.

Dorabji, in the meanwhile, was visiting the local district office to inform them that they were winding up their project, when he spotted a map of the Geological Survey of India pasted on a notice board. He saw the map marked with dark spots at certain places, indicating iron ore deposits. On closer inspection, Dorab was pleasantly surprised to find that the places marked were merely 140 miles from Nagpur and rushed to give Weld and Jamsetji the good news. The places shown on the map were in nearby Durg district.

Once there, walking uphill, they could feel their heels hitting iron-rich soil. Their initial inspection proved them right, the soil had over 60 per cent iron ore content. But there was no source of water nearby, Water was an important element among the requirements for setting up a steel plant. Their efforts, abandoned then, were not completely wasted. Nearly fifty years later, Durg would become famous for the Bhilai Steel Plant, a Government of India undertaking set up in 1955.

However, fortune favoured the persistent, and Jamsetji soon received a letter from geologist P.N. Bose, who had earlier worked in

Durg and was now posted in the princely state of Mayurbhanj in Bengal province. Bose's letter stated that not only did the state have rich iron ore reserves but that the Maharaja was willing to give favourable terms to anyone who would set up a plant.

Work began in right earnest. It was rough terrain, with wild elephants roaming without a care and jungles populated by Santhal tribes. Once digging began, they struck a solid piece of iron, just a few feet below the soil! The group was overjoyed. The soil had 60 per cent iron ore concentration, well over 3.5 crore tonnes of it! Their search for water, a crucial commodity, ended soon when they discovered two large rivers nearby. A railway station, Kalimati, was also close at hand. All the elements had come together. Like children finding long lost toys, the group hugged each other in joy!

The birth of India's steel manufacturing was about to happen.

Jamsetji was so confident of his dream project that he wrote to Dorab, five years before actual production began at the steel plant, asking him to ensure that the roads in the town where the plant would be set up should be wide and laid well. He said that the roads would see a lot of truck traffic and hence needed to be built with care. He asked Dorab to plant a lot of fast-growing trees along the roads and in the villages nearby as the steel plant would generate a lot of heat and the green cover would offer some respite. He even directed him to build football and hockey fields and temples, mosques and churches for the benefit of villagers.

Jamsetji's instructions to his son were reminiscent of those of the great Maratha warrior Shivaji, who was known for laying down detailed rules of how his men should behave when on or off duty.

THE TAJ MAHAL HOTEL

Bombay, meanwhile, had been battling the scourge of the dreaded bubonic plague for three consecutive years, from 1896 to 1899. In 1898 the death toll in the city exceeded 18,000. Of those attacked by the disease, no less than 91 per cent succumbed. In 1897, a Russian doctor, Professor Waldemar Haffkine, had introduced inoculation against the bubonic plague, but it was met with jealousy from doctors and with superstition and mistrust generally. Stories went round that leprosy and smallpox had resulted from the serum. But Jamsetji, whose knowledge was practically encyclopaedic and who was always ready to devote himself to the thorough study of any current problem, was not to be fooled. He did whatever was possible to fight this disease in the interest of the community's well-being. He went through every piece of literature he could find on the subject in order to familiarize himself with the history and treatment of different kinds of plague, and to find the best methods of preventing the spread of infection. He was quick to see the value of Haffkine's discovery. Jamsetji underwent inoculation himself and ensured that all his servants did likewise. This was the same Haffkine who was later appointed the director of the Plague Research Laboratory in Bombay, which today goes by the name of the famous Haffkine Institute.

By the turn of the century, Bombay was growing fast, leading to a divide between the 'bada sahibs', or the whites, and the 'chhota sahibs', the local gentry. There were just three hotels to cater to visitors: Esplanade Mansion near Kala Ghoda for the brown sahibs and the Great Western Hotel and Apollo Hotel for the white sahibs. The rooms were small and claustrophobic, with mosquitoes adding to the menace. There is an apocryphal story about Jamsetji being refused entry into one of the two hotels meant for whites and how that led him to build a far superior hotel. But no one knows how true the story is. The fact is that Jamsetji wanted to build a world-class hotel in Bombay as none of the three existing ones were of that standard.

At this time, Bombay was witnessing the construction of some of its most iconic buildings—Victoria Terminus; the building which today houses the Mumbai municipal corporation's head office; and the headquarters of the Bombay, Baroda and Central Indian Railway (BB&CI, which later became the headquarters of Western Railway), which is familiar to us today as Churchgate railway station.

The architectural engineer responsible for these marvels was F.W. Stevens and he was being helped by two Indians—Raosaheb Sitaram Khanderao and a Parsi gentleman, D.N. Mirza. Jamsetji hired the two Indians for his hotel project. He had already chosen 2.5 acres of land lying between the Naval Yacht Club and the dockyard at Apollo Bunder, and had signed a ninety-nine-year lease. The Gateway of India was yet to be built. Land reclamation was in full swing and Jamsetji was convinced that he had chosen the perfect location for his hotel.

His sister, hearing of the hotel project, asked him whether his plate wasn't already full running the spinning mill, a steel plant and other things. Why would he build an 'eating house' of all things, she wanted to know. But Jamsetji wanted to build his Taj Mahal for the people of Bombay.

Without any fanfare, following just a simple pooja, work began on 1 November 1898. Jamsetji had told his family that his personal finances would be used to build the hotel. He would visit the construction site each day, involving himself completely. Digging the foundation to a depth of more than 40 feet was a difficult task, as it was very close to the sea. But Jamsetji had a vision: each of his rooms must face the sea, making the guests feel like they were floating on the water itself.

He was personally involved in all purchases, whether electrical appliances from Dusseldorf or chandeliers from Berlin. He ordered washing machines, fans and soda-making machines from America, while iron pillars were shipped from Paris. Jamsetji had seen the impressive Eiffel Tower and was convinced about the longevity of iron pillars from France. Even today, parts of the hotel are supported by these pillars. Jamsetji spent nearly ₹25 lakh on the furnishings—all his own funds, as promised. The hotel opened its doors to the public on 16 December 1903, though not yet fully completed.

INDIAN INSTITUTE OF SCIENCE: A PROJECT PROPOSED

Along with the Taj Mahal Hotel, Jamsetji had also been actively following up another dream project of his, something that would make India grateful to him forever. In pursuance of this project, and about a month before George Nathaniel Curzon landed in Bombay as the new Viceroy of India, he wrote a letter to Swami Vivekananda on 23 November 1898.

Tata and Vivekananda had met in 1893 on the passenger ship *Empress of India*. Tata was on his way from Japan to Chicago, where Vivekananda was going to attend the World Parliament of Religions. They got a lot of time together and their friendship and mutual respect grew. Now, Tata wanted Vivekananda on board for his new dream project.

The winds of scientific progress were now reaching the shores of India from Britain. The year 1851 had seen the arrival of the telegraph. It was the same year the Geological Survey of India was established and its first task was to measure the height of Mount Everest. The opening of the Suez Canal in 1869 had increased trade considerably. The Meteorological Department had been established in 1875, and the year after that saw the opening of the Indian Association for Cultivation of Science (half a century later, C.V. Raman, working here, would bag the Nobel Prize for Physics). The Imperial Bacteriological Laboratory was opened in Poona in 1889. Higher education was thus available for Indians at their doorstep. The Protestant Mission established Wilson College in Bombay while the Jesuits started St Xavier's. Universities were established in Lahore and Allahabad to compete with the University of Bombay. The number of colleges had reached 176. But Jamsetji had in mind the Royal Society of England. He wanted something similar in India.

Therefore, on 31 December 1898, the day after Lord Curzon landed in Bombay, Jamsetji, along with a delegation of teachers, met the new viceroy to impress upon him the need for an Indian centre of excellence in science for research and learning. Curzon was reputed to be an intelligent man. However, he failed to show much enthusiasm for the proposal. He was not sure if an institute of such repute would get an adequate number of students in India, and, even if it did, he wondered what they would do after graduating from such an established institute.

Jamsetji was not one to be disappointed at this lukewarm response. He wrote to the Secretary of State for India, Lord Hamilton, who gave him a patient hearing and asked the principal of the Royal Society of England, William Ramsay, to study the proposal. Prof. Ramsay came to India for a quick ten-day tour and concluded that the proposed institute could be set up in Bangalore. He also noted that the institute would have the potentital to contribute to the setting up of certain industries in India. He constituted a committee, which recommended that 'an institute on a less ambitious scale may be set up'.

Jamsetji donated £8,000 for the proposed institute, the equivalent of nearly ₹1.25 lakh at the time. He was not going to allow the idea of a 'small institute' to take root. He had also formed his own committee to advise him. One of its members was Mahadev Govind Ranade. Jamsetji was confident that many industrialists would come forward to donate for such a cause. The then Maharaja of Mysore donated 371 acres of land, made a one-time contribution of ₹5 lakh and promised to further donate ₹50,000 each year. Contrary to Jamsetji's hopes, the royal families of Baroda, Travancore and other princely states did not come forward to donate. It was only the state of Mysore that recognized the value of his enterprise. Hearing of the donation pledged by Mysore state, industrialist Chabildas Lalubhai from Bombay announced that he would equal Mysore's share. He had a huge land bank of 18,000 acres. Soon, many donors started pouring in.

Lord Curzon, however, was adamant about not allowing the project to take off. Jamsetji, not willing to give up, met Lord Hamilton during his visit to India, much to the annoyance of Lord Curzon. He believed the project was doomed to fail from day one, and any money spent towards it was a waste of resources. But Jamsetji was hell-bent on making it happen. He was a tired old man. He wrote in his will, 'In case the institute does not come up in my lifetime, my personal wealth may be used to build the same.' He sold seventeen of his buildings in Bombay to generate funds for the project.

His single-minded efforts eventually were to lead to the formation of the Indian Institute of Science (IISc), one of India's most prestigious research institutes. Sadly, Jamsetji was not to see it completed, just as he would not see his other pet project, the Tata Iron and Steel Company (TISCO, now Tata Steel), completed. Jamsetji passed away on 19 May 1904 in Bad Nauheim, on a visit to Germany.

A man like Jamsetji, whose dreams were always bigger than anyone else's imagination, would have required ten lives to see all of his dreams take shape. It was these dreams and the efforts he made towards turning them into reality that laid the foundation of a strong and independent India. Laying the foundation for the Taj Mahal Hotel, he had said he had no interest in owning the place; he just wanted to show the world that Indians were capable of building such a hotel. He wanted it to be an inspiration for others. The India of today has emerged from the dreams he sowed in the minds of Indians during his lifetime.

3

The Glow after the Sunset

Jamsetji's death was acknowledged by the British government in an official note that stated that it was indeed a sad day for the country to have lost such a great and large-hearted soul. The *Times of India*, then a British-owned newspaper, carried an item the next day, on 20 May 1904, saying that Jamsetji combined humility with pride, never berating his juniors but not kowtowing either to his superiors, and that it was a mark of his greatness that he never did anything with an eye on honours or fame; he had just one mission: to put India on the road to prosperity. The tribute was testimony to the remarkable respect Jamsetji commanded.

THE INDIAN INSTITUTE OF SCIENCE: A DREAM ACCOMPLISHED

Cognizant of the prestige now associated with the Tata name, the British government enquired after the progress of the construction of the IISc and offered its support to Jamsetji's sons. Taking advantage of this turnaround, Dorabji and his younger brother Ratanji decided to meet Lord Curzon, who had earlier dismissed the idea of IISc as unviable. The meeting proved to be a damp squib as Lord Curzon's views were unchanged. Dorabji told him curtly if the government was not keen on supporting the cause, the Tatas would drop the idea and look to put their money elsewhere. That chastised the viceroy a bit and he said he would look into it.

Dorabji's confrontation with Lord Curzon had its effect. Until then, the government, which had agreed to give the IISc project a mere £2,000, now agreed to put in each year half of whatever the others contributed. But Curzon later changed his stance once again and sent word to Dorabji to gather funds for the venture on his own rather than begging the government. Dorabji decided to meet him once again to explain his father's vision. It appears that Lord Curzon was under the impression that the Tatas were eager to put their name on the proposed institute. Dorabji made it quite clear that the Tata family had no such intentions.

In the meanwhile, the newspapers had picked up the story, much to the irritation of Lord Curzon. Dorabji further assured Curzon that he was willing to put the entire money promised by his father into a trust which would work exclusively for the creation of IISc. Finally, the government and Lord Curzon agreed to amend the law to allow such an institute to be established.

A year after Jamsetji's passing in 1904, Lord Curzon was ignominiously informed of his retirement without prior notice. He resigned, hoping that the government would be shocked into reconsidering its decision. After all, he was credited with having established the Archaeological Survey of India and laying the foundation for higher education in India. He was taken aback, however, when the government readily accepted his resignation; Curzon returned to England embittered. His successor, Lord Minto, approved the IISc project and gave his sanction, leading to the passing of a vesting order by the government on 27 March 1909 that marked the foundation of the institution.

It was Jamsetji's dream that the name should display its 'Indian-ness'. It was his large-heartedness that, despite having played a significant role in its formation, he had no ambition to have his name anywhere on it. He was a reticent man who preferred not to be in the public eye.

The Institute has been the backbone of scientific progress in India. Not many know that stalwarts like Dr Homi Bhabha and Vikram Sarabhai were attached to the IISc in the early part of their careers.

HYDROELECTRICITY FOR BOMBAY

Jamsetji's ability to dream beyond what an ordinary man could even dare to has left us with gifts we will cherish for generations to come. Most of us travelling on the Mumbai–Pune route today would be enamoured by the twinkling lights in the valleys below, imagining stars shining on earth. There is Jamsetji's hand in it.

He had seen the Narmada fall from a height near Jabalpur and believed it was the right site for an electricity generation project. Unfortunately, a swamiji, whose ashram was on the land proposed for the site, refused to move. The government, not wanting a religious dispute on its hands, did not support Jamsetji, who had to give up his plans grudgingly.

It is important to note that Jamsetji saw the potential for hydroelectric energy well before the world witnessed such a project come up. He dreamt of it six years before the Wisconsin hydroelectric project, the world's first, was set up in 1882. By the time he set his eyes on the Dudhsagar Falls on the Goa–Maharashtra border, a hydroelectric plant had also been set up at the Niagara Falls on the US–Canada border.

Jamsetji planned to generate electricity and sell it in Bombay. The spinning and weaving mills, running on coal-generated electricity, would be ready customers for the project, he surmised. The black soot from the coal plants, an added nuisance, would also be done away with. Jamsetji's dream was to light up the entire city of Bombay. He sought the help of an architect, David Gosling, who visited the Dudhsagar Falls, but was not convinced of the viability of the project.

Gosling, who spent the summers in the hill station of Khandala close to Poona, would often travel to Lonavala. He noticed that the tall peaks of the Sahyadris offered an opportunity for the generation of hydroelectric power. The only challenge was to create a dam to store water. In the case of Niagara or Dudhsagar, the natural flow was enough to work the turbines, but it wasn't so here. Jamsetji visualized a dam that would store water and then, through artificial channels, let the water run down towards Khopoli, where the turbines would generate electricity. He selected a suitable spot at Valvan, en route to Poona from Bombay, just after Lonavala, where he found a narrow gorge suitable for a dam. He was well aware that it was going to be a feat of engineering to construct such a dam. He had to get water down from a height of nearly 1,800 feet. Generating electricity was challenging enough, not to mention ensuring its transportation to Bombay. But challenges were the intoxicant that propelled Jamsetji's work.

Jamsetji decided to set up a company with the help of Gosling. Taking a few companies associated with the East India Company as partners, he made two proposals—one for the British and the other for the Portuguese government since both were related to a river originating near Goa. Electricity generated in the Portuguese territory would be supplied to British-ruled Bombay.

Jamsetji was in a hurry. There were niggling health problems and the British government was sitting on the fence, unable to take a decision. There was no precedence anywhere in the world for such a project, where an artificial lake had been built and the water flowed down a natural slope to generate electricity. But Jamsetji felt compelled to get on with the project for the sake of the country's progress.

He met Secretary of State Hamilton once again. Lord Hamilton was familiar with Jamsetji's zeal regarding both the steel project and the proposed IISc. Jamsetji sent a detailed letter explaining the rationale behind his plan; the ever-increasing demand for electricity in Bombay; the need for it to power more businesses; for it to act as a catalyst for the entrepreneurial spirit of the city; and, last but not the least, to keep the Taj Mahal Hotel bright and shining! His confidence in the project was so high that he doubled the size of the lake which would hold the water behind the dam.

Lord Hamilton consulted the then Governor of Bombay, Lord Northcot, who was impressed by the idea. Hamilton's office wrote to Jamsetji saying that his idea was impressive and if he could get it to fruition, it would be a proud moment and he would take the lion's share of the credit for its success.

Unfortunately, Jamsetji did not live to see his dream come true.

A few days after Jamsetji's demise, Lord Sydenham was made Governor of Bombay. He was an engineer by profession and was quickly drawn to Jamsetji's idea of hydroelectric power generation. He loved the idea of creating an artificial waterfall from water stored in a man-made lake. He decided to fully support the idea, giving immense encouragement to the Tatas. They added two more lakes, apart from Valvan at Khandala, borrowing money from abroad and reaching out to the mill owners in Bombay asking them to participate in the venture.

Ironically, only two mill owners, David Sassoon and Sir Shapoorji Bharucha, agreed to buy electricity from the Tatas, while the rest believed that it was not worth their while. It was Lord Sydenham who felt that the project needed speeding up. At a function in Solapur he urged the public to support it financially and make it a truly Indian project. The winds of swadeshi were beginning to blow and Sydenham's appeal was received well, allowing the Tatas to raise a capital of ₹2 crore*, a mind-blowing amount in those days.

By 1911, the Valvan project was completed, with Dorabji Tata having been knighted just the year before, making him Sir Dorab. Inaugurating the project, he remembered his father, who never had any personal ambitions for money or fame but worked for the cause of uplifting India's industrial and intellectual property. He said it was his pleasure that he was able to fulfil his father's dream. Lord Sydenham, present at the function, added that the project was a fine example of India's increasing self-respect which would inspire others to dream the impossible and make it happen.

---

*   1 crore = 10 million or 10,000,000

More than 7,000 men worked on the project. Getting pipes nearly seven feet in diameter up the steep terrain was not an easy task. But the men worked diligently to complete the project. The quality of the work speaks for itself; the pipes did not spring a leak at any place for years. The pipes were imported from Germany while the turbine blades came from Switzerland. The turbines were American while the wires carrying the electricity were from England. The project was completed in a year. Lord Willingdon pressed the switch to start the turbines, illuminating the Simplex Mills complex in Bombay. The other mills and businesses, sitting in denial till then, began queuing up for electricity from the Tatas. One of them was Bombay Electric Supply and Tramways, which we know as BEST today.

Lord Willingdon complimented the Tatas in his speech, saying that it was a shining example of a tribute paid by a son to his father. The tribute would be paid many times over. In the eastern part of the country, in Bengal, a steel factory was taking shape.

TISCO TAKES SHAPE

Having discovered iron ore reserves, it was time for the mines and the factory to begin their work. The biggest challenge, as always, was to raise adequate capital. Jamsetji used to say that an Indian investor, unlike his American counterpart, is not happy with a return of 5 or 6 per cent; he wants more! There was also an inherent disbelief in the ability of Indians to set up a steel plant, let alone run it. Those who doubted were not at fault; they had never seen a project of such magnitude in India.

Sir Frederick Apcott, then Chairman of the Indian Railway Board, sarcastically remarked, 'You mean a steel plant in India? Well, if that is to happen, I promise to buy all my steel from there.' Others were equally pessimistic. Sir Thomas Holland, then head of the Geological Survey of India, trashed the project saying that it was a classic case of misplaced love for the country and it was destined to die a premature death due to business realities. In the meanwhile, the Tatas had already invested ₹5 lakh but the question of raising sufficient capital still loomed large.

Dorabji stationed himself in London, meeting investors, bankers and anyone willing to listen to his story. He got a lot of encouraging words but no money! London and the world markets at large were in a bear phase and all investors were shy of investing in long-term capital. Dorabji was not in favour of foreign investors to begin with. The winds of nationalism were blowing strong in 1906-07 thanks to the fiery speeches and writings of leaders such as Lokmanya Tilak. Dadabhai Naoroji, having returned from Britain, stoked the idea of using the manganese ore mined in India for Indians rather than it being sent to England. Aurobindo Ghosh was busy igniting the fire of the Swadeshi Movement.

The overwhelming angst against Indian resources being used to make the British rich was spreading across Bengal. This woke up the handful of rich businessmen in India to the need of supporting the Tata project. Dorabji rode this wave of patriotic fervour and appealed to all Indians, 'Don't you want to participate in the first such project in India?' He formed a limited company on 26 August 1907 and opened a public issue worth ₹23 crore. His own investment was nearly ₹25 lakh. The shares available to the common man were worth ₹15 crore.

The very next day saw long queues outside the Tatas' Navsari Mansion in Bombay. The rich picked up their lots while the common man invested in small amounts. Nearly 8,000 people had invested within two weeks. The news reached the Maharaja of Gwalior, who put in a princely sum of £400,000! Dorabji was convinced that his father's dream would see the light of day. He said, 'It feels so nice that for the first time in our country we are seeing a project that is for the Indians, by the Indians and of the Indians.'

It was the first time the name Tata was being used for any of the group's businesses. The company was named the Tata Iron and Steel Company (TISCO; Tata Steel today). The earlier businesses were Empress Mills, Swadeshi Mills and Indian Hotels Company Ltd; they did not have the Tata name. But from 1907, the Tata name was to be intrinsically linked to steel.

That Christmas saw the inauguration of the mining project at Mayurbhanj. Soon, trucks would be ferrying iron ore, trundling in a jungle where tigers roamed. One can imagine the difficulties of mining in a dense jungle full of carnivores and swamps all around. The elephants would at times charge, angry at the noise the machines were making. Two workers lost their lives to a tiger, and a bear gave birth to her cubs in a deserted office room. Geologist Srinivas Rao spent time roaming the jungles on horseback and soon, just as he expected, he found a huge source of water—the River Subarnarekha, where it crossed the Bengal–Nagpur border. Unfortunately, his efforts took a toll on his health and he did not survive long.

Despite the hurdles, the workers put in their best. Charles Perin got his men to help. His engineers were to direct the men in the construction activities. The locals, till then used to seeing the white man as an administrator in the British government and not dirtying his hands at work, received the engineers with great fanfare. By the time real work began, it was February 1908. Makeshift huts and offices were ready. A board at the entrance to the site proudly proclaimed, 'Tata Steel Company'. There was a sense of excitement in the air. They all knew they were creating something big. They had no idea when the journey would end. Nor did they know the scale of the project. They had, after all, never seen anything like it before!

Finally, the day arrived in February 1912 when the first steel ingot rolled out of the factory. A wave of cheers spread across the plant. But Dorabji Tata was not one to get overwhelmed. His address to his men warned them not to be swayed by emotion. He likened the factory to a newborn infant, which would face challenges as it grew, whether teething or running a fever. He advised them to be like responsible parents who did not give up but ensured the right attention. He concluded by saying that they would have to manage carefully and that they were going to be tested henceforth.

Not that his speech dampened the spirits of those celebrating. The news spread like wildfire across India and people flocked to Mayurbhanj just to see what a real factory looked like!

TISCO STEEL MEETS WORLD WAR I DEMANDS

The imminent threat of war hung over Europe and, in August of 1914, it broke out. It soon spread to West Asia, centring around the Suez Canal and from there to the Mesopotamian region, now called Iraq. World War I had begun. Britain was heavily involved and looked towards its colonies for men and materials. Britain needed cars and trucks, which required transportation through the railways. It was a dual challenge; there were no such ready railway tracks and, to build the tracks, you needed steel. German U-boats were making life miserable for the British navy, and to build ships the country needed steel. And this was where TISCO came into the picture.

The demand was overwhelming. The Mesopotamian region required huge amounts of steel, which was sourced from TISCO. The two-year-old company worked day and night to meet the demand, which was a staggering 1,500 miles of steel tracks. World War I became its first customer, so to speak. It grew the Tatas' business. Dorabji said, while addressing his shareholders in 1916, 'We have a massive demand for our production, keeping our factory busy for the next few years. It is only thanks to your faith in us that we are able to see such remarkable progress.' Dorabji had not forgotten the condescension with which Sir Frederick Apcott had commented, 'I shall have all the steel for my breakfast.' Now Dorabji remarked, 'I hope he does not visit us; for he is likely to suffer from indigestion!'

Well, we don't know whether Sir Frederick visited TISCO but Jawaharlal Nehru, Mahatma Gandhi and many other leaders came to pay homage over the years. Subhas Chandra Bose stepped in to provide support and sort out issues with labour. Gandhiji spent a night there. Charles Perin, the person responsible for building the plant, visited it again in 1935. The water did not suit him, in all probability. He suffered from stomach ailments and, despite many attempts to treat him, he finally succumbed to a long-drawn illness after two years.

The workers had worked day and night during the war, not taking a single break. The guns finally fell silent on 11 November 1918. The war had ended. The then Viceroy, Lord Chelmsford, visited the factory to express his gratitude for the role played by the Tatas in the war. He said, as he stood on the steps of the bungalow built for the resident engineer:

> … I wanted to come here to express my appreciation of the great work which has been done by the Tata Company during the past four years of this war. I can hardly imagine what we should have done during these four years if the Tata Company had not been able to give us steel rails, which have been provided for us not only for Mesopotamia, but for Egypt, Palestine and East Africa.

He proceeded to rename the town 'Jamshedpur', after Jamsetji, and the railway station became known as Tatanagar.

It was ten years after Jamsetji's death that the factory had taken shape. The sky continued to be illuminated brightly while the sun had set long back. It was not going to be dark soon.

4

Son of the Sun

'The market for this company is not going to be just Bombay or this country. Its target is to capture the world.'

Once upon a time in India, Diwali would begin in the wee hours of the morning, when people would rub their bodies from head to toe with a sweet-smelling reddish oil before washing it off with soap. The tradition was followed on the day of Naraka Chaturdashi. One's hair would smell of the oil for a few days while the sweet smell of sandalwood would permeate the body. This was thanks to a brand called Moti, a round sandalwood-infused soap packed in a square box. Moti was for special days like Diwali, while the rest of the year people used a more ordinary soap called Hamam. There was a slab called 501 for washing clothes. All these brands, including the oil, came from the Tata stable.

The man behind all of these was Burjorji Padshah, a loyal employee of the Tatas and also related to them. His father and Jamsetji had been close friends and Jamsetji cemented the relationship by marrying off his daughter to Burjorji. Those were the days of child marriage.

Unfortunately, the little bride died at the age of ten. Burjorji's father too died when Burjorji was young and the responsibility of managing the family was taken up by Jamsetji.

Burjorji was a very bright child, clearing his matriculation exam by the time he was thirteen. He enrolled in Elphinstone College, bagging scholarships all through. After studying mathematics at Cambridge University, he took up a job as an assistant professor at a college in Karachi. Jamsetji sent his own son, Ratan, to study under him there. Later, when Burjorji learnt that a British national had been given preference over him for the post of professor, he resigned in protest and returned to Bombay. His mind turned to social work and he wanted to support Gopal Krishna Gokhale's Bharat Sewak Samaj. However, Jamsetji convinced him to work for him.

Aware of Burjorji's academic brilliance, Jamsetji told him to travel the world. We want to create a world-class institution of science, he said to him, and I want you to see the world and learn from the best. So, Burjorji travelled to many great institutions and reported back. It was he who suggested that the proposed institute be modelled on Johns Hopkins University in the US, and IISc was duly built on the lines suggested by Burjorji. Eventually, he became Jamsetji's right-hand man in all his projects. His ability with numbers was well known and he was the man to approach in case anyone wanted to understand the complex economics of any project. His presence was of great help to Dorabji and Ratanji after Jamsetji's death.

He remained responsible for all factory purchases and travelled extensively across the world searching for the best equipment. World War I had just ended and everyone was scrambling to get global business and economics in order. Everyone was keen to get things stabilized as soon as possible. A trip of Burjorji's during that period took him to Japan from America to assess business opportunities now that peace had been established. On the long sea journey, he befriended one Edward Thomson, who was an advisor in the area of cooking oil production. Burjorji recalled Jamsetji commenting once, 'We must get into the business of cooking oil. After all, we produce millions of coconuts but we do not produce the oil from it.'

Thomson proposed starting a factory for coconut oil, describing factories in the Philippines that produced coconut oil, adding, 'The Americans love this business. It has high margins of nearly 70 per cent.' Burjorji promptly suggested Edward submit a detailed project plan, since he knew it had been Jamsetji's wish to start a factory that produced coconut oil. Edward's enthusiasm knew no bounds. He suggested three factories instead of one. He insisted there was huge demand from America. He also suggested creating downstream products from the solid residue left after the extraction of oil.

The Tata management, dreaming of the new project, was unaware that Edward had hidden a critical aspect which could turn the dream into a nightmare. America had invested a lot of money in the Philippines, which was under their control. India was a British territory and the Americans naturally preferred to do business within their own dominion. Besides, their investments in the Philippines were about to flower. Edward had waxed eloquent about American demand but had failed to mention it would primarily be met by coconuts from the Philippines, not so much from India.

Meanwhile, the Tatas had, as suggested by Edward, set up their factory in Kerala, the heart of coconut land. The company was Tata Oil Mills (TOMCO), and Edward was hired as an advisor on contract with the Tatas.

TATA OIL MILLS VS LEVER BROTHERS

TOMCO was a turning point of sorts for Kerala. The first cooperative movement began after the factory was set up. Small producers, dependent on selling their produce locally, could now dream big. It was the first time women were employed in a factory. And what a ruckus it created! The Tatas were quite taken aback to find protests against women being employed—in a state that prided itself on its matriarchal society. TOMCO appointed a woman clerk, to the loud protests of the employees there. But the Tatas stood by her and gradually the protest died down. One must admire that, way back in 1917, the Tatas showed that they could manage social issues while creating wealth and setting up factories.

But the business was struggling. America was not really dependent on Indian coconuts and, on top of it, levied a huge import duty on coconuts sourced from India. The Tatas had run into rough weather at the very outset. Edward, scouting the world for purchasing all the machinery, was least worried about the problems back home and went about buying things, including a fancy boat for himself. The Tatas had no option but to terminate his contract.

Next, the Tatas focused on just one product: extracting oil from coconuts, for which there was huge demand in Kerala itself. There were local extractors but there were fluctuations in both price and quality. The first Tata product was launched under the brand name of Cocogem, which established itself fairly quickly as a reliable product. The next in line was a bathing soap. Till then, a lot of households used a combination of milk and gram flour for bathing, with the husk of a dry coconut acting as a brush. Soap was rarely, if ever, used for bathing.

The first instance of bathing soap manufacture in India was in 1879 but it hardly got any traction. Washing soap usage too was not very different. The first batch of washing soap was imported to Calcutta in 1895 under the name of Sunlight soap. The label proudly said: 'Made in England by Lever Brothers.' Lever Brothers, which later became Hindustan Lever and is now Unilever, made its entry into India with Sunlight soap. Lever Brothers set up Hindustan Vanaspati Manufacturing, producing the Dalda Vanaspati oil. The company expanded to all parts of India over the next few decades. Many today believe it to be an Indian company!

The Tatas faced a lot of resistance from Lever Brothers when they tried to introduce soap in the Indian market. Lever Brothers was aware of the stiff competition the company would face if the Tatas were to enter the soap and detergent market. The Tatas had already entered the electricity generation market, and there was nervous excitement about the steel factory being set up in the eastern part of India. Bombay was proud of its first five star hotel, the Taj Mahal, as it was of Swadeshi

Mills, while Empress Mills in Nagpur was running to full capacity. Lever Brothers had reason to worry.

The Tatas launched their first bar of soap at ₹10 for 100 bars and named it 501. The history behind the name is quite unique. Levers was a British and Dutch company. The Tatas did not want a name which would associate them with the British. At that time, a French soap brand called 500 was a serious competitor to Levers. So, Tata chief executive Jal Naoroji, the grandson of Dadabhai Naoroji, decided to name their product 501.

Levers retaliated by using a classical ploy to kill competition. They reduced their price to ₹6 for 100 bars of soap. It was a price that did not even cover the cost of raw material used to manufacture the soap. Tata distributors and employees urged Naoroji to follow suit too, but he stuck to it, saying, 'Let us wait and watch. I wonder how long Levers can last with this price.' And after three months, Levers were forced to revert to their original price.

TOMCO was growing fast. Its oil and soap business was doing well. The Tata empire was growing. In Jamshedpur alone, many companies had taken birth: Tata Pigments, Special Steel Limited, Tata Metal and Strips, Tata Davy, Tata Mann, Tata Aquatic Farms and many more. But the Tatas were not content with creating companies in just one geography or any one area. They wanted to be in every area that could take the country ahead. Dorabji Tata, like his father, was very clear in his vision on this account. While the oil factory was taking shape, he laid the foundation for a cement plant in 1912 under the name of India Cements. By then the warning bells of World War I were already audible. By the time the war began, the demand for Tata products hit the roof. When the war ended, the business had already gained momentum.

TATA INDUSTRIAL BANK AND NEW INDIA ASSURANCE

The Tatas were now keen to enter into the world of finance, and a bank thus emerged—the Tata Industrial Bank. The thought behind the formation of a bank was simple: an independent source of capital to propel the industrial growth of the nation. It was the same thought which led to the formation of the Industrial Development Bank of India (IDBI) more than a century later.

Dorabji was very clear that money from the bank would not be used to fund the Tata companies. His integrity was seen in one more instance, when the bank's directors, seeing that the bank was doing well, mooted a plan to raise more capital by issuing new shares at higher value. The existing shareholders were quite upset and the complaints reached Dorabji, who said the shareholders' complaints were genuine. The bank had not yet yielded a single dividend, yet its directors expected more people to put their money into the bank. If at all the bank decided to raise more equity, it must be done at the same valuation and not more. When many of the directors protested quoting market sentiment, which was willing to pay more, Dorabji promptly offered to resign. To him this was a matter of principle. Unfortunately, the bank did not survive for long and in 1923 changed hands to become the Central Bank of India.

The next big business in the financial services area from the Tata stable was New India Assurance. The Tatas put in a substantial initial capital of ₹20 crore in 1919 when the company was formed. One can imagine the amount in today's terms. Quite naturally, it was soon the largest insurance company of India. Even now it is, the only difference being it is owned and run by the government.

Dorabji was confident while launching the company that it would be a success. As he had predicted, by the time the company was nationalized in 1956, it had spread its wings to forty-six countries! Many other businesses like Tata Constructions and Tata Electrochemicals had also sprung up in this period. Not that all were planned. Many were created as part of the ever-growing Tata empire. But the end of World War I in 1918 was soon to test the Tata empire and Dorabji Tata's business acumen.

POST-WWI RECESSION

The sudden relaxation of the tension created worldwide due to the war led to a sort of vacuum. Unemployment soared by 1920. Millions of soldiers, previously occupied in the business of war, were now returning home fearing unemployment. It was worst in America—in 1918, the number of soldiers on active duty was 29 lakh. It fell to 15 lakh the following year and fell drastically further to 3.8 lakh by 1920. The number of people in the job market had increased by a whopping 4 per cent in a single year and it was impossible for all of them to find a job, leaving the Federal Reserve confounded. The American economy, already depleted due to the war, faced the added problem of unemployment. Capital was more expensive now, leading to another spiral in inflation. The cycle was to continue for nearly eighteen months.

Indian industries were affected badly too. Murmurs of disgruntled workers were beginning to make their rounds in Jamshedpur. Tata Steel's only regular customer, Japan, was shaken up by an earthquake, leaving demand drastically reduced. Production was reduced to such a low that there was a question of finding money to pay wages to the workers. When the Imperial Bank of India (State Bank of India today), banker to Tata Steel, refused to extend a loan to the Tatas, the prospect of closing down Tata Steel loomed large.

Dorabji's actions at this time were exemplary. Not only did he put his personal assets for sale, but he asked his wife Meherbai to pawn her jewels. He managed to raise ₹1 crore and got another crore as a loan from the Maharaja of Gwalior. The Diwan (Prime Minister) was a Parsi gentleman called F.E. Dinshaw. The Gwalior royal family had invested earlier in Tata Steel and were willing to extend a helping hand. Dorabji's single-minded pursuit was to ensure that no worker should get his salary late. His uncle RD stood by him shoulder to shoulder, giving support. At a shareholder meeting in 1924, when a group suggested selling the company, RD stood up and shouted, 'Never! Never will the company get sold till I am alive!' Saying so, he banged his fist on the table and stormed out of the meeting.

The Tatas had barely managed to overcome the problems in the post-war era when another one in the form of imports from England cropped up. The British had begun using India as a market to save their own domestic industries in the post-war period. It was becoming obvious that the British government would buy steel produced in Britain rather than from a colony such as India.

It was Jawaharlal Nehru and Muhammad Ali Jinnah who came to the rescue. They shared a common link with Jamsetji, whose cousin RD was a friend of the Nehrus and also of Jinnah. Nehru and Jiinah now clamoured to the British government, asking it to levy duties back home on British steel exported to India. Undoubtedly, the British firms were not going to support such a proposal. Luckily, the British government agreed to the demands raised by Jinnah and Nehru. This is the only example where the government ruled in favour of a local Indian company instead of those back home.

Tata Steel was back on track but there was more trouble brewing. At that time, the company employed nearly 55,000 workers. Of these, nearly 23,000 worked in the mines. With such a huge number, it was quite expected for a workers' union to be formed. The birth of the union took place in 1920, when the company was facing its worst crisis, with its first secretary being C.F. Andrews, a close confidant of Mahatma Gandhi.

Subhas Chandra Bose too took active interest in the affairs of the union, his main grouse being the fact that Tata Steel was appointing foreigners in leadership roles. 'Don't you find anyone in India suitable for these posts?' was his refrain. Later, he would occupy the post of secretary. Leftists started taking a keen interest and a few anti-social elements also meddled in its affairs. A lot of political leaders were curious about Tata Steel by then. Rajendra Prasad was from Bihar, so he had a natural affiliation for Jamshedpur. Mahatma Gandhi visited the factory in 1924.

Dorabji was quite close to the political leaders of that time but he never used his friendship to benefit the Tata business. In fact, he did not like the political leadership and its varying philosophies, especially the socialist approach of the Congress Party. And when the Tatas were criticized for splurging money on unnecessary things like a fancy township, R.D. Tata replied that they were spending money to build houses, hospitals, schools and playgrounds for the workers and their families, but were instead accused of splurging unnecessarily. He said he pitied the narrow mindedness of such critics. The company was not merely building houses but was raising a modern, well-equipped town which would serve as an example to the rest of the world.

The problems at Tata Steel had begun quite a while ago. Tata shareholders had not received a single paisa as dividend for nearly twelve years. Addressing the shareholders, RD told them to imagine trying to dam the ocean. Building the company was similar and they had to put in whatever effort they could to build the dam. Even a small hole in the dam could cause it to collapse, he said. Likewise, he added, they would have to ensure that they ploughed back all money they made into the company to create a future which would be long lasting. He hoped they would not bicker about small things like return on investment at such a crucial point in time. Eventually, the persistent efforts of Dorab and RD resulted in a whopping profit of ₹65 lakh in 1925. As promised, they invested the entire money back into the business.

The very next year, R.D. Tata died at the age of seventy. He had stood staunchly behind Dorabji, whether it had been handling problems at Tata Steel or setting up the hydroelectric project. To the extent that when he received a telegram saying his wife was very ill in France, he chose first to resolve the crisis at hand that was plaguing the ailing Tata Industrial Bank. As soon as things improved and he bought a ticket on the next steamship, he received the cable, 'Sooni no more!'

RD left behind a legacy befitting the Tata name. He used to say, while addressing shareholders, that they had merely scratched the surface; there was so much to do that the company could not rest on its laurels. India needed a lot more, he would say, and if the company and its shareholders did what had to be done, future generations would lead a far better life. He would ask whether the economic rejuvenation of India should not be the sole purpose of the company.

Following RD's death, Dorabji had to now fight his battles alone. He knew his father Jamsetji had left a lot of responsibilities for him to shoulder; he had to bring to fruition the grand designs his father had dreamt of, and he felt proud of it.

DORABJI'S LEGACY

Not many know that it was Dorabji Tata who spearheaded the movement to get Indians to participate in the Olympics. Despite Tata Steel going through turbulent times in 1920, it was Dorabji who sponsored the Indian contingent to the Antwerp Olympics that year. He facilitated the participation of four athletes and two wrestlers. As president of the Indian Olympic Council, he financed the Indian contingent to the 1924 Paris Olympics as well. Quite naturally, when the Indian Olympic Association was formed in 1927, he was made its secretary. He believed India had a great future and that Indians needed to invest in it. Dorabji would also say in jest, of his own love for cricket, that he might not be able to recall how many tonnes of cotton the company exported, but he could recall in detail each and every century hit by legendary English cricketer W.C. Grace.

Despite his love for sports, Dorabji never took his responsibilities or his father's dreams lightly. In fact, it would not be an exaggeration to state that Dorabji brought Jamsetji's dreams to life.

Speaking of his personal life, Dorabji had once gone to Mysore for some work related to IISc and met Dr Hormusji Bhabha, the first Indian Inspector-General of Education of Mysore state. We are not sure whether the task for which he had gone was accomplished or not, but we know that Dorabji married Bhabha's daughter, Meherbai, in 1897, at the age of thirty-eight.

Unlike most girls of her time, Meherbai had no interest in being stuck in the kitchen or managing household chores, and was an excellent tennis player to boot. She would take up issues on behalf of other women and be supported wholeheartedly by Dorabji. She died of leukemia in June 1931 in England. Dorabji ensured that his own burial place was booked next to her grave. And since there were no facilities for treating cancer patients in India, he set up the Lady Tata Memorial Trust, putting in ₹75 lakh of his personal money. The whole idea was to utilize these funds for cancer research and help needy patients.

Dorabji wanted to set up a facility of international standards for the treatment of cancer in India, but he passed away before this dream could be fulfilled. As a tribute to him, his successor and cousin, Nowroji Saklatwala, Chairman of the Tata group from 1932 to 1938, took up the work of setting up the Tata Memorial Hospital in Parel, Bombay. Established in 1941, the hospital had all the facilities for treatment, surgery and post-surgical recuperative care. The best of doctors in Bombay were sent abroad on scholarships for training in the treatment and care of cancer patients.

It was a noble cause and the Government of Bombay contributed ₹1 lakh towards it. The Tatas' emphasis on charity was reflected in the hospital: more than 75 per cent of the beds were reserved for those who could not afford treatment. The cost would be borne by the Tata group. In the initial years, Sir Dorabji Trust contributed ₹1 crore towards the funds. Today, Tata Memorial Hospital is considered one of the world's leading hospitals in cancer care.

Indeed, Dorabji set up various trusts, donating his entire wealth to them. He had no children of his own. Ignoring requests to give money to various Parsi organizations, he donated his wealth for public causes. This had been his father's wish too. He had once bought a ruby in London for a whopping ₹30 lakh. He donated that too to the trust. His favourite tie-pin made of pearls also went to the Sir Dorabji Trust. The Tata headquarters, Bombay House, was constructed by Dorabji Tata. Moreover, the trust has played a vital role in encouraging and supporting the education of deserving students. One such example is that of the illustrious Narlikar father and son duo—physicist Vishnu Vasudev Narlikar and his son, the astrophyscist Jayant Vishnu Narlikar.

In 1932, Dorabji sailed for London with the intention of praying at his wife's grave on the occasion of her death anniversary but died of a massive heart attack en route, just two weeks before her death anniversary. As per his wish, he was buried next to his loving wife.

5

The Dawn of the Industrial Age

Jamsetji Tata was lucky as far as his sons were concerned; Dorabji and Ratanji were both illustrious in their own ways. Dorabji spent his life completing the projects his father had either dreamt of or started, be it the steel factory, hydroelectric project or the IISc. Jamsetji had dreamt these three big dreams, which were duly fulfilled by Dorabji.

Ratanji was different. He was a diehard romantic, with a pointy beard, sharp nose and dreamy eyes. Art, sculpture, archaeology, these kinds of subjects interested him. He stayed on the outskirts of London at Richmond upon Thames, in a stately home called York House. He had a stature of his own among the well-heeled of London society. Dorabji was busy adding to the industrial and national wealth, while Ratanji would give the wealth a social standing. Amongst the Tatas, the idea of social welfare was most intensely present in Ratanji Tata. He was inspired by Gopal Krishna Gokhale.

The two brothers, influenced by different philosophies, worked for the benefit of the nation. While the elder was keen to contribute to the national GDP and improve its wealth, the younger was of the belief that the country needed a more aware social consciousness. Ratanji firmly believed in giving all his time and effort for the cause of Bharat Sewak Samaj, the Servants of India Society, formed by Gokhale. His contribution to the society was publicly acknowledged by Gokhale in 1909.

Ratanji supported Gokhale in many areas. One of Gokhale's disciples who was to benefit from Ratanji's largesse was Mohandas Karamchand Gandhi. While Gandhi, then not yet known as Mahatma, was fighting apartheid in South Africa, Ratanji supported him with a whopping contribution of ₹1.25 lakh!

Not many people are aware that when the funds needed for the excavation of the ruins of Harappa and Mohenjo Daro fell insufficient, Sir Ratan donated generously. It can be said that the history of the Indus valley civilization is revealed to us thanks to him. Even the historical excavations in Pataliputra, close to modern-day Patna, were made possible only courtesy of Sir Ratan Tata. He donated ₹75,000, a large sum in those days. It enabled the discovery of the pillared hall of Emperor Ashoka's palace.

He was simultaneously concerned with the health and wellness of the common man. A tuberculosis centre was set up for preventive treatment in Bombay with his funds. The idea of creating a beautiful seaboard from Bandra to Cuffe Parade was also his. He had allotted ₹8 lakh to be donated to various social and academic institutions post his passing away.

Ratanji had a keen desire to study the reasons for poverty. He was intrigued that many were wealthy without putting any effort, while millions suffered despite working hard. He set up a chair at the London School of Economics (LSE) for the study of this phenomenon, setting aside a donation of £1,400 each year. The contribution was recognized by LSE, which later set up a separate foundation and department in honour of Sir Ratan Tata to identify scholars each year who would benefit from the scholarship. The department was extremely popular and, in an advertisement for the post of its head in 1913, the department shortlisted two names: Clement Atlee and Hughes Dalton. Finally, Atlee was selected for the post. He would, thirty-two years later, go on to become the Prime

Minister of Britain and under his prime ministership India would become independent.

Coincidentally, Dalton, who was not selected then by LSE for the post of its head, became the finance minister in Atlee's cabinet. The work done by the department over the years has produced concepts such as the school nutrition programme. In those days, the research done on unorganized workers had significant impact on labour laws.

Ratanji Tata was spiritual in nature. Events in life had made him that way. Once, while sailing to England in 1916, his ship was torpedoed by German U-boats, and he survived by hanging on to a wooden plank for nearly twenty-four hours, before being rescued. His orientation in life was not so much to merely create wealth but to find ways to put it to long-term and permanent use for the benefit of mankind. He wanted to build a memorial for his father in his native Navsari and helped build a community centre, a library and a town hall there in memory of his father, donating a sum of ₹25 lakh. The Sir Dorabji Tata Trust too contributed. Both the brothers were equally inclined towards charity and had given strict instructions that the trusts should not allow religion, caste or such considerations to cloud their decision while deciding the beneficiary.

Ratanji Tata had written in his will, 'If I were to die childless, my entire wealth should be used for the purpose of education, especially areas which focus on improving human life and those that work towards alleviating pain and suffering. The grant should go for original research work, one that combines science and fundamental knowledge.'

In 1918, Ratanji Tata died at the mere age of forty-eight, leaving behind a childless widow, Navajbai. She survived him for another forty-four years. He had kept aside a sum of ₹81 lakh for the explicit purpose of donating to various institutions. (The generosity behind this can be better understood if one takes into account, by comparison, that the construction of the Viceroy's House—which became the Rashtrapati Bhavan in independent India—in those days had cost a little over ₹1 crore.) A part of that was used for setting up the Ratan Tata Industrial Institute, involved in teaching vocational skills to poor children. The institute also worked on providing support to the homeless poor suffering from illnesses, and helped the blind find a living. Ratanji Tata's huge collection of exquisite paintings by celebrated painters was donated to the Prince of Wales Museum in Bombay. Later, the museum opened a separate wing in honour of Dorab and Ratan Tata.

NAVAL HORMUSJI TATA BECOMES NAVAL RATANJI TATA

At birth, Naval Hormusji Tata and Jehangir Ratanji Dadabhoy (JRD) Tata were just thirty-two days apart. Naval might have been born in the Tata family but that is where the similarity ended. There was a world of difference between the two families. JRD was born with a silver spoon while Naval spent his childhood in a foster home. His father Hormusji was a spinning master in Advanced Mills in Ahmedabad. Naval was just four years old when his father died. The household was steeped in poverty. He had two elder brothers. As Hormusji didn't have a pension or a life insurance plan, it was impossible for the family to manage. For a while, the extended Tata families in Navsari took care of them. Eventually, Hormusji's widow moved with the children to Surat, making ends meet by taking on embroidery and stitching work.

Some time later, a chance meeting with Dorabji, during his visit to Surat, changed their destiny. The two older boys were put into J.N. Petit orphanage while Naval, much younger then, was admitted after a year. Naval's mother was not able to pay the subsidized fees for him. The orphanage luckily agreed to waive the amount. It was a hard life for the 300-odd children there. All came from very poor backgrounds. The only entertainment was a visit to the garden once every three weeks. Little did the children know that the life of one of them was about to change dramatically. The lucky boy was Naval.

In 1918, Ratanji died suddenly in London. Like Dorabji, he too did not have any children. The question of the last rites came about and led Dorabji to think of adopting a child as his late brother's heir. He recalled that three children from his extended family resided in the J.N. Petit orphanage. Dorabji's and Ratanji's mother Hirabai—the wife of Jamsetji Tata—was the sister of Hormusji's mother. Quite naturally, Dorabji thought of one of the three boys.

He liked Naval the moment he saw him, and introduced the child to Ratanji's widow Navajbai, who agreed to adopt him. The fate lines on the young Naval's palm had suddenly been altered. Naval Tata once said that it was like a fairy princess waving her magical wand at him—in an instant, his life changed completely.

But Naval was not allowed to leave the orphanage. The rule stated that such children who were being housed free of cost had to complete their matriculation exam before being allowed to go. So, Naval joined the Tata household after completing his matriculation. He had been catapulted from the orphanage to the immensely wealthy world of the Tatas.

He later graduated from Bombay University in economics and then proceeded to London for a short course in accountancy. When he returned to Bombay, it was 1930, and he joined the Tata group as an executive.

Naval Ratanji Tata's forte lay in labour laws and labour welfare and he was known as an expert worldwide on these two subjects. He represented the unions in the International Labour Organization (ILO) for a period of thirty-eight years. He was later the Vice-Chairman of the Tata group. Like the other Tatas, he was interested in sports and held senior offices in social, educational and welfare work. He was President of the Indian Hockey Federation for fifteen years and was at the helm when the Indian hockey team won the Olympic gold in 1948, 1952 and 1956. He never forgot his humble roots—the fact that he had stayed in orphanages in his early childhood. He would always be ready to help deserving but poor students, a trait which he passed on to his children as well. The Tata flag was to fly high. And it was to be carried by his eldest son Ratan Naval Tata. However, all that was still decades away.

CHAIRMAN NOWROJI SAKLATWALA

Following RD's death in 1926 and Dorabji's passing in 1932, the man chosen to take over the reins of the Tata group was Nowroji Saklatwala, Jamsetji's nephew—the son of Jamsetji's sister Virbai and her husband Bapuji Saklatwala. Nowroji, not the least bit nervous, took it in his stride.

After all, despite not being a direct descendant of the Tata family, he had worked long enough with Dorabji to have imbibed the group's values.

Nowroji Bapuji Saklatwala had joined the group immediately after graduating from St Xavier's College. He worked with Dorabji on all his projects. Like his cousin Dorabji, he was also fond of cricket and was the captain of the team at Parsi Gymkhana. He did a lot for the game of cricket. One of his major contributions was the formation of the Cricket Club of India. The CCI later constructed Brabourne Stadium, which too was with the support of Nowroji.

Two years after he took charge, a massive earthquake ravaged Munger in Bihar. It was the Tata group that took the lead in providing help and sent a special relief train to Munger, carrying workers who constructed a temporary hospital to take care of the wounded. More than 400 people were treated and medical workers also ensured that diseases like chicken pox, cholera and typhoid did not spread. The massive earthquake had attracted the attention of the Viceroy, Lord Willingdon, who visited Munger with his entourage. To his surprise, the Tata workers had already set up camp and were busy taking care of the wounded. Upon his return home, the viceroy sent a telegram to Jamshedpur congratulating the Tatas with a message, 'The Tatas have won splendidly ... Willingdon.' It is therefore only befitting that Nowroji Saklatvala was also the person responsible for the setting up of the Tata Institute of Social Sciences (TISS) in Mumbai.

A social organization called Nagpada Neighbourhood House, located close to the Bombay Central railway station in south Bombay, was run in the 1930s by one Dr Clifford Manschardt, an American. The science of social work was not yet well established. Dr Clifford believed that social work was a subject that needed to be taught. He believed that independent India would need a large number of social workers and that there was a need to teach the subject formally. He presented his ideas to the Tata group—naturally, it was accepted wholeheartedly.

The group, under the chairmanship of Saklatwala, decided to contribute towards making this a reality with funds from the Sir Dorabji Tata Trust, which led to the setting up of the Sir Dorabji

Tata Graduate School of Social Work in 1936. Nine years later, it was rechristened as the Tata Institute of Social Sciences.

Saklatwala's main job was to run the Tata companies, in which he had the support of a young man, a family member, whose cabin was next to his and whose job was to look at all papers going to and from Nowroji's desk. The appointment of the young man turned out to be fortuitous. Just six years after taking over the group, Saklatvala died of a massive heart attack in 1938. The job now fell on the shoulders of the young man: Jehangir Ratanji Dadabhoy Tata, just thirty-four years of age. It was the birth of the industrialist of the century—J.R.D. Tata.

6

Jehangir's World

The Champs-Élysée in Paris is one of the most impressive avenues in the world. There are tall buildings on either side, and the footpaths have well-manicured grass. Chestnut trees line the avenue, reminding one of disciplined schoolchildren standing to attention. Shops display the best brands. There are coffee houses, pubs and high-class nightclubs.

On one end of the Champs-Élysée is the Place de la Concorde, which has the Arc de Triomphe honouring those who fought and died for France in the French Revolutionary and Napoleonic Wars. The construction began in 1806 and was completed thirty years later. But Napoleon died in 1821. His dead body was kept at the then under-construction Arc for a while. Following the death in 1885 of famous writer Victor Hugo, the author of *Les Misérables*, his body was also kept there for public viewing.

As one travels in the direction of the River Seine, one comes across a beautiful garden. Turning left, one reaches a lane called the Rue Halévy known for its Opera House. The second house on this lane is what we are interested in. It is easily recognizable with its huge, arched doorway. The house stands as beautiful as it did in 1904. It was here that Sooni Tata gave birth to a boy on 29 July 1904. Her husband RD was still grieving the loss of his beloved cousin and Tata family patriarch Jamsetji, who had passed away just two months earlier in Bad Nauheim in Germany on 19 May. RD had been with Jamsetji in those last days.

Jamsetji, despite having had a heart attack, was desperately holding on to see his eldest son Dorabji once more. Comforted by that fact that his cousin RD and son Dorabji had mended their differences and were working together, Jamsetji told RD that he wished they would be able to preserve, if not build on, whatever he had created. He also gave RD his wristwatch. It was a solid gold Patek Philippe and the dial had an image of Jamsetji's mother. RD, overwhelmed by the gift, was also acutely aware that Jamsetji had little time left. He was worried that Dorabji had not yet reached Paris, from where he and his wife would drive down to Bad Nauheim.

Dorabji and his wife Meherbai had left Bombay for Paris but, by the time they reached on 18 May, Jamsetji was slipping in and out of consciousness. They tried to wake Jamsetji, who opened his eyes a bit and smiled weakly, mumbling incoherently. Dorabji and RD tried to decipher his words but to no avail. Jamsetji died the next day. RD recalled that it was just two years earlier that he had visited Bombay with his wife Sooni and had been welcomed by Dorabji and his wife Meherbai. Sooni had till then spent all her life in France and had been overwhelmed and a little nervous in Bombay, in the midst of a large Parsi family and its traditions. On top of it, she had no one to speak French with. RD had managed to get a French-speaking household help from Pondicherry. They had five domestic helpers then, one of them being Japanese.

We learn a lot of this from the letters Sooni used to write to her mother. To pass the time, she would write a letter each day. The letters reflect the social life of the time. 'These Parsi men dress quite strangely,' she writes in one of them. 'They wear a strange cap over their largely western dress.' She was quite taken aback seeing the men wear a dress similar to the saree worn by the ladies. She did not know that it was a traditional dhoti which the men were wearing. It was quite a culture shock for her to see the British, Portuguese, Arabs and the many Indians wearing turbans, which she had never seen before, and that they mingled and lived alongside each other.

It was the year after she landed in India that the celebration on account of the coronation of England's Emperor Edward VII took place. Sooni describes it in her letters. 'Bombay has been decorated like never before ... you have to see the Elphinstone College building to believe it. The building, built in the Gothic style, is looking exquisite with all the lights burning brightly, as if it is the sole representative of the British supremacy.' Sooni's letters were also an indication of her settling down in Bombay.

A major reason for her to be able to do so was her adoption of the Parsi religion. It had never happened before. Not only was she from a different religion but a foreigner to boot. It was a shock to all other Parsis. But it was RD's idea. He was quite religious and wanted his wife to adopt his religion. Sooni agreed. She would get up early morning and learn the Zoroastrian prayers. She learnt, despite initial troubles, to wear the saree the Parsi way. She learnt to wear the Parsi blouse and put the pallu over her head.

The big day finally arrived. Despite a little resistance and some tension in the air, she was initiated into the Parsi religion in the presence of the religious heads. But many elders who opposed the idea had boycotted the ceremony. Meherbai stood behind Sooni, giving her moral support. RD was aware of her habit of writing letters. He warned her, 'You may write whatever you want to, except for one thing.'

Sooni knew what that exception was. She never confided in her mother about her having tasted the holy water. Meherbai had advised her earlier, 'You can just act as if you are sipping the water. Don't actually drink it.' The vessel containing the water was brought to Sooni, who was repulsed at its smell. Her face fell but she somehow managed to make a show of having drunk it. Later, she asked, 'What was that anyway?'

RD answered, 'It is cow's urine ... and for heaven's sake, don't mention this to your mother.' Funnily, much against the advice of

RD, Sooni did write to her mother warning her, 'Don't ever let Ratan know that you know ... I don't want him to feel that we are insulting his religion. Now I too am a Parsi. You cannot imagine how happy I am. It gives me great pleasure that I could do this much for someone who loves me so immensely.'

Sooni was pregnant when she was inducted into the Parsi religion. Soon thereafter, they left for France. 'I will knit sweaters and socks for him,' she had said. But the baby turned out to be a she and not a he, and was named Sylla. The small family of three returned to Bombay later. Sooni was pregnant for the second time when Jamsetji died on 19 May 1904. She delivered a beautiful, fair boy on 29 July the same year but RD was not in France then. He blessed his newborn son, saying, 'He will win the world; just the way Jamsetji did ... he will be a conqueror ... let us call him Jehangir.' And Jehangir spent halcyon days growing up in France.

JRD: THE EARLY YEARS

Two little boys sat talking about India, unaware of the success of the Tata family, as they lounged about on a beach in northern France. One boy's father was Louis Blériot, whose claim to fame was that he was the first to fly a plane over the English Channel in 1909. From where they sat, the boys could see Adolphe Pégoud carrying out some aerobatics in a family-owned plane. After a while, Pégoud landed the plane on the beach, much to the astonishment and delight of the boys. Young impressionable minds do not forget such incidents easily and these often play a role in determining the future.

The younger of the two boys was surely impressed by Pégoud and secretly wished to become an ace pilot one day—to do something big in the field of aviation. His name was Jehangir.

Jehangir would recall his childhood with great clarity in his later years. Apart from his elder sister Sylla, he had a younger sister Rodabeh and two brothers, Darab and Jimmy. His father shuttled between France and India. His mother Sooni took care of the five children untiringly, travelling continents without complaining.

Sooni was an independent-minded woman, with a fair sense of humour. She was quite adept at painting, photography and making French cuisine. She was also a beautiful, blue-eyed blonde. Jehangir wrote in one of his memoirs that his mother was so beautiful that heads would turn whenever they entered a hotel; people would let out a deep sigh as she vanished out of sight and they had to get back to their meals. She was delighted that the eyes of her fourth child, Darab, were blue but unfortunately they later lost their bluish tinge! Sooni was quite disappointed.

Sooni had no servants back home in France, unlike in Bombay. Except for the help of a cook, she would manage everything on her own. RD liked staying in France; he was attracted to their art and way of life. But there was too much work waiting for him back in India for him to have the luxury of staying there for long. He decided to build a holiday home in France and selected a place in the seaside resort town of Hardelot.

Once he started building his house at Hardelot, he realized he could build an upscale colony, which he did subsequently. One of the owners, incidentally, was Loius Blériot. He would land his plane on the beach and park it in a shed in the garden. Young Jehangir's imagination had already taken wing watching Blériot and Pégoud fly.

Meanwhile, the children spent half the year in Bombay and the other half in France. The medium of instruction in Bombay's Cathedral and John Connon School was English, and in France the children solely used French. Shuttling between France and India was taking a toll on the children's education. Realizing this, RD decided to let Sooni and the children live on in France and young Jehangir took quite naturally to French manners and society. He enjoyed his studies in art and science, both of which received the same kind of respect there.

But things were to change soon. War loomed large on the horizon, threatening to disrupt everything. When World War I began, ten-year-old Jehangir and his siblings were in Switzerland with their grandmother. When they returned to France, they were surprised to find their mother in a nurse's uniform. Sooni, at the request of the French government, had joined the medical corps. Warning bells would sound, announcing the arrival of enemy aircraft. Jehangir, instead of hiding in the bunkers, would be on the rooftop, watching the planes in fascination. He would watch for hours the planes dropping loads of bombs like eggs, while the anti-aircraft guns, perched on top of the Eiffel Tower, tried to shoot them down. These experiences added to his love for flying.

The war effort was doubling each day, adding to Sooni's work. She was being stretched to her limits, managing her house and children and her job in the medical corps. To cap it all, it was discovered that she had tuberculosis. RD was in Bombay at that time and had to decide whether to let his wife and children stay on in France or move them to Bombay. He decided to bring them back even though it was dangerous to sail, with the German U-boats torpedoing whatever they could. The family reached Bombay safely and RD housed them at the Taj Hotel.

However, Sooni found the humid weather very difficult to cope with. RD was tempted to move them to the nearby hill station of Panchgani, where a new health facility had been set up on land donated by Jamsetji. But RD also had a lot of business connections in Japan and finally decided it would be best to move the family to Yokohama, taking up a big house on rent there. There was an English school in the city, which the children joined. Sooni found the weather suitable and the family settled down, despite the occasional earthquake and cyclone at times shaking the wooden house! But luckily, no one was hurt.

Jehangir enjoyed his schooldays in Yokohama. He was fourteen and befriended an eighteen-year-old French girl whose family was staying in Yokohama. Later, she married a French military officer. JRD, even in his late seventies, could recall her telephone number in Japanese. He did meet her once later.

Sooni and the children spent all of 1917 in Yokohama. Seeing that her health had improved considerably, RD decided to move them back to Bombay. It seemed safe enough in 1918 to sail from Japan to Colombo though the war had not yet ended. The family set sail on the Japanese passenger ship *Hirano Maru* and Jehangir spent hours learning to type on a Remington typewriter that he borrowed from someone on board. The ship reached Colombo and then finally arrived in Bombay via Madras, before continuing onward to England. A few days later, they received the news that German U-boats had destroyed the *Hirano Maru* and sent all its passengers into a watery grave.

Sooni was comfortable in the Bombay winters but the monsoon unsettled her again. On 11 November 1918, World War I ended with the signing of the armistice, and RD decided to move the family back to France. The country was limping back to normalcy under Prime Minister George Clemenceau. The Treaty of Versailles was signed under Clemenceau, imposing punitive territorial, military and economic provisions on defeated Germany.

Jehangir, now fifteen, closely observed the events unfolding in France. He spent a lot of time reading books on history. His nationalistic fervour arose the more he read, and he was convinced that British rule in India had to end one day. The years in Europe had been opportune, giving him the chance to observe and see many world-changing events at close quarters. It was an education in itself and shaped his personality. Jehangir wanted to go for further studies to Cambridge. It was a common belief then that one's education was incomplete if one did not spend some time at Oxford or Cambridge. But RD was against the idea and wanted Jehangir to spend time with his mother.

By 1922, after three years in France, Sooni's health had improved considerably. RD wanted her to move back with him from France to Bombay and started building a house for them on Malabar Hill. The house, overlooking the sea, was to be built in the French style. An excited Sooni started buying furniture for her new home and they decided to move to Bombay the next year. But it was not to happen. Sooni's health deteriorated suddenly and, by the time 1923 came around, she was in bad shape. Unfortunately, it was also the time that Tata Steel, back in India, was going through a severe crisis. Cheaper steel from Britain was creating serious competition. RD used all his political connections with people like Motilal Nehru, M.A. Jinnah and others to help the business. To make matters worse, the death knell of the Tata Industrial Bank also sounded in 1923.

A wife battling death, a banking business that changed hands, and a steel business on the brink of collapse—RD was truly in the thick of it. In the midst of all this he received a telegram informing him that his wife's condition had deteriorated further. His wife and family needed him in Paris; the business needed him full-time in India.

It is a testimony to his mental strength, endurance and integrity that he promised Dorabji that he would leave for Paris only when things improved a little on the business front. Dorabji needed his help badly and he was not going to shy away. He managed to raise the required funds and matters were a little more stable when he bought a ticket for France. But death does not wait for anyone. RD had boarded the ship when one of his office assistants brought him a telegram they had just received; Sooni was no more.

She was only forty-three years old. She had so much to look forward to. Jehangir was to win the world. RD had built a bungalow for her so that she could stay in Bombay. She had been looking forward to shifting there. But her life was too short for her ambitions and dreams. After all, she was a Tata too, and their dreams always far exceeded their lives.

RD was unable to spend the final moments with her. She was silent forever now. In her memory, he named the house Sunita. He was unable to reach Paris in time for the last rites and she was buried in a prestigious burial ground much before his ship reached Paris. The Père Lachaise is a garden cemetery, with trees shading the tombs, including those of many celebrities such as Jean de la Fontaine, Oscar Wilde, Alfred de Musset and Molière. With a little breeze, flowers shower down on the graves. The fallen flowers were to be drenched that day by the tears of RD.

With Sooni's death, the responsibility of raising the children fell on RD and his mother-in-law. RD spent a week in Paris arranging for the family to move to Bombay. Jehangir wanted to study engineering at Cambridge and RD decided to move him to England for a year to study at a Grammar school before he sought admission for engineering studies. Dorabji had given a hefty donation of £25,000, which would help Jehangir to secure admission to the college of his choice. But Jehangir was not destined for Cambridge. That year, the French government came up with a new rule—one year of compulsory military service for the eldest boy of each family. As a citizen of France, JRD had to enlist in the army. In between the Grammar school and his time in the army, he spent a brief spell at home in Bombay.

Once in Bombay, the children were beginning to realize just how strict a disciplinarian their father was. RD, trying his best to tutor the children, was very particular about time. The car to take them for tuition arrived at 8.30 a.m. sharp, not a minute late. They dared not run to the car, breakfast in hand. A cold stare from their father was enough to stop them in their tracks. At the stroke of half past four every afternoon, they would return home. RD followed this schedule so that he could spend more time with the children and also reduce the burden on their grandmother, Mrs Brière.

They would often go for picnics. One such picnic was to the nearby hill station of Matheran. The train dropped them at Neral, where a car waited to take them to Matheran. They would reach their destination, Dinshaw Petit's bungalow, in two hours. Dinshaw was in the textile business. It was here that Jehangir's sister, Sylla, met Fali, the Petits' older son. Sylla was an accomplished tennis player, learning under Jal Naoroji, who happened to be Dadabhai Naoroji's grandson. It was a lovely gathering at Matheran. Later, Sylla married Fali.

JEHANGIR AND THE FRENCH ARMY

The French government, in the meanwhile, sent Jehangir a reminder about compulsory military service. Jehangir, who knew how to ride a horse and was keen on learning polo, thought it over and decided to use his grandmother's good offices to try and enrol into one of the cavalry services. By mid-1924, thanks to his grandmother's referral, he was accepted into a cavalry unit but it turned out to be an Algerian one! The horses there, unlike the French, were pure Arab ones—fast and big. The saddle too was strange, rough and pointed at both ends. Barely two days into the unit, Jehangir had bruises on his backside. When he consulted his senior officer, he assured him that his body would get used to it and that he could try sitting in a water container, similar in design to the saddle.

Little did Jehangir know that the moment he immersed himself in the cold water, it would sting his sensitive skin no end! Luckily for him, the unit was looking for someone to type and Jehangir volunteered. He was immediately taken in to assist the captain of the unit in typing out letters and other correspondence.

A year passed by. Thanks to his dedicated work and the skill he showed in horse riding, Jehangir was selected for promotion by mid-1925 and had to complete a special training course. He requested his father for permission. RD was upset. 'Are you mad?' he wrote. 'Enough of your army training.' Jehangir knew he had no choice but to decline the training and return to India. It proved to be a lucky coincidence. A few days after his departure, the entire cavalry unit was killed after it was deployed in Morocco. Each and every soldier in the unit was killed by the bandit leader Abdul Kareem and his men.

Jehangir's dream of going to Cambridge to pursue his studies in engineering was also not approved by RD. He wanted Jehangir to help him in business and asked him to return to India and work with him. It was a request Jehangir could not refuse. And so Jehangir reached Bombay and started working with his father.

7

Baptism by Fire

When Jehangir joined the business, the Tata headquarters were housed in a building called Navsari Bhawan in Fort. Bombay House, the prestigious headquarters we know now, had not been built then. The construction of Bombay House was given to George Wittet, who had built the magnificent Gateway of India. By the time Jehangir returned from the army in 1925, the building was ready. He was introduced to the Managing Director of Tata Steel, John Peterson, by his father the day he reported to work.

Peterson was a retired British ICS officer who had worked in the supplies department during World War I. He came in contact with the Tatas as he was responsible for getting steel supplies to England. He was diligent in his job without being cynical. He was disciplined yet practical. RD liked his dedication and offered him a job with the Tatas, an unprecedented act. A British officer was being asked to work for an Indian company! To RD's pleasant surprise, Peterson accepted the offer and joined as Managing Director of Tata Steel, but based at the Bombay office.

RD introduced Jehangir to him and said his son would be working with Peterson. Peterson's office was a simple affair, with just a few wooden chairs and a wooden table. Jehangir had a similar small office next to Peterson's. His job was to look at all the correspondence going in and out of Peterson's office. Peterson was particular about the language used for correspondence. He had his views on how to advise someone, how to praise another without exaggeration, and such. It was a trait JRD was to pick up.

After working for a few months under Peterson, Jehangir was asked to move to Jamshedpur. The year was 1926. RD readily agreed. Jehangir boarded the train run by the Great Indian Peninsula Railway (GIPR), on which he would journey for another thirty-two hours before reaching his destination.

Jamshedpur was already famous as the Mecca of Indian industry. Many famous personalities including Gandhiji had visited the place. Jehangir had heard a lot about the factory, how his father had managed many difficult situations there. Jehangir had been put up in town administrator J.K. Sondhi's house and his job was to spend a day in each department and understand its workings. He spent his evenings reading a book called *The Shaping of Steel*. It was the story of TISCO. Soon, two months passed by and summer arrived. Normally, RD would spend time with the family in Paris. Jehangir's siblings were even now in France with Mrs Brière. But RD wanted Jehangir to stay back and learn. He felt Jehangir had just got into the rhythm and that it would be best for him to continue learning about TISCO.

So RD, aged seventy, went to Paris alone and took the family to their holiday home at Hardelot. One evening, Sylla requested her father to dance. Not wanting to refuse, RD agreed. After a while, he felt tired and lay down. He had mild chest pain. When he got up to go to the bathroom, he collapsed there. It was a severe heart attack which turned fatal. There was no time to call the doctors. Ratanji Dadabhoy Tata, aka RD, was no more. RD, who had supported his cousin Jamsetji Tata since the very beginning of the Tata business, had left the world without any warning.

The message of his father's death reached twenty-two-year-old Jehangir camped at Jamshedpur. It was a shock difficult to bear. The burden of responsibility was enormous. He had four siblings and a grandmother to look after. This was the beginning of the transformation of the young Jehangir into JRD.

RD'S DEATH: THE PASSING OF AN ERA

By the end of that year, JRD, now the head of his family, had also been appointed the head of the Tata empire. He made the long journey by train to reach Bombay, and then a longer journey by ship to reach France. RD was buried next to Sooni.

The news of RD's death spread across India. Jamnalal Bajaj, founder of the Bajaj group, said, 'If all businessmen in India were even partially as nationalistic as RD, our country would reach tremendous heights.'

JRD had to return to Bombay after his father's death. During the long and seemingly unending journey back to Bombay, JRD wondered whether his father had had a premonition about his death and had therefore not permitted him to study in Cambridge, but insisted he return to India.

Upon his return he was in for another shock. RD had built homes in Bombay, Panchgani, Poona and Hardelot, and opened offices in Hong Kong and Singapore, while his companies were undergoing losses. An agent based in London, responsible for investing in markets, had syphoned off profits and left further losses for the company to bear. Most of RD's lenders were happy to waive off their loans, but not Dorabji Tata, from whom RD had borrowed money personally as well.

Clearly, the first issue JRD had to tackle was the financial mess. He announced that each rupee would be returned, and began by shutting down all loss-making businesses. He also sold 'Sunita', the house RD had built for Sooni and the family. Another house to be put on the block was a bungalow in Ganeshkhind, Poona. The holiday home at Hardelot was the next to go. He moved, along with his siblings, into the Taj Mahal Hotel.

However, RD had signed an agreement stating JRD would join the Tata group at a salary of ₹750 per month. JRD, thus, continued to work under Peterson, learning the ropes of the business. Having made the resolve to focus completely on the business, he gave up French citizenship. It wasn't as easy a decision as it may sound. His mother tongue was French. His mother was French and JRD would think in his native language! To replace all that with English was a daunting task. Just recently, his father had been awarded the highest civilian award by the French government. It was not easy to break ties with France.

Above all, JRD was young, had lost his father, was learning the ropes and had great ambitions; all this needed a counsel and moral support, which Peterson provided. 'He took the place of my father,' JRD writes. Once, Burjorji Padshah, an old hand at the Tatas working since the time of Jamsetji and having played an important role in the setting up of IISc, sent a proposal to Peterson. JRD, reviewing the proposal, pointed out many errors. Peterson counselled him saying that RD had once sent a proposal back asking it to be written in English, but while such sarcasm coming from RD was acceptable, it would not befit JRD.

He carried a notebook with him which had 'JRD' engraved in a beautiful font. His love for French poetry saw him noting many poems in it; writers and poets like Victor Hugo, Alfonse de Lamartine, Alfred de Mussay and Charles Baudelaire were his constant companions in his readings. His favourite topics were love and death. JRD would go on to become a legendary businessman but his love for poetry did not drown in the pursuit of wealth creation. He did not allow the romantic dreamer in him to die.

JRD was often ill at this time but would spend his time in bed reviewing correspondence and giving instructions. His youngest sister, Rodabeh, who was taking care of him, said, 'Don't you see you are getting weaker by the day? Why don't you rest and recover first?' JRD, the man in a hurry, said, 'I have to prove that I am a Tata first!'

MARRIAGE AND AN AIR RACE

RD had not allowed JRD to buy a motorcycle. Like all youngsters, JRD too was fascinated by the two-wheeler and bought for himself an old one for ₹100. He later bought himself a Bugatti convertible. JRD, zipping on the roads, would cover the distance from Poona to

Bombay in just two and a half hours. But he was careful when he drove in Bombay. He loved to take a slow drive on Peddar Road, which had lovely bungalows on either side, with the sea close by, in the evenings when the municipal lamplighter would be busy illuminating the roads.

JRD loved the evening hours and, on days when the roads were free of pedestrians, he would race with his friends. He lost his friend Russa Mehta during one such race. The accident took place on Peddar Road when the car hit a lamp post.

The police arrested JRD based on a false witness who stated that it was JRD who was driving the car. JRD sought out lawyer Jack Vicaji, recommended to be the best. Incidentally, Vicaji lived just behind the Taj Mahal Hotel. JRD started visiting Jack's house to discuss the case and, luckily for him, Jack argued the case successfully and dismissed the eyewitness produced by the police. The judge not only held JRD innocent but rapped the police for producing a false witness.

Another happy outcome of the case was that JRD fell in love with Thelma, Jack's beautiful niece. Her parents were separated. Her mother was in Italy while her father toured the world, thus leaving the responsibility of her upbringing to her uncle Jack.

The Vicaji household had been an extremely rich one, once known to be lenders to someone as wealthy as the Nizam of Hyderabad. However, the Nizam refused to return a large loan taken from the Vicaji family. Despite their appeal to the British government, they lost their case. The later Nizam, Salar Jung, took pity on them and offered a monthly pension which the proud Vicajis declined. Jack Vicaji thereafter moved to Bombay and started practising law. Thelma was under his care and was now hopelessly in love with JRD! The young couple got married on 23 December 1930. Thelma's mother sent her best wishes for the marriage from Italy. It fell upon Jack Vicaji, as expected, to get everything done.

THE AGA KHAN AIR RACE

JRD had got his pilot's licence just a year earlier in 1929, three years after his father's death, and was so proud of his Flying Club membership card showing 'Member Number One' that he carried it for ages with him! In 1930, the Aga Khan, the religious leader of the Shia Muslims, announced an award for anyone who would fly solo from England to India in the month of May. Though a religious leader, he was one of the wealthiest men in the world. The award for the winner was £500.

JRD put his name down for the race. Another Indian participating in the race was one Manmohan Singh, who began his journey from England towards India. He was a good pilot but his navigation was not as good. Planes in those days lacked today's navigational aids; pilots had to manage with maps. Singh got lost in Europe for a while and returned to England dejected. This happened twice. The joke doing the rounds then was that Singh's plane, *Miss India*, was so named because he had a habit of missing India!

A third Indian was also in the fray, eighteen-year-old Aspy Engineer. He was to fly from England to India, while JRD chose to do the journey in reverse—from Karachi in India to England. It was coincidental that they both met at the Alexandria airport in Egypt. Seeing a worried Aspy, JRD asked what the problem was. He replied, 'I don't have a spare spark plug which I badly need.'

JRD gave his spare spark plug to Aspy, who touched down in Karachi before JRD could land in London. Aspy, while accepting the reward, conveyed his gratitude to JRD for the spare spark plug. JRD shrugged it off, saying he never considered anyone a competitor and that he was bound to help a person in need.

Winning at any cost was not on JRD's mind. He believed in fair play. This large-hearted man was to gain world reknown but his humility remained intact. Aspy Engineer later went on to join the Indian Air Force and rose to become the Chief of Air Staff, while JRD went on to become India's best-known industrialist. Meanwhile, another benefit of this race held in May 1930 was that JRD's participation in such a prestigious air race and earning a name for himself endeared him to Thelma even more.

SETTLING DOWN TO MARRIED LIFE

After they got married in December 1930, Thelma and JRD moved to their house in Colaba. JRD's siblings were grown up now and loved to fly. His younger brother Jimmy was a very good pilot and JRD had no doubt that Jimmy would play an important role in any aviation company that JRD would launch.

Soon after getting his licence in 1929, JRD also met British pilot Neville Vincent, who had come to India with the intention of popularizing air travel and was offering free rides. JRD knew how to fly and Vincent, while talking to him, said, 'You run such a large business. Why don't you start your own airline?' JRD decided to start an aviation company in partnership with Vincent. JRD trusted him completely. Vincent was an ace pilot who had flown in World War I. Once during the war, he had to force-land his plane in the desert of Arabia. Since it was already dark, he and the co-pilot could not take off. By then the Arabs had surrounded them on all sides. Daredevil Neville, realizing that he had only one gun attached to the nose of the plane, told his co-pilot to take charge of the gun while he, holding the tail of the plane, spun it around as the co-pilot fired at the attacking Arabs. The Arabs vanished quickly and, having spent the night in the desert, the two pilots flew back the next morning.

JRD, who trusted Neville Vincent's courage, initiative and resourcefulness, duly broached the subject of starting an airline with Dorabji Tata, who was not quite as excited.

Where Jamsetji, Dorabji's father, had been open-minded and willing to take risks, Dorabji was more prudent. Dorabji had gone through bad financial times, when he had raised money by selling off his personal wealth. He was thus not in favour of investing in a risky venture like an airline.

Quite obviously, JRD was not in agreement with Dorabji. JRD persisted, 'We don't need much capital to begin with, maybe 2 lakhs or so.' Finally, Dorabji seemed convinced; it was not a large amount. He agreed and JRD immediately converted a dirt road in Juhu into a landing strip for his small De Havilland Puss Moth aircraft. In those days there was no equipment to support flying, including runways. There were no radios, and the 'autopilot' was decades away. Despite the obstacles, JRD was focused on getting his airline off the ground.

BIRTH OF TATA AIRLINES

The new aviation company was christened Tata Aviation Services and was to be inaugurated on 15 September 1932 at Bombay's Juhu aerodrome. But incessant rains over the previous few days made the airstrip unfit for the plane to take off. The inauguration was thus postponed and the take-off venue changed; it was now Karachi. The flight took off on 15 October, in the presence of the Karachi postmaster and the municipal commissioner. JRD was dressed in white trousers, a white half-sleeve shirt and a pair of goggles. The winds were against him, making the journey a little tough. He stopped at Ahmedabad for refuelling. The bullock cart ferrying the aviation oil filled four gallons of fuel into the Puss Moth's tank. He landed at Juhu that afternoon at 1.30. The *Statesman* reported the landing the next day. JRD was asked as he landed, 'What do you plan to do now?'

'I intend to start a regular Bombay to Karachi postal service,' he replied. The airline started services soon, flying Karachi–Bombay–Madras. Why did JRD choose Karachi? Well, the British postal service planes serviced the Indian subcontinent up to Karachi only. JRD decided to connect his plane service from Madras to Karachi via Bombay.

Tata Aviation Services was known for its prompt service and not a single minute of delay. In the monsoon, the plane would negotiate its way through the mountainous region of the Deccan plateau, yet arrive in time at Madras. The Tatas would have felt proud that the British, known for their efficiency and fastidious nature, asked their employees to look to the Tatas as their role model when it came to punctuality and service standards.

The Tatas had approached the British government for funding, which was denied. They then approached the people sending their goods regularly for loans. They managed to collect enough funds and the services ran regularly for three years.

In 1936, Jimmy lost his life in a freak air accident in Vienna. He was only twenty-one years old. It was a massive shock for JRD and a huge tragedy for the entire family. He decided to bury his brother in France next to the graves of his parents. JRD could hardly find time to grieve his brother's death as the aviation business was booming. Within a year, the company started making profits. JRD soon bought a bigger plane and started a Delhi–Bombay service.

Meanwhile, Nowroji Saklatwala had taken over as Chairman of the Tata group in 1932, filling the void left by Dorabji's death earlier that year. Nowroji's main job was to run the Tata companies. And he had the support of JRD, whose cabin was next to his and whose job was to look at all papers going to and from Nowroji's desk. On the face of it, the job was tedious and boring but JRD worked diligently. It was a great learning and gave him insights into the workings of the Tata group.

Saklatwala was hardworking and studious by nature, but he took a conservative approach, not venturing into anything new. He was fond of cricket; many people recalled his holding a ball in one hand and a 555 cigarette in the other! He was more than sixty years old when he took over as the group head. Within six years of taking charge, Saklatwala died of a sudden heart attack in 1938, while on tour to Europe. He was the third Tata chief to have died on European soil.

8

J.R.D. Tata: Chairman, Tata Sons

An emergency meeting of the Tata board was called on 26 July 1938. Those present included JRD, Jamsetji Tata's fourth sister's son Sorabji D. Saklatwala, Ardeshir Dalal and Hormasji Pherozshah Mody. The board was chaired by Sorabji Saklatwala. They paid homage to Nowroji Saklatwala with a two-minute silence before they began the proceedings. Saklatwala then presented the next item on the agenda: to appoint JRD as the Chairman of Tata Sons. Ardeshir Dalal seconded the same. At the young age of thirty-four, JRD was given charge of the entire Tata group.

In JRD's appointment an important role was also played by Naval Ratanji Tata, who, prior to his adoption by Ratanji Tata's widow, had been Naval Hormusji Tata, a relative of the family. After adoption as the late Ratanji's son, he was sent to England for higher studies and returned to join the Tata group on 1 June 1930. His job title was 'Despatch Clerk and Assistant Secretary', his monthly salary ₹150. He got his first promotion three years after joining and was transferred to the aviation company as an executive. After five years he became a manager.

By then, JRD had progressed well. No doubt, in 1938, when Nowroji Saklatwala died, JRD was the automatic choice for the top job. Compared to JRD, Naval was not as successful. His forte was labour laws and labour welfare and he was to be known later as an expert worldwide on these two subjects, eventually representing the unions in the International Labour Organization (ILO) for a period of thirty-eight years. Now, Naval himself proposed JRD's name for the chairman's post. JRD's name was also fully endorsed by Naval's adopted mother, Lady Navajbai. It is admirable that she did not bat for her own son.

There was no doubt in anyone's mind regarding JRD's candidature. Naval's mother only requested that Naval be made a Director, which was easily accepted. Naval was well deserving of it, in any case. Later, he managed the textile business for the Tata group.

THE BUSINESS OF AVIATION

By 1939, when the Tatas' fledgling aviation business had just begun to take off, World War II forced the British government to seize all planes. There was nothing JRD could do. Vincent came up with an idea: 'Why not build planes while we cannot fly them?' The British government supported the idea and soon a factory was planned to be set up near Poona. The company was christened Tata Aircraft Limited. The Tatas had started hiring manpower but suddenly, to their surprise, the government changed its mind and permission to build planes was abruptly withdrawn. JRD was disappointed, but sadly his troubles were not to end here; another tragedy was round the corner.

In 1943, Vincent flew abroad on business, careful to take flights that used air routes where there was no shelling. However, on his return journey to India he boarded a bomber instead of a passenger aircraft. The pilot was a friend from his flying days. Vincent invited JRD along, saying, 'You may join me if you wish.' These were his last words to JRD, as the bomber was shot down over the ocean. It was a blow JRD found difficult to accept. His younger brother first, and now his dear friend and partner; both had died in plane crashes. JRD felt terribly lonely. He also missed his mentor Peterson, who was no more.

TATA STEEL: THE SILVER LINING

However, a silver lining appeared as the demand for steel rose during the war, requiring Tata Steel's Jamshedpur factory to run overtime. Tanks, made of steel from the Tata factory, were called Tatanagar. They were very popular thanks to their tough frame and body. The tanks would sustain some dents but never did one see the tank ripped apart due to bombshells.

The company flourished. After JRD's arrival, changes were evident not only in business but in the way things were done. Earlier, there were a lot of perquisites which the senior management enjoyed. For example, there was a lift meant only for the managing director of the company. JRD stopped the privileges of a separate dining room or toilets for the top personnel. Everyone was treated equally. Earlier, the Chairman of Tata Sons held the chairmanship for all the group companies. This prevented the next level leadership from blossoming, nor did other top executives see a growth path for themselves. JRD took the bold decision of having a chairman for each company who would take decisions independently. Having established some stability from an administrative point of view, JRD explored new avenues for growth. Within a year, a mega company began to take shape.

THE BIRTH OF TATA CHEMICALS

The British government in 1929 had announced through the Tariff Commission that if India were to lead in industrial development, it needed to invest in chemical processing. This was a valid point as critical chemicals like soda ash and caustic soda were imported then. There was no chemical processing business to speak of in India. Even common salt for cooking had to be imported. Large multinationals, whether British or German, controlled and dominated the markets.

They were reluctant to share the processes with others, making it impossible for any new aspirant to compete.

It was coincidental that the need to start a chemical factory was expressed by the then Maharaja Sayajirao of Baroda state, who wrote a letter to JRD, saying, 'Why don't you start a chemical plant here?' While the two stalwarts were discussing the idea of setting up a chemical plant, another person entered the fray. His name was Kapilram Vakil. He was studying chemical engineering at Manchester. The large domestic cottage industry around the massive coast of India produced salt for consumption in food, and Kapilram asked himself why chemicals could not be produced from the same. After touring extensively, he came to the conclusion that waters off the western coast of India had a larger concentration of salt compared to the waters off the eastern and southern coastlines. Now, it was a question of deciding the place for the manufacturing plant.

Mithapur lies at the western extreme end of Kutch region, nestled between Okha and Dwarka. The region was under Sayajirao Gaekwad as part of the Baroda state. Sayajirao liked the idea proposed by Kapilram and put it forward to Tata, whom he admired. JRD immediately agreed. The experts concurred with Kapilram's observation about the salt content. It was decided that a factory would be set up at Mithapur. Sadly, the proposal to build a factory and the start of World War II coincided.

In such a scenario, to start a factory at the farthest end of Kutch was a daunting task. To reach Mithapur using rail and road was akin to circumnavigating the globe! But JRD was determined. A few foreign experts wanted to know why he was pursuing such a mad enterprise; it did not look sensible from a commercial point of view. JRD simply said they were used to doing such things. He pointed out that people had ridiculed their earlier projects too, which were now running just fine. He said he expected the same outcome here as well.

It was a test of JRD's industriousness. The war had disrupted the movement of goods and it was a challenge to get machinery for the factory. Despite the hassles, JRD placed orders for the plant and machinery. The ship carrying the machinery was attacked and sank, leading to a huge loss. JRD then decided to order the machinery from a country that was not participating in the war. He chose Sweden. The machinery was to travel via Russia. Till then, Russia had not entered the war. From Russia, the ship would sail to India. But as luck would have it, Russia soon entered the war.

JRD had to start the procurement process all over and turned to the US. When the ship left the US port, JRD received a message that the ship that was stuck at the Russian port too had sailed for India! Soon the ship reached the West Asian region safely, finally docking at Bombay. The fate of the ship and machinery that had left the US is not known to date.

Meanwhile, the machinery that reached India was shipped to Mithapur. It had a capacity of producing 200 tonnes of soda ash daily. JRD was keen to double the capacity to 400 tonnes. The question was of finding the right technology and process expertise. He started discussions with a Japanese company but they were unwilling to share their expertise. Then he heard of an Indian, who was returning after studying chemical engineering in the US and looking for a suitable opportunity to work.

JRD sent him a message while he was still on board the ship. The message told him to make a stopover at Germany and learn the technology before landing in India. He could not find much support in Germany and reported that to JRD as soon as he landed in India. That man was Darbari Seth. He was thirty-one years old then.

He said at his very first meeting that there was no point depending on these German and American companies. He said they could set up a plant which would produce 400 tonnes of soda ash daily. JRD asked him to present his case to the executive committee. Darbari Seth presented his ideas to a team of sixteen members. Most of them dismissed his ideas. The only one supporting him was JRD. He fully believed him. Ignoring the comments of the fifteen others, JRD gave Darbari Seth complete freedom to set up the plant the way he had envisaged.

It was the birth of Tata Chemicals. If Jamshedpur is the steel capital of India, Mithapur is considered the Mecca of the chemical industry.

The credit goes to Darbari Seth and, of course, to JRD, who gave him his complete support.

The simple water purifier Tata Swach we see today is a product of Tata Chemicals. The company expanded, with a fertilizer complex at Babrala in Uttar Pradesh and Haldia in West Bengal, and a detergent manufacturing plant at Pithampur in Madhya Pradesh, which was later sold to Jyoti Laboratories.

TATA AIRLINES BECOMES AIR INDIA

While the chemicals business took off, JRD had not forgotten his dream to pursue the aviation business. He requested the British government for Sir Frederick Tim's help. Sir Frederick was heading the civil aviation department and was JRD's friend. The British government agreed to release him from his assignment and allowed JRD to pursue his aviation business, saying, 'The war is going to end soon. You may start preparing for the business.'

The year after the war ended, JRD launched Tata Airlines. It was earlier a division of Tata Sons. JRD decided to issue shares distributing the ownership between the Tatas, the government and the public at large. It was also rechristened and a new airline was born—Air India.

JRD was deeply involved in his plans for Air India. He was keen to buy more planes once the war ended. It was during this time that the logo for Air India was decided.

A few years earlier, an Oxford-educated young man had approached JRD for a job. The young man, Bobby Kooka, impressed Vincent and JRD. When asked about his salary he said, 'Whatever you will pay me.' Vincent agreed to pay him a monthly salary of ₹100. This was in 1938.

Bobby Kooka eventually retired as the Commercial Director many years later. During the time Bobby was recruited, the ticketing of Air India was being managed by Thomas Cook and Company. The advertising agency was J. Walter Thomson, whose artist, Umesh Rao, was Bobby's friend. Bobby asked him to create a mascot for Air India: 'Someone who defines the Indian man. Holding a hookah in hand.

We want to show how relaxed an Air India traveller is and how royal the services are.'

Umesh created the image that we know today as the Maharaja. The Maharaja began merely as a rich Indian potentate, symbolizing graciousness and high living. And somewhere along the line, his creators gave him a distinctive personality: his large moustache, the striped turban and his aquiline nose.

JRD was now eager to spread his wings westwards. He wanted to start a Bombay–London service. He realized that India was positioned uniquely from a geographical perspective. Today, companies like Boeing talk of the geographical advantage of India, but JRD had sensed the opportunity to serve the regions around India, including the Far East, Australasia and China on one side and Europe and the Middle East on the other. He was waiting for the right opportunity to begin.

9

Independence Dawns

Dear Jawaharlal,

On this day my thoughts go to you, whose steadfast and inspired leadership have brought India to her goal through these long years of struggle and suffering. I rejoice that you who have always held so high the torch of freedom are the first Prime Minister of free India and I send my heartfelt wishes for success in the heavy task of guiding her to her great destiny.

Jeh

14 August 1947

That JRD would remember his friend on the eve of India's Independence was quite natural. They were dear friends. Their fathers, Motilal Nehru and R.D. Tata, had been good friends. Motilal had helped RD a lot during the time when he was setting up Tata Steel. It was quite logical that the friendship continued into the next generation.

They had similar traits, Jawaharlal and JRD. Both had spent their childhoods in Europe, which allowed them to be open-minded. They had both returned to India and had struggled to adapt to the Indian way. There was an invisible bond between the two. But that never tempted JRD to enter politics. He believed that those engaged in the business of wealth creation should focus their energies on the business. He wasn't interested in dabbling in politics, running a newspaper or other such activities. JRD differed in this respect from other prominent businessmen like Ghanshyam Das Birla, who did not find anything wrong in mixing business and politics. But JRD was a vocal supporter of the cause of Independence nevertheless. On 5 August 1942, four days before the Quit India movement began, Birla and JRD had written a letter to the then viceroy, stating, 'There is no option for you but to give complete Independence to India.' JRD had categorically stated that 'if you want India to remain peaceful, it is better that you grant her the Independence she deserves. It would save a lot of bloodshed'.

JRD was sure that the economic burden after World War II was crippling England and that it had no option but to eventually leave India. He had, even in his younger days, talked of his dissent against the British rule and he had never lost a chance to decry the British rule and oppose their dominion over India.

It was during his honeymoon in Darjeeling. Thelma and JRD were stuck in a traffic blockade for a long time. The police had held back the traffic to allow the passage of the then Bengal Governor Stanley Jackson's car. Seeing Governor Jackson's car arrive, JRD stepped forward and shouted, 'What do you British think of yourselves? Aren't you ashamed of holding hundreds of Indians on the road for your comfort?' Seeing JRD shout at the governor, Thelma started shouting too, sticking her neck out of the window. The road cleared and the traffic moved forward. JRD's and Thelma's act was the talk of the town in Calcutta and Bombay for a while!

JRD was sure that war-crippled Britain would not survive in India for long. But he had no comments to make on post-Independence politics. He was worried about the economy and the business climate, for he was sure that the Congress leaders had no clue about running an economy. According to JRD, there were only two leaders who had some idea of the nation's economy: one was Gandhiji and the other Nehru.

That made him even more nervous, for he was not a follower of Gandhian economics. There had been an argument between the two on the subject earlier. A delegation of Indian businessmen were to visit England and the US in May 1945. The war had ended and the informal delegation's objective was to understand the technical aspects of a few businesses. Just before the delegation left, Gandhiji felt it should not go till the British government released many of the Congress leaders from prison.

'We need to show solidarity,' he said. 'All Indians need to stand together and express their protest wholeheartedly. The business delegation thus should hold their plans for a while and not dare to oppose the sentiment of the people of India.' This was a threat to the delegation and its mission. JRD wrote a personal note to Gandhiji, apart from his public reply to Gandhiji's appeal:

My dear Gandhiji,

You must have seen my statement to the press on the communique you issued couple of days ago on the subject of our forthcoming visit to England and America.

I cannot tell you how hurt I was by the views you expressed about our trip and by the strong language you used.

What made it worse was that I, or some other member of the group, was not given an opportunity of removing the misapprehensions which you evidently entertained about the purpose of our trip. In the circumstances I was driven to issuing my statement to the press in order to make my position clear.

I am leaving on Friday morning and expect to return some time in August when I hope I shall have an opportunity of discussing the matter with you.

With kind regards and sincere wishes,

Yours sincerely
J.R.D. Tata
9 May 1945

JRD was not someone who would get bogged down by public opinion. In fact, Gandhiji's reply to JRD is a testimony to the respect Gandhiji had for him. He wrote on 20 May from Mahabaleshwar:

Bhai Jehangirji,

I have your angry note, if you can ever write anything angry.

If you have all gone not to commit yourselves to anything, my note protects you.

My answer is to the hypothetical question. If the hypothesis is wrong, naturally the answer is wrong and is therefore protective of you all. There was no question of my referring to any of you, as I was dealing with an assumption. I hope I am clear.

M.K. Gandhi.

JRD was convinced that Gandhian economics would not be right for the country and that it would not lead India to prosperity. At the same time, he was a little worried about Pandit Nehru's love for Russia. I hate the word 'profit', Nehru had said once while talking to JRD. The discussion was regarding how to run public sector units profitably. JRD was of the opinion that Nehru's love for Russian socialism was a disaster in waiting for the industrial economy. He realized he could not put his faith in Nehru to make India prosperous.

He realized that it was the industrialists who needed to chart a course for the country. He did not believe in following the British methods. The politicians were not capable and were busy with politics; it was best that the industrialists took it upon themselves to formulate a body which would influence policymaking.

J.R.D. Tata had definite ideas about the path independent India ought to take for the fruits of progress and modernity to reach its unwashed masses. He got together Sir Shriram from Delhi, G.D. Birla from Bombay, Sir Purshottamdas Thakurdas, the textile tycoon, and Kasturbhai Lalbhai. The others who joined the group were Sir Ardeshir Dalal, A.D. Shroff and Dr John Mathai.

After several rounds of discussions, they came up with an economic development plan for India. JRD presented it in his address to the Bombay Rotary Club. The first plan was to double the standard of living of the people of India in fifteen years. This would require industrial output to increase by three times and would need significant investment. Those present at the meeting were in agreement but it was decided to let John Mathai present it to the political leaders. The meeting had generated a lot of debate and some even suspected the motives behind the plan. As expected, nothing came of the plan, though it became very popular and the group began to be known as the Bombay Club. It was probably the only instance of JRD sharing his thoughts directly with political leaders.

10

Air India and Free India

After the end of World War II, airlines such as KLM (Royal Dutch Airlines), Air France, BOAC (British Overseas Airways Corporation) and others started services to India. After India's Independence, Pan American and Trans World Airlines also began flying to India. Air India's prestige can be judged from the fact that when Vijayalakshmi Pandit, a diplomat and Nehru's sister, flew to Moscow after Independence as India's ambassador, it was Air India which took her there. She wrote in glowing terms about the service standards of the airline. JRD was keen that the first ambassador from India should travel Air India. He replied in response to Vijayalakshmi's letter:

My dear Nan,
Thank you very much for your kind letter...
I was very happy to know that the flight to Moscow went off smoothly, and that you were satisfied with the manner in which Air India carried it out. The pride and happiness at flying the first

Ambassador of free India to the USSR was really ours, and it was doubly so for me because you were Ambassador...

Thelly joins me in sending you our sincerest wishes.

Yours affectionately,

Jeh

But the foreign trip was an exception.

JRD was keen to start the services abroad but India was under serious economic stress after Independence. Partition had created huge problems, which were unlikely to be solved soon. JRD had proposed to the government that they start an international service under a sister concern, Air India International. He had proposed that the ownership be divided between Air India, the government and the public. He even intended to take the company public at a later stage. To JRD's pleasant surprise, the government accepted his proposal! The government had no option. It was not in a position to start a new airline as it would require a lot of capital, and giving the opportunity to the Tatas, who would run it efficiently, made a lot of sense. The shareholding pattern decided was as follows: 49 per cent with the government, 25 per cent with the Tatas and the rest with the public.

Air India International's first flight to London took off in June 1948. JRD was himself present on board. His sisters Rodabeh and Sylla came to see him off on the occasion. It was a proud moment for JRD. Rodabeh, now married to Colonel Leslie Sawhney, wrote to JRD:

Jeh darling,

It seems only yesterday that we were all waiting for you in Juhu hangar, and you appeared as a little dot on the horizon, carrying the mail with the first Indian airline. Twenty-five years have passed since and they seem to have flown by swiftly. You especially have been very busy during that time and your life has been full of achievements which you can look upon with pride. The creation of a great airline is not the least of them.

I still remember when in 1929 you told me of your dream to start an airline, it seemed fantastic to me. But when I waited for you in the Juhu hangar, I knew that through your tenacity and faith you had made your dream come true and that your airline would have a great future.

A few years later you spoke to me of starting an international airline. I knew that you would do it but nevertheless, when the first Air India International plane took off one night from Santa Cruz, taking you on its first flight to London, Sylla and I held hands and shed a few tears of emotion and pride in our brother's achievement.

Since then you have gone through much disillusion, heartache and maybe moments of loneliness, but one thing you must never forget is that millions of people in India and in many parts of the world are giving you freely and willingly their respect, trust and affection.

This is the greatest of your achievements you can wear proudly as a crown, for you have not acquired it through meanness, deceit or false brilliance but through selflessness, integrity and hard work.

And so, darling, the purpose of this letter was just to say, Gold bless you always and for many many years to come.

Love,
Rodabeh

JRD had his entire family's support, allowing him to immerse himself completely in running the airline. He had been closely involved in the first flight, even to the extent of selecting the curtains for the windows. Whenever he travelled, he would make notes in his diary and then hand over his observations and suggestions to the local manager. The suggestions and comments would be about the curtains, the behaviour of the air hostesses or about the food served on the flight. JRD would send his comments to the regional head or even the general manager.

He wrote to K.C. Bakhle, the managing director, once: 'If you serve beer with high alcohol content, the stomach feels heavy. Please serve light beer ... the tea and coffee on this flight looked the same ... please look into it ... some of the chairs did not recline properly ... please get them corrected.' He wrote once to the general manager: 'Please see that all the lights are on when dinner is served. I have often noticed that the overhead lights are not switched on. It is far more enjoyable with all the lights on; more so, our silver cutlery would shine in the lights, giving the customer a further satisfaction.'

He was involved in every minor detail. He had recommended to the then International Airport Authority chief, Air Marshal Y.V. Malse, about baggage handling. He had instructed his staff on how the announcements made inside the aircraft should be similar whether in Paris or Bombay.

Those were the days when brands were not given much importance. JRD, on the other hand, would be constantly thinking of how to make the Air India brand one to reckon with. He knew he could not compete with foreign airlines when it came to spending money. His focus was thus on service and punctuality. He would tell his people, 'Let us focus on being the best. Only then the best will come out of us.'

Air India was becoming popular and the government too was keen to see it grow. Rafi Ahmed Kidwai, an Independence activist and politican, suggested a postal service from the four corners of India, with Nagpur as a hub for overnight sorting. The idea in itself was good but JRD pointed to the fact that there was a need to first set up night-landing facilities before Air India could look into the proposal. The government, as usual, was adamant. The differences between them were growing with each passing day now.

JRD was losing patience fast with an adamant minister like Kidwai. The American government, after the end of the war, had offloaded the Dakota aircraft into the market, making all kinds of industrialists jump into the aviation business, with or without any prior experience of running such a company. In India, where barely a few companies could survive, more than a dozen airline companies came up. JRD called for a meeting of all the four airlines then in India—Air India, Air Services of India, Airways (India) and Indian National Airways—and decided to jointly oppose the idea of overnight postal service suggested by Kidwai. Seeing all the four competitors come together upset

Kidwai. He concluded that JRD was trying to form a union against the government's policies.

Despite his proximity to Nehru, JRD felt that Nehru was living in some sort of socialist utopia and would not intervene on this issue. Kidwai was hell-bent on starting the service and asked JRD in no uncertain terms to look into it without any further delay. JRD knew that no amount of correspondence was going to convince Kidwai. The minister went ahead and launched a new service called Himalayan Aviation in 1948. He declared how profitable the venture was going to be. It was a snub to Air India. JRD came out with an open letter to the minister, dismissing all his claims about profits.

JRD's open letter created a storm of sorts. The very next day, Kidwai's deputy minister Khurshid Lal came to meet JRD's representative in Delhi. 'Let us stop these arguments. It would lead to nothing,' was the refrain.

Nehru finally intervened but Kidwai, adamant that he would teach the airlines a lesson, raised the issue in Parliament. He labelled the companies as bloodsucking profit entities who were not bothered about public service. He said that except for Air India, all other companies were willing to support the postal initiative, and that Air India was the only airline which had not reduced its passenger fares while others were doing so. He personally targeted JRD over the issue.

Finding things going out of hand, Nehru stepped in and publicly declared that the Tatas were doing a fine job and that Air India had been praised widely for its efficient and friendly service. Given the Tata expertise, he suggested setting up a committee to look into the proposal given by JRD. The formation of a committee was a nice way to diffuse the situation without coming to any conclusion.

Nehru knew that JRD was a blunt man and would not hesitate to air his views on the economic policies of the government. It was quite daring of JRD to take up cudgels with the leaders. It had been just two years since India had become independent and the public's attitude towards leaders like Nehru was quite worshipful. To criticize such men required courage of conviction. But JRD was not one to be swayed by their contribution to Independence. He was a strong critic of the government's economic policies and would not hesitate to comment whenever the need arose.

JRD continued to receive support for his views. The *Times of India* wrote in an editorial on the parliamentary debate started by Kidwai that the arguments put forth were sans logic and not becoming of Kidwai's seniority as a minister. This was enough to anger Kidwai further. In Parliament, while JRD was being publicly humiliated, Nehru chose to remain silent. JRD knew that he could not afford to be a mute spectator while Air India was being questioned. The future was at stake. He wrote a letter in direct and plain language to Nehru and sought Sardar Vallabhbhai Patel's help. He said, 'What does Kidwai know about the aviation business?' As always, Patel listened to JRD with an eye closed and pursing his lips. He did not comment but heard him patiently.

Nehru formed a committee under the chairmanship of the then Bombay High Court Chief Justice, G.S. Rajadhyaksha. The differences between Nehru and Patel were growing by the day. Patel had discovered that Kidwai was collecting money from some businessmen for the Congress mouthpiece *National Herald* in return for favours granted to them. When he presented the facts to Nehru, Nehru's impulse was to protect Kidwai. JRD, on the other hand, was only worried about saving the aviation sector in general and Air India in particular.

The Justice Rajadhyaksha Committee report was scathing in its appraisal of the government's decision and recommended reverting to the earlier status. It reprimanded the government for having issued licences without thinking of the economic feasibility. 'Where four companies cannot survive, indiscriminately issuing licences to a dozen more is arbitrary,' it said. JRD's stand was vindicated.

The initial feasibility study after World War II had suggested that a maximum of four companies enter the airline business. Yet, when the sector was opened up, then Minister for Communications Abdur Nishtar of the Muslim League gave licences to fourteen companies in total. Many of them did not have the capacity to raise capital, yet were awarded licences. JRD, keen to save the sector from dying a premature death, met most of the businessmen who had entered the fray. One of them was Ghanshyam Das Birla. After hearing JRD out, he agreed to think things over, then wrote back to JRD, saying, 'I understand your logic and I too am not in favour of entering this sector but my son is insistent. Secondly, I am not here to make money. I want to serve the country.'

JRD was worried, and rightly so, that if all the companies started faltering, the government would nationalize the companies. In fact, even before Independence, one Sardar Mangal Singh had proposed that the government create a separate department of aviation. In other words, he had proposed nationalizing the private companies involved in the aviation sector. Sardar Patel had dismissed the request, stating, 'It is not right to come to such conclusions unless we have carried out a detailed study.'

But the clamour for nationalization reared its head once again after Independence. JRD had, in an interview with Associated Press, stated his views clearly: any sector being nationalized was not good for the country. He believed it led to politicizing the sector, which in turn was disastrous. He believed the bureaucrats working for the nationalized companies reported to the ministry concerned and could never take independent decisions.

JRD had sent a copy of his interview with Associated Press to Nehru. He believed that it was not in the government's interest to enter into a sector which was capital intensive. Unlike the roads or railways, the capital required here was thirty-five times greater, JRD pointed out. He believed the government was better off not being involved in this sector, and should avoid wasting time, money and energy. But Nehru would not stop the issue of licences, and the possibility of nationalization became a distinct reality by 1949. JRD had made it clear that:

> any airline needs to run its aircraft for a minimum of 2,500 hours. The current situation allows a plane to fly for not more than 500 hours. This makes the entire business unviable. While India requires twenty-five to

thirty Dakota planes, we have an over-supply here by more than five times. Air India or any other airline would not be profitable in such a situation.

As feared, two of the companies, Ambica and Jupiter, declared bankruptcy. JRD wrote to G.D. Birla, requesting his support to prevent companies from going belly up, but Birla did not heed the request. He wrote back saying that as many players as possible should be allowed, and that those who could not run the business would fold up eventually.

For the first time, JRD felt disenchanted. Finally, the day arrived in 1952 when all the aviation companies were to be merged into one and run by the government. Nationalization was at the doorstep now.

JRD suggested forming two companies: one for the domestic sector and the other for international travel. He was worried that all companies would be measured by the same yardstick and Air India and Air India International would lose their status. He did not want the Indian aviation industry's name to be ruined outside India. But the government, including Nehru, was not interested in listening to his proposal. All companies were merged into a corporation. JRD appealed to the government to appoint an independent committee to compensate the companies which were being merged. That too was rejected, leaving JRD totally disturbed.

The new Minister for Communications, Jagjivan Ram, invited JRD, who went along with Homi Mody, hoping to see his proposal through. Unfortunately, contrary to his hopes, Jagjivam Ram did not even bother to ask him for the proposal. This enraged JRD no end. He challenged him, saying, 'Do you think it is easy to run an airline just the way you run other departments? You will see it for yourself.'

Jagjivam Ram coolly replied, 'It may be a government department but we want your help to run it.' This was rubbing salt into JRD's wounds. Firstly, the government had happily gobbled up private enterprise and now they wanted JRD to run it. JRD was furious and the meeting ended without any conclusion. Nehru tried to pacify JRD by inviting him for a dinner meeting. JRD said, 'If you have already decided, why the farce?' JRD had returned to Bombay when Nehru's letter arrived:

> My dear Jehangir,
>
> I was very sorry to notice your distress of mind when you came to lunch with me the other day. You told me that you felt strongly that you or the Tatas, or at any rate your air companies, had been treated shabbily by the Government of India. Indeed you appeared to think that all this was part of set policy, pursued through years, just to do injury to your services in order to bring them to such a pass that the government could acquire them cheaply.
>
> You were in such evident distress at the time that I did not think it proper to discuss this matter with you. Nor indeed am I writing to you today with any intention to carry on an argument. But I feel I must write to you and try, in so far as I can, to remove an impression from your mind which I think is totally wrong, and is unjust to the government, to me as well as to you.
>
> Yours affectionately,
> Jawahar.

JRD replied in detail. He advised the government on how they should deal with industries and businessmen. He said, 'All my efforts are to produce a world-class airline in independent India. I just wish the shareholders and the employees do not get a raw deal in the decisions taken by the government.'

But unfortunately, nothing of what JRD had suggested was implemented. All that was being discussed was the compensation to the airline owners. JRD was least interested in those discussions and negotiations. He felt bad that his close friend Jawaharlal Nehru had been at the helm of affairs. JRD had no option but to hand over his child, his favourite business, to the government. For JRD, the wound inflicted by Jawaharlal would never heal.

JRD no doubt spent nearly two-thirds of his time on Air India. JRD had been most troubled by Air India but he had always maintained that it was not for profit or making money that he had started this airline. He wanted to make it an example of Indian efficiency and something India would be proud of. He was fighting a battle with the government but he never took an approach of non-cooperation. But a situation would arise soon which would test JRD's approach.

11

New Ventures

While JRD was busy fighting his battle for Air India, that did not stop him from expanding the Tata business in other domains.

LAKMÉ IS BORN

Cosmetics were an import item then. Thanks to the rising price of the dollar, the government decided to curb imports, affecting the business of importing cosmetics. Quite naturally, a lot of women customers were incensed. Many women's groups made representations at Nehru's residence, where they were received by his daughter Indira, who was responsible for managing Nehru's office. Indira, convinced by the appeal made by the groups, asked her father to look into the matter.

One of these groups confronted Nehru on his way to office, just outside his residence. A few women actually started sobbing, telling him of the trials and tribulations caused by living without imported cosmetics! Nehru asked his private secretary, M.O. Mathai, to look into it. Mathai took it casually but when he found Indira insistent, he asked if it was a critical issue. It is, Indira replied, and there were no companies making the products in India.

Mathai reached out to the Tata resident representative in Delhi, A.D. Naoroji, who was asked to consider starting a cosmetics factory. We will give you whatever support you need, Mathai assured Naoroji. JRD was quite amused at the assurance. On the one hand, the government was keen to nationalize Air India and, on the other, was giving the Tatas assurance that it would provide all help to start a new business.

Tata Oil Mills was already in the business of making hair oil, detergents, bathing soap, etc., competing with Levers. JRD started a new company specially for the purpose of making beauty products. It was given a French name, Lakmé. It meant the goddess of wealth (Lakshmi, pronounced the French way). The company and the brand were to become a household name very soon.

Simone, Naval Tata's wife, who was born in France and studied in Switzerland, was given the charge of running Lakmé. Their son Noel runs Trent now, which owns the Westside stores. In 1996, Lakmé was sold to Hindustan Lever and the proceeds were used to create Trent.

THE TATA INSTITUTE OF FUNDAMENTAL RESEARCH

A young Parsi boy, Homi Bhabha, once wrote a letter to JRD. His mother Meherbai was the granddaughter of Sir Dinshaw Petit, while his father Jehangir was a barrister in England. Born in 1909, Homi had done his initial studies in Mumbai and then gone to Cambridge for higher education, getting admitted at the young age of fifteen, instead of the usual eighteen! He had earned an Isaac Newton scholarship, thanks to his academic performance there. His first paper was published when he was just twenty-four.

Not wanting to take up an offer to teach at Cambridge, Homi had returned to India. By then, World War II had just broken out, hence the question of returning to England did not arise. A special post was created at IISc in Bangalore for Homi. His family was close to the Tatas, his father being an advisor on many companies. Within two years of joining, Homi was promoted and was able to work independently on cosmic rays.

Homi realized that there was no independent institute working exclusively on the subject. Those were the pre-independence days but Homi was aware that if India were to make rapid strides in technology and innovation, there was a need to fund such an initiative. No one other than the Tatas could do that. It was then that he approached JRD.

If you write what you specifically want in a detailed proposal, JRD wrote back, I can get you support from the Dorab Tata Trust as we believe in supporting fundamental research. JRD also requested Sorabji Saklatvala, who headed the Dorab Tata Trust, to look into the matter.

Homi's proposal was discussed by the committee under the Dorab Tata Trust on 14 April 1945. Many of the members did not believe that a poor country like India could afford to spend money on fundamental research, but JRD was keen. He believed that arts and science were as important as business. He managed to convince the members to approve a fund to set up a department for the study of cosmic rays at IISc.

Soon, the work at the department grew at a rapid pace and, with JRD's support, the Tata Institute of Fundamental Research (TIFR) was born on 1 June 1945. The members who had earlier opposed the idea soon came to appreciate JRD's vision. The atomic bombing of Hiroshima and Nagasaki in Japan jolted the world and the need for an organization like TIFR was felt acutely. The institute began at a bungalow called Kenilworth on Peddar Road in Bombay and then shifted to the Yacht Club near the Gateway of India. On 19 December 1945, it was formally inaugurated by the then Governor of Bombay, Sir John Colville. It was housed in a separate building at Colaba. JRD would personally go there every day to supervise its construction. It was inaugurated by Pandit Nehru.

FORAY INTO LOCOMOTIVES

There was a small factory in Jamshedpur run by the railways. JRD bought it for ₹45 lakh and redesignated it as the Tata Locomotive and Engineering Company Limited (later changed to TELCO). It began production of steam engines running on coal. Soon, they were making more than a hundred engines a year. The only problem was that it had a single customer, making the business dependent on its arrogance and whims. There were payment delays and, more importantly, the British government was not willing to part with the intellectual property associated with the production of steam engines. JRD was desperately looking to find a way to reduce his dependence on that single customer.

The opportunity arose in the form of the German car manufacturing giant Daimler-Benz. Ford and General Motors had shut shop in India after they failed to find an adequate market. To add to it, the British government did not trust them. Daimler-Benz was looking for the right partner to start a factory in India which could be the supply base for the whole of Asia. It was an opportunity JRD was waiting for. And to help him was a young man with a vision which matched his talent.

It so happened that a year before JRD took his proposal to Daimler Benz, a young man had returned to India after getting a degree in engineering from England. He was unable to find a suitable job, when a company called CP Cement Works, located in the western end of India at Dwarka, accepted him on one condition—they would take care of his boarding and lodging but would not pay him a salary.

The young man accepted the offer! The year was 1929. He started at a salary of ₹250 per month from the sixth month onwards, but that did not deter him from giving his best. Soon, word about his capabilities spread and one of the companies to offer him a job was Associated Cement Company (ACC), part of the Tata stable. ACC had been set up in 1912. The young man was to show his talent during World War II.

He was posted in Bihar to start a new factory but the war broke out, leading to stoppage of supply of machinery which had been ordered. The man said, 'I can ensure we get all the machinery made in India. We need not worry about the imports.' This man was Sumant Moolgaokar. JRD adored his dedication and love for machines. Even while travelling abroad with a delegation, he would spend the whole day with the delegates but skip the evening cocktails to spend time in some factory.

Sumant Moolgaokar: A Tata Legend

JRD once said to Moolgaokar while he was at ACC, 'How long are you going to spend your life producing something which sticks two bricks together!' Moolgaokar was keen to leave but Sir Homi Mody, the managing director, was not willing to relieve him. JRD persisted but Sir Homi denied his request. Finally, JRD had to use his position as the chairman of the group to ask him to be relieved!

In 1949, Moolgaokar came to Jamshedpur to take charge of a new business. The foundation for the Indian automobile industry was being laid there. The period was just after Independence and the tremors were still being felt. The Pathan workers had all quit. Not that much was being produced but Moolgaokar would keep the factory spic and span such that visitors coming to see Tata Steel would be shown TLECO too. Someone joked that 'the Tatas could make money by converting TLECO into a tourist spot'.

Not that such a situation was anticipated. The very next year Daimler-Benz came scouting for a partner. JRD, along with his advisor J.D. Choksi and Moolgaokar, went to Germany. But despite three days of negotiations, things did not move forward. Most of the conditions put forward by the German company were not acceptable to Choksi. 'Daimler may be a giant, but that does not mean we are going to be beggars,' was his refrain.

Finally, the MD of Daimler asked JRD to ignore his legal advisor's comments and put forward what JRD felt was important. The new draft was more or less agreeable to both the parties. A new phase was to begin soon. But JRD was worried about the permission from the Indian government. The government believed that most of the heavy industries and those producing basic commodities should be run by the state. He already had an inkling of the fate Air India was likely to meet. He decided to meet the industries minister, T.T. Krishnamachari.

Both Moolgaokar and JRD were sceptical of getting any support from TTK. To their surprise, having hardly heard them, TTK said, 'Oh! That is wonderful. Go ahead.' JRD and Moolgaokar looked at each other and were about to say something when TTK repeated, 'Very nice. You must start as soon as possible.'

JRD said, 'It is not about your best wishes. We need the necessary permissions from you.' True to his words, TTK ensured that there was no delay in giving the clearances. A new company was born—TELCO, the Tata Engineering and Locomotive Company. The earlier company had been called TLECO—Tata Locomotive and Engineering Company. The name was changed as manufacturing steam locomotives was not going to be the mainstay for the company. The main product would be trucks and other machinery.

TELCO was the first engineering company in India. JRD had written to the then World Bank chief, George Woods, saying that TELCO would play a critical role in creating the new India. That was in 1949. It took a few years for JRD to do what he had written but he did make it happen. He gave complete charge to Moolgaonkar. He mentioned in one of his memoirs that he soon realized Sumant was not one to work in a crowd; he needed to be left alone. JRD would allow Sumant complete freedom. JRD said once, 'Sumant is doing a wonderful job. I may have steered the company in a different way but Sumant's approach too is fine.' A lot of directors believed in expanding, but Moolgaokar believed in going deep first and then expanding. JRD, true to his words, did not interfere and allowed him to run the company the way he deemed fit.

Both JRD and Moolgaokar, while similar in many ways, were poles apart in many other areas. Both loved engineering and would tinker with something or other in their workshops. Both loved speed; JRD drove a car while Moolgaokar liked to ride a motorcycle. Both were diligent and fastidious in their work. JRD was forgiving but not Moolgaokar. Both could not tolerate shoddy work. Moolgaokar would say that Indians should be the best in whatever they did in order to compete in the world market.

Moolgaokar was not satisfied simply setting up a plant. He wanted to do something new. His mind was that of an engineer but he was an artist at heart. He would thus create an ecosystem and not just a plant. Nanabhoy Ardeshir Palkhivala (better known as Nani Palkhivala) said once of him, 'He was not creating a plant. He was creating India.'

An exceptional engineer who focused more on research and innovation than on market forces, Moolgaokar was truly the architect of TELCO. However, there were many other facets to his personality. He was an engineer with a reformist mindset. Being the head of TELCO, he had umpteen opportunities to throw his weight around but never did. He was not conceited. He was the recipient of several prestigious awards from reputed institutions globally. But Moolgaokar remained his modest self despite all the recognition. His wife and family were equally simple and down to earth.

His wife Leela Moolgaokar was well known as an independent social worker who pioneered volunteer blood transfusion service in India. Not many people today are aware of her contribution. It was due to her efforts that the Indian Lepers' Act of 1898 was modified. She had met Indira Gandhi in 1984 and led the efforts to abolish the Act. Whether it was the Koyna earthquake of 1967 or the famine in 1972, Leelatai was at the forefront when it came to social work. She had no airs about being the wife of the managing director of a company like TELCO. As Sheriff of Bombay in 1975-76, she tried to improve the lives of women prisoners.

For thousands of workers in TELCO, the Moolgaokar household was no less than a temple. Moolgaokar died in 1989 while Leelatai passed away in 1992.

TELCO's Akurdi Plant Comes Up

Moolgaokar convinced everyone that if TELCO were to make everything from engines to spare parts, it needed to get out of the shadow of TISCO and set up a separate plant elsewhere. He chose Akurdi near Poona. A lot of land was available at low cost. He planted a few thousand trees the moment they decided on the land. To others it looked like madness, for the trees needed water, but Moolgaokar went ahead and built two artificial lakes. The whole thing then cost ₹15 lakh! Those were tough days for the Tatas to raise capital and such extravagant expenditure was quite naturally opposed by many. JRD stood behind Moolgaokar like a rock. He said:

I completely agree with what he is doing. It is not about building a manufacturing plant. Look at how we have built Jamshedpur and Mithapur. We cannot have just a dry brick and mortar building as a plant. We need the entire ecosystem around it.

As it turned out, when the plant was fully ready, the trees added to its glory. So much so that migratory birds would flock to the lakes and bird lovers would be seen spending hours there with their cameras. Once a man who loved hunting, Moolgaokar was now a bird lover, spending all his free time there!

The trucks manufactured in the Poona plant were in great demand. The 407 model was a huge hit. Even truck manufacturing giants like Mazda, Mitsubishi or Nissan had not been successful in making a slim and strong truck like the Tata 407, which captured more than 70 per cent of the market. Customers were willing to pay a hefty premium of ₹40,000 for getting one out of turn. But, despite the suggestions by many in the management to take advantage of the situation and raise prices, both JRD and Moolgaokar were against the idea.

Profits were an important part of business, they maintained, but profits could not be earned at the cost of taking advantage of the scarcity in the market. In the long run, fleecing the customer could never be good for business.

TELCO Tries to Enter the Passenger Car Market

In the 1960s, JRD and Moolgaokar decided to enter the passenger car market. Except for the government-run Ambassador and Walchand group's Premier, there were hardly any other car manufacturers in India. In order to convince the government, the Tatas got a few cars imported from Daimler-Benz and gave them to influencers and decision-makers such as Commerce Secretary K.B. Lal and Defence Minister V.K. Krishna Menon to try out for a year. These cars are just fantastic, was the feedback, but the licence to manufacture was never given. Eventually, Daimler-Benz grew frustrated and abandoned its plans for setting up a plant in India. Instead, the company turned its attention to Singapore. Ironically, India imported many of its cars from Singapore, spending precious foreign currency!

12

Air India Is Nationalized:
A Devastating Decline Begins

There was little consistency in the way the government behaved; it had treated the airline industry in the same manner. It was a sad state of affairs. JRD had been fighting a losing battle with the government on the compensation for Air India. Despite his insistence that the government set up an independent compensation committee, the government continued to dither. Then, at a meeting, Nehru rejected the idea of an independent commission and instead handed over charge to the secretary for communications. A bureaucrat working under Communications Minister Babu Jagjivan Ram was to decide what compensation the Tatas deserved!

The compensation being proposed to JRD was trivial. In fact, it was less than the amount deposited with the government towards fuel import! And yet the government had the gumption to request JRD to continue running the airline as its head. JRD agreed solely because his love for Air India would not let him see the airline suffer. His disappointment was further deepened as he believed his own friend Nehru had let him down.

In India JRD may not have got the kind of respect and recognition he deserved but he was recognized at the international level. In 1952 he was listed among the top 100 most influential people in the world. And in 1951 JRD had been praised by *The Sunday Times* of London, which said that JRD had not allowed success to spoil him, and his humility and compassion were genuine. It added that he listened to the other person's point of view and did not force his on others, and that for a person who was responsible for the jobs of more than twenty lakh people, he was truly a simple man.

But JRD was untouched by such praise. He was focused on dealing with what he had been served.

Air India's style of functioning, as expected, changed the day the government took it over in 1953. It was counted amongst the best-run airlines in the world, but soon after nationalization it began to slip in the rankings. A couple of accidents added to its rapid decline. The first occurred in 1955, just prior to the Afro-Asian Conference that was to be held in Bandung in Indonesia from 10 to 24 April.

Nehru was keen that Air India fly Chinese Premier Chou En-lai from Hong Kong to Bandung, as Chinese planes at that time could not fly such long distances. Air India's *Kashmir Princess* was made ready for the trip and flew to Hong Kong to pick up the Chinese leader. After waiting for a few hours on the ground in Hong Kong, there was still no sight of Chou En-lai, but some junior Chinese bureaucrats and technicians did come on board the aircraft and the captain was asked to fly them to Bandung.

About five hours into the flight, when the plane was over the South China Sea, a time bomb placed aboard the plane exploded, causing a fire in the rear baggage compartment that rapidly spread to the right wing. Captain D.K. Jathar and chief stewardess Gloria Berry tried to manage the situation without panicking, the captain's main aim being to try a controlled ditching and bring the damaged craft on to the water's surface as gently and as fast as he could. But the fire on the right wing precluded anything of the sort and the crash into the sea took the lives of sixteen of the nineteen on board. Among those killed were Captain Jathar and Gloria Berry. Miraculously, there were three Indian survivors.

JRD was shattered and went to meet Captain Jathar's wife in Bombay. He also told Captain Vishwanath, who was originally supposed to have operated the ill-fated flight, to take another aircraft and leave immediately for Singapore to reach the crash site. During the relief work, Chou En-lai got in touch with Captain Vishwanath. He asked him, 'Were you not warned?'

'No,' Captain Vishwanath replied.

'But the New China News Agency warned us,' Chou En-lai said.

'Then why did you not inform us? And why did you risk the lives of the crew and eight of your own citizens?' Captain Vishwanath asked. He did not receive an answer. Despite all this, the Nehru government arranged for another special aircraft to fly Chou En-lai to Bandung.

Two years later, when the nation celebrated the silver jubilee of Indian civil aviation on 15 October 1957, President Rajendra Prasad praised JRD for his contribution in placing India firmly on the world aviation map.

It was ironic—on the one hand, the government was doing everything possible to create hurdles for JRD, while on the other the President sang his praises. JRD wrote back to him, assuring him of his complete commitment to the cause of Indian aviation. That year, the government also felicitated JRD with the Padma Vibhushan, the nation's second highest civilian honour. To add to JRD's happiness, Aspy Engineer, who had once competed with him in the Karachi-to-London air race, and was now the deputy chief of the Indian Air Force, was present on the occasion.

However, the day-to-day running of Air India was another, and rather dismal, story. Bureaucrats and paper pushers sat on the Air India board with no clue about running an airline. Meetings would last as long as two days, with nothing being achieved, frustrating JRD no end. Members of the new board acted as though they owned the airline. Finally, JRD, unable to take it any more, wrote a letter to the Minister of State for Civil Aviation Prof. Humayun Kabir on 23 January 1958, bringing to his attention the waste of government time, machinery and money ever since the nationalization of Air India. He pointed out how meetings would run for an hour at the most when the Tatas ran the airline for seven years but, after it was nationalized, they started stretching for two or three days, with every member insisting on having 100 to 150 pages of matter printed. He said that the government needed to decide how to run the business—either take it over completely or allow individuals like him to run it the way it was earlier.

However, the situation did not change.

Five years later, on 15 October 1962, JRD planned to fly a Puss Moth from Karachi to Bombay to celebrate thirty years of Indian aviation. However, no Puss Moth could be located and he had to opt for an equally vintage Leopard Moth, which he boarded with enthusiasm. At fifty-eight, his energy remained unflagging. Accompanying him was Captain Vishwanath. They hit some rather bad weather and strong winds en route. Unperturbed, JRD only wanted to know if they had enough fuel to land, as the winds were slowing them down a bit. They landed at Juhu, many surprised at JRD's enthusiasm. Someone asked, 'Isn't that a little too much daredevilry at this age?' JRD said he thought it unlikely he would be around to celebrate the golden jubilee and had decided he might as well celebrate when he could.

However, four years later, in 1966, JRD was given cause to grieve when he lost two of his closest aides—Dr Homi Jehangir Bhabha and Gianni Bartoli—when Air India's *Kanchenjuga,* on a routine flight from Bombay to New York via Geneva, crashed into Mont Blanc in the Alps.

Bartoli, an Italian by birth, was a daredevil pilot who was once forced to land in the Egyptian desert by the British army. He managed to land his plane safely and walked out casually, much to the amusement of the soldiers who had accosted him. When asked what he was doing there, he replied, 'Nothing. Just taking a walk.' He was arrested and sent to India as a prisoner of war. Later, when released, he stayed back in India. His love for planes meant he eventually met up with JRD. They became friends and soon Bartoli fell in love with Kitty, JRD's wife's sister, and married her. He went on to join Air India, managed the Geneva office and was known for his administrative capabilities.

His last message was to Minoo Masani, a politician and a leading figure of the Swatantra Party, who had invited him for dinner on that fateful day. 'I am sorry,' Bartoli had written to him, 'but I have bookings to do. I cannot make it that day. We will plan for some other day.' But that day never came. The Air India Flight 101 crash killed all 117 on board, including Dr Bhabha and Bartoli.

13

Stressful Times

The 1950s was a stressful period that challenged JRD in various ways. He was opposed to Nehru and his team over their socialist views. The very successful airline that the Tatas had built was being strangulated by government control even as the government invited the group to get into diverse businesses. Industries Minister Harekrushna Mahatab had written to JRD asking him for his help in the development of steel and other sectors. He wanted his guidance in raising capital, technical knowhow and setting up industries.

Defence Minister Baldev Singh had gone a step further. He was keen to set up Hindustan Aircraft Limited in Bangalore and wanted JRD to chair the board. JRD was not keen as he did not believe that the government should enter into the business of manufacturing aircraft. Moreover, he felt that as the Chairman of Air India, he would be indirectly competing with the new organization. Meanwhile, Girija Shankar Bajpai, the Governor of Bombay State, was requesting JRD to head a delegation to the United Nations.

JRD, with his characteristic humility, declined all these requests. He doubted the government's intentions behind these overtures. His experience had shown that the government believed that capitalists made money by looting the common man and were committing a crime of sorts.

JRD also met Morarji Desai in the early 1950s when he was the Chief Minister of Bombay. JRD was accompanied by the Managing Director of Tata Electric Company, Homi Mody. The discussion was regarding the supply of electricity to Bombay. JRD and Homi believed that the demand in the coming year would exceed supply and there was a need to expand capacity.

Morarji summarily dismissed the view without allowing Homi to speak further. JRD stood up, signalling the end of the meeting, much to Morarji's surprise. He said that he did not wish to waste Morarji's time or his own by continuing with the meeting when the politician had come to a conclusion without even bothering to look at the figures they had presented. Morarji at once asked JRD to sit down and then heard them out patiently. The Tatas got their permission to expand capacity. But the interactions had left a bitter taste in Morarji's mouth and the duo later shared a very cold relationship.

NATIONALIZATION BEGINS

The socialist mindset of the government got a further boost when Parliament passed a resolution in December 1954 that its economic policies would follow the socialist path. This was reflected in the Industrial Policy Resolution adopted by Parliament in April 1956. According to it, industries were classified into three sectors. The first was purely government-run and included the railways, civil aviation, defence and so on. The second group was of private companies which had to be nationalized, such as insurance companies, and the third was the private sector. This list was the shortest.

As part of the nationalization programme, the government conveniently swallowed the New India Assurance Company, a well-run company of the Tatas set up in 1929—and a profitable one at that. The Tatas had set up the insurance company at a time when Indians were not even aware of the concept. And now, while nationalizing these companies, not only were the founders and owners not adequately compensated, but the government also did not feel the need for even an apology of any sort.

Within four years, the government had gobbled up three high-performing Tata companies—Air India, Air India International and New India Assurance. JRD called this decision a 'fraud'. JRD's only contention was that the government should allow a fair playing field. He firmly propagated the idea that the government should not give undue favours to the companies it ran. He was afraid that the government, suspicious of other shareholders, would land up becoming the largest shareholder in most businesses, thus making the playing field an uneven one.

He endorsed Gandhiji's views that opposed the government holding unlimited powers. JRD wrote to his colleague Dinshaw Daji once in 1953, criticizing the government's policies:

> In the almost universal cry for nationalization in this country, no one seems to think of the potential danger of concentrating enormous economic power into the hands of a small political-cum-bureaucratic minority ... Socialism, to most of them, boils down merely to the ownership by the State of all means of production and no differentiation is made between socialism, communism and state capitalism, nor is it realized that full-scale socialism or state capitalism is inherently incompatible with democracy as understood in the West. The concentration of all economic power and patronage into the hands of a few at the top of a national pyramid must ultimately lead to a similar concentration of political power and therefore to a totalitarian regime. Few realize that in fact capitalism with suitable safeguards is one of the most democratic forms of economic organization as it is based on wide diffusion of economic power.

Unfortunately, Nehru declared that the government would be controlling the economy of the country at the highest levels now. The bureaucrats were functioning as lords with the blessings of their respective ministers, and together they looked down upon businessmen with disdain. Nehru's views seemed to prove JRD's worst fears.

JRD spoke about the future at the annual general body meeting of the shareholders of Tata Steel in 1956. He said that he didn't agree with most of the economic policies of the government; he thought they were decadent and out of sync with reality and the basic principles of economics.

Moreover, the Communist Party won the election in 1957 from Jamshedpur. The leftists started eyeing the Tata Steel workers' union. Even before Independence, JRD had urged the management at Tata Steel to form a department to look after welfare. This was even before terms like HRD and Personnel Departement had come into vogue. JRD's futuristic thinking was to come to his aid now.

TATA STEEL: THE GENERAL STRIKE THAT WASN'T

The communists, led by Comrade Shripad Amrit Dange, had put forth three demands: a 25 per cent increase in salary for all workers, an immediate increase in dearness allowance, and dismissal of the existing workers' union of Tata Steel. The demands had no logic to them. The Tata workers were happy. They were well taken care of, and the kind of facilities being provided to them were far superior to what other organizations could think of.

The communists were able to make their way into other Tata companies in Jamshedpur, namely, TELCO, Tinplate and Indian Tube. But these companies were newer and smaller than Tata Steel. When the Jamshedpur Mazdoor Union of the Communist Party managed to make a space for itself in these three companies, JRD was quick to take action and summoned his colleagues J.D. Choksi and Michael John from Bombay while discussing the developments with the Government of Bihar. The workers had got a raise totalling to ₹22 lakh just the previous year. JRD announced a further raise totalling to ₹45 lakh. Encouraged by this, the communists increased their clamour to de-recognize the workers' union at Tata Steel.

Dange announced a strike and tried to threaten the workers with dire consequences if they dared to ignore the call. Despite this, work at Tata Steel continued as usual. The leftists, now enraged, called for a general strike at Tata Steel on 28 April.

JRD met the workers' representatives, urging them to consider the strike illegal. He explained in clear, logical terms why the strike was not beneficial to anyone. The workers agreed, leaving the leftists defeated but further enraged. They started threatening the workers at the factory gates. Most ignored the threats and continued their work as before. Dange and his team then entered the factory by force to disrupt production there. They started destroying property, forcing the management to stop production and declare a shutdown. JRD announced that it was a precautionary shutdown and not a lockout. The leftists, itching for action, took to the streets, raiding shops and forcing them to shut. Buses were burnt.

After a gap of two days, JRD sent a notice to all workers, calling them to the factory for work. It was an unexpected move. Much to the disappointment of Dange, nearly 9,000 workers came forward to work. The much publicized general strike had failed. The foundation for workers' welfare and the kind of policies laid down by the elder Tatas were visible. JRD was following in the same footsteps. The workers were more willing to trust their management than follow an outside union which promised a steep increase in their wages.

While the Tata Steel issue was settled for the time being, JRD was increasingly disturbed by the overall business climate created thanks to the government's socialist approach. He had an inkling of things to come. The year 1958 was the golden jubilee year for Tata Steel, but JRD was not in a mood to celebrate. His letter to the shareholders that year reflects more bitterness than excitement as he pointed out that, over the past fifty years, the company had produced nearly 2.5 lakh tonnes of steel, got a revenue of ₹70 crore for the government, spent nearly ₹175 crore towards wages and given a cumulative dividend of ₹45 crore to the shareholders, while, in the process, saving precious foreign currency for the government, and showing that not every private enterprise was greedy for profits alone.

Those were times when unfortunately the image being created by the government was that private businesses were unethical, crooked and created for the express purpose of looting the public.

BUTTING HEADS WITH MORAJI DESAI

Morarji Desai, who was India's finance minister from 1958 to 1963, did not get along with the Tata group. The Tatas were planning to raise capital from the secondary market. At that time, an increase in share capital required government permission. JRD sent his proposal to the government stating his intention to come out with an 'at par' issue without any premium, thus making it more attractive. Tata Steel shares had slipped considerably in those years, coming down to ₹100 per share from a high of ₹200; it was not exactly a time to attract premium for a secondary issue. Profits too had declined by 2 per cent. The proposal to issue the shares at par was thus logical. But Desai put his foot down. It was very much the company's decision as to what price they wanted to offer the shares at, but Desai had his views and told JRD to price shares at ₹170 per share instead of ₹100. JRD replied sarcastically:

> In a matter where the government has no role to play and is not responsible in any manner, I am surprised that you are getting into the finer details of the issue. Earlier, such decisions were left to the individual businesses. I hope I have the liberty to rue the fact that we lost those times.

But such instances were to unfortunately continue.

RUN-IN WITH BUREAUCRATS

In the late 1950s, Transport Secretary M.M. Philip challenged JRD's authority over Air India. All matters related to finance and all the top appointments were his prerogative, no longer JRD's; he would bypass JRD while making senior appointments in Air India. A frustrated JRD reached out to Civil Aviation Minister Prof. Humayun Kabir, bypassing Philip. 'Should the chairman not be told of the changes you intend to make?' he asked the minister. Kabir took the bureaucrat's side, and said, 'It was his prerogative as per the new policy. It is the government's responsibility, after all.'

JRD was also upset about the fact that the government was contemplating a steep rise in the salaries of the bureaucrats when they had delivered nothing. He was not upset at the bureaucracy per se. He knew they were simply being dictated to by their political bosses, no matter which government was in power. However, he was once truly stumped by the level to which they could go. Some senior officers demanded that they be allowed to fill petrol in their cars at the petrol pump inside the Air India premises, arguing, 'We are given government vehicles but we don't get a separate allowance for petrol. How do we use these cars then?'

SWITCHING ALLEGIANCE: SUPPORTING THE SWATANTRA PARTY

Around this time JRD got a chance to meet C. Rajagopalachari, who was once the Governor General of India and was then the Chief Minister of Madras Presidency. Rajaji was contemplating the formation of a new party to counter the Congress. He had thus decided to form the Swatantra Party. JRD was in favour of such a thought. The alternative to the Congress then was the Left, which he did not like. Minoo Masani, one of the senior executives in the Tata group, was a supporter of the Swatantra Party and was keen that JRD support it too.

While JRD did not approve of Nehru's economic policies, he still believed that Nehru was his friend and thus decided to inform him of his decision to support the Swatantra Party. He did not want any misunderstandings between them. In a letter, JRD wrote to his friend:

In these circumstances, and after many, many hours of thought and discussion amongst ourselves, we have come to the conclusion that it is indispensable in the national interest that the effort should be made to displace the Communist Party as the second largest party in Parliament. The only party which, it seems to us, offers any possibility of developing ultimately into a responsible and democratic opposition is Swatantra Party, which, after all, consists mainly of people who have been fostered by the Congress, have spent many years within the

Congress and, while conservative in outlook, are not reactionary or communal or extreme rightist.

I personally doubt that the Swatantra Party can achieve anything substantial in the coming elections, but we believe there is a good chance that they could make sufficient headway to replace the Communist Party as leaders of the opposition, however small in relation to the Congress their Members in Parliament may be. If they were totally to fail, they would have no alternative but to disappear altogether from the scene, leaving the field, however limited, to extremist parties. I will not pretend that we are not to some extent influenced by the fact that the economic views or policies of the Swatantra Party are nearer to those of the business and industrial community than those of any other party in the country, not excluding the Congress, but I hope you will believe me when I say in all sincerity that this is only a secondary consideration.

Nehru replied, saying:

It is your prerogative to decide which party your group should extend support to. But your belief that the Swatantra Party could be a good alternative is false. The roots are not, as you believe, originating from the Congress and they are deprived of modern thinking. I am sure you would be quite disappointed with them.

Nehru's assessment of the Swatantra Party turned out to be right. The party did not succeed, but at the same time JRD's estimate of the economic policies of the Congress was not wrong either. The 1960s and 1970s would together see three wars and years of political turmoil.

CHINA AND PAKISTAN: THE 1962 AND 1965 WARS

India was involved in a military conflict with China in 1962. The Chinese leadership had been miffed since 1959, when the Dalai Lama was given refuge in India. But Nehru and Defence Minister V.K. Krishna Menon were unable to read the signs. The result was the Chinese invasion into Indian territory.

JRD promptly offered all support possible. Unfortunately, the government, confused by the sudden development, could not take advantage of the offer. But one positive outcome of the conflict was a request by the new defence minister, Yashwantrao Chavan, to form a high-level committee, including the three service chiefs, the defence secretary and JRD, to come up with a ten-year road map on India's preparedness and need for military aircraft and other requirements. The report included requirement of radar, signalling and other equipment, including spare parts manufacture.

JRD's passion and experience with Air India came to his help. He put all his energies into understanding the current situation and suggesting a comprehensive plan. The report was so detailed that it is used even today as compulsory reading for a new air chief when he takes over. JRD's unrelenting passion and selfless contribution to the work can be seen in a telegram he received on 4 October 1966 from Sarvapalli Radhakrishnan. It said that Radhakrishnan was pleased to appoint him as Honorary Air Commodore in the Indian Air Force for his selfless contribution and excellent service to the country.

It was the highest honour JRD had received till then. It was the same honour the British government had bestowed on Winston Churchill for his leadership of the nation during World War II. When Air Chief Marshal Arjan Singh mentioned this to JRD, he replied that he was a little taken aback at being compared to Churchill. He said that his contribution was merely in preparing the detailed report for the air force and, to add to it, not a single recommendation of his had been implemented, and so he was hesitant to accept such a big honour.

Unfortunately, JRD's report remained only on paper and was not really put into practice. Once the Chinese conflict had ended, the urgency to act on the recommendations also died down. Nehru died in 1964, when JRD turned sixty, and Lal Bahadur Shastri took over as Prime Minister.

When the conflict with Pakistan began in 1965, JRD rushed to the Prime Minister's Office to express his desire on behalf of the entire Indian business community to extend all support possible. He asked his senior engineers to be available in Delhi for any support required in the manufacture or procurement of equipment. JRD appealed to Shastri, stating how expensive imports were not only hurting the country but depriving the local industries of a chance to manufacture them. Shastri responded saying, 'Your recommendations to loosen the controls put on the manufacturing sector are being considered and we will surely revert.'

But Shastri died soon thereafter, and Nehru's daughter, Indira Gandhi, was made Prime Minister. JRD had excellent relations with Indira. In fact, in 1942, Nehru had personally informed JRD of his only daughter's marriage and asked that he and Thelly be there to bless the new couple. JRD, aware that there would be too many people attending the marriage and that his friend would be inconvenienced trying to host him, did not attend the wedding. Instead, he sent an affectionate letter expressing his inability and sent his and Thelly's blessings to the newly wedded couple. He was a kind of foster uncle to Indira.

THE MRTP ACT, 1969

As prime minister, Indira Gandhi too pushed through populist socialist policies. JRD had been repeatedly appealing to the government that while it was dangerous to allow industrialists to have complete freedom, it was equally or more dangerous to allow the government to dictate all terms. But he had realized that the government was only keen on holding the reins to industry. In 1969, the Monopolies and Restrictive Trade Practices Act (MRTP) came into force. All businesses with a net worth of more than ₹20 crore were included under it. The Act stipulated that any company having more than one-third of the market would be considered monopolistic in nature. In short, what an industrialist could produce, in what quantity and where he could invest were now to be decided by the government.

JRD was disappointed but could do nothing. He mentioned in his annual shareholders' meet in 1972 that if the government was going to decide how much to invest, where to invest, what salaries to pay and the bonus policies, amongst other things, what rights did the owners carry then? He said that there must be no business in the world as big as that of the Tatas with as little powers. The government had every right to interfere in and stop businesses which were illegal and those creating artificial scarcity, but to impose such conditions on businesses which were legitimate and trying to create a market for themselves was unjustified.

But Indira Gandhi was not receptive to such arguments. New laws affecting the board structures came into effect. Tata Sons, which would bail out companies making losses, was now not able to do so. The representative of the Tatas in Delhi, whose visiting card used to refer to him as the representative of Tata Industries, was now not allowed to do so. He had to write the names of all the eighteen companies he was representing.

Meanwhile, other business houses started outperforming the Tatas. The Birla group, with a consolidated net worth of ₹1,065 crore, was ahead of the Tatas, who had a net worth of ₹975 crore. The Birla group turnover of ₹1,309 crore was also ahead of the Tatas' ₹1,180 crore. Even in net profits, the Birlas were ahead of the Tatas (₹130 crore against ₹107 crore). Grasim and Hindalco were ahead of Tata companies like TELCO and Tata Steel.

INDIRA GANDHI DECLARES EMERGENCY

The political highlight of the period, though, was the Allahabad High Court's ruling declaring the election of Indira Gandhi null and void. It created a panic situation. The entire nation expected her to resign. JRD wrote to her extending his full support. In fact, it was JRD's lawyer Nani Palkhivala who represented Indira Gandhi in the Supreme Court, challenging the decision of the high court.

He placed his arguments cogently in the Supreme Court on 23 June 1975. Indira won the case. Many believed that Palkhivala should not have been sent by JRD to argue on behalf of Indira Gandhi. Unfortunately, proving Palkhivala's critics right, Indira declared the Emergency just three days after the Supreme Court's decision. Palkhivala was enraged and no longer wished to be associated with or represent Indira Gandhi. However, JRD requested him not to take such a step.

JRD personally appeared to be in favour of Indira's decision regarding the Emergency. In a newspaper interview, he said he had been positive about the Emergency to the extent that it would bring discipline into the country. He said nearly 60 crore Indians were more worried about whether they would get their next meal or not than their freedom of speech. He said that he looked at the Emergency from a perspective different from that which was popular.

JRD and Palkhivala also had further differing political views. JRD was in favour of a presidential form of government while Palkhivala believed that it would not make any difference. 'Till we change our political DNA, no change will make a difference,' Palkhivala would say.

According to some, though, JRD had supported the Emergency out of fear of a backlash on the group. Many did not like the open support JRD gave to Indira. However, she stated at a meeting attended by JRD and his senior director Ardeshir Sabavala that there were many in the Tata group who were trying to destabilize the government. JRD was hurt hearing such baseless insinuations.

The Emergency remained hugely unpopular and Indira and the Congress suffered a massive defeat in 1977. In a personal note to Indira Gandhi, he wrote that he stood by her in those difficult times and prayed that she would have the strength to bear them.

PRIME MINISTER MORARJI DESAI

JRD's next major challenge was now staring him in the face. The defeat of the Congress meant that the government was now headed by Morarji Desai. It was going to be a tough battle for JRD, as the two men had never got along well when Desai was the commerce or finance minister.

His very first decision after taking over as the prime minister in March 1977 was to remove JRD from the Atomic Energy Commission. With a stroke of his pen, Morarji severed a relationship that had existed since 1948. The next year, on 3 February, JRD received a call from the chief executive of the Tata group's Indian Tube Company, P.C. Lal, former Indian Air Force chief, who said he was being asked to take over Air India. It was evident that Morarji wanted JRD to step down. He had got his cabinet to approve a change of guard at both Air India and Indian Airlines. When Lal asked what JRD's role would be going ahead, Morarji said that JRD had been handling the two for quite a while. The message was clear.

JRD 'Dismissed' from Air India

JRD heard of his dismissal, and of the formation of a new board, on the news on radio that evening. The next day, the *Indian Express* reported that Tata had been ousted from Air India in a hush-hush move. The airline's managing director, K.G. Appusamy, and his deputy, Nari Dastur, resigned. The employees' union of both the airlines expressed their anger.

On 7 February, JRD received a letter written by the PM on the fourth of that month. It said:

My dear JRD,

We have had under consideration the question of reconstitution of the Boards of Air India and Indian Airlines. After taking into account various considerations which were relevant to the importance of securing efficient working of the two airlines, we came to the conclusion that there should be one Chairman of both the undertakings. We have, therefore, decided to appoint Air Chief Marshal P.C. Lal, who is already part-time chairman of Indian Airlines and who we thought could be spared by you, as the Chairman of both the airlines. You know P.C. Lal very well and I do hope you will agree with our choice. Let me assure your that we are very sorry to part with you as Chairman of Air India. We fully appreciate the distinguished services you have rendered to Air India during your long association with it and the great contribution you have made to its build-up ... I am expressing these views particularly because I do not wish you to entertain any impression that we have in any way made this change because of any lack of appreciation of your conspicuous work.

With best wishes and regards
Yours sincerely
Morarji Desai.

JRD replied stating the conditions under which he had taken charge of both the airlines. He also reminded Morarji of the meeting they had had on 24 January and expressed sadness that while they had discussed various issues, they had not touched upon this subject.

Morarji replied in detail, trying to explain the rationale behind his decision. But as far as JRD was concerned, the matter was over. He was deeply hurt and the wound was not to heal quickly. Next, a letter arrived from Indira Gandhi, similar in tone to Morarji's. JRD was not surprised. By then, he had realized that successive governments had found ways to not encourage entrepreneurship.

All these events were being keenly observed by a young man who had been inducted into the Tata group as a junior executive in 1962, when JRD was celebrating the foundation day for Indian aviation. He was learning the ropes and did not mind the oil stains on his factory overhauls. He was preparing to take charge of the entire Tata group after a while. His name was Ratan Naval Tata, and he was Naval Ratanji Tata's son.

14

Naval Ratanji Tata and JRD

JRD and Naval Ratanji Tata were quite different personalities. Naval was a tall, handsome man and would look dashing in stylish sunglasses and a T-shirt. JRD was not outgoing or flamboyant; besides, the two had different styles of working. However, the Tata family values and upbringing would never allow them to speak against each other either in public or private. When asked about Naval, JRD would readily say that they did not agree on many issues related to business but that did not mean they had any differences with each other.

Naval too would respond in a similar vein, saying that what JRD was doing for the group was exemplary—his own job was to follow the instructions of the group and he did so with all his heart. Naval respected the hierarchy and never allowed his differences to show in his work. He performed his duties behind the scenes with great integrity and dignity. He was known for his cool demeanour and rarely lost his temper. Even his instructions to his secretary would be a gentle request, not an order! He never forgot his past; it kept him humble and grounded.

Often, those who have suffered in their childhood or early life are bitter towards others despite being remarkably successful themselves. Not Naval. He performed his duties, doing whatever he was asked to do, staying outside the limelight and never aspiring for the top job. His interest in labour laws was recognized by the International Labour Organization (ILO), where he later represented India, and a lot of credit goes to him for getting India on the world labour map.

Naval observed the way JRD was struggling with the government and its policies. Indira Gandhi, who otherwise never lost a chance to praise the Tata group, scuttled their proposal to expand capacity at Tata Chemicals in Bombay. But he never stepped into the battle personally. In fact, his flamboyant personality took a back seat and he never crossed the line with JRD, allowing himself to work behind the scenes for the group.

It was once—and only once—that Naval Tata would step out to take centre stage. No one before or after him from the Tata family has taken such a step.

NAVAL RATANJI TATA'S POLITICAL FORAY

Naval Tata decided to fight elections and enter politics. He nominated himself as an independent candidate from Bombay in the 1971 Lok Sabha elections.

What was JRD's reaction? Probably fed up with politicians and the bureaucracy, he might have felt that someone like Naval could make a difference. But he did not openly support Naval's nomination from the South Bombay seat, nor did he oppose it either. There were three candidates in the fray—Naval, the independent candidate, being backed by the newly formed Shiv Sena's head Bal Thackeray; a young candidate from the Congress party; and seasoned trade unionist George Fernandes, who was seen as a shoo-in since he had defeated a prominent Congress nominee, S.K. Patil, in the earlier election. Naval was seen as the businessman fighting against a known labour leader, not really a strong position to be in.

Fernandes had a lot of respect for JRD as a businessman and as an individual and they shared quite an informal relationship, which itself has an interesting history. Once, George Fernandes was beaten up badly just outside the Taj Mahal Hotel. JRD felt very bad about this and sent Leslie Sawhney to meet him. Leslie had retired from the army and was married to Rodabeh, JRD's sister. When George visited JRD at his residence, JRD said, after the initial introductions, 'Call me Jeh. Don't be formal calling me Mr Tata.' So, thereafter, George would address JRD as Jeh. They met once again in 1969 at the Tata guest house in Delhi, where JRD had invited him for a discussion about the situation in Jamshedpur.

The communists, not being able to make inroads into the Tata employees' union at Tata Steel, were quite annoyed and were trying to use political influence. JRD was worried that they might finally be able to penetrate the union and he needed a young, dynamic and fearless leader. He asked Fernandes whether he would head the employee union. Fernandes, taken aback, had laughed, saying a leader should be one who is easily accepted by the workers. He refused JRD's offer. JRD, probably dismayed by his response, chose not to react.

We do not know how JRD felt about Naval standing against Fernandes. It was quite an interesting contest. The outcome of the election was a complete shocker—George Fernandes lost his deposit; Naval lost but didn't have to forfeit his deposit; the winner was the Congress nominee. The rumour mills worked overtime, alleging that the party had arranged for the use of disappearing ink on the ballot papers, having learnt the art from the Russians, to make their candidate win.

Whatever the truth, Naval's experiment with politics turned out to be a damp squib. JRD had earlier supported Rajagopalachari, when he had formed the Swatantra Party, against Nehru's Congress. That had failed miserably. Now, Naval too had lost. JRD realized that politics was surely not his cup of tea and he was better off leaving it to others. He wanted to be away from politics, but politicians were not willing to leave businesses and businessmen alone.

Plagued by political interference, JRD was trying to stay focused on his work and keep the essence of the group alive. In his many battles, the support of Nani Palkhivala proved most invaluable to JRD. How Palkhivala, one of India's brightest jurists and economists, came to be part of the Tata family is an interesting story. The Forum of Free Enterprise in Bombay had organized the first of his annual budget lectures in 1958. (These lectures went on to become legendary over the years, with people packing up the hall where they took place in large numbers to listen to his sharp analysis of the budget.) In attendance was Tata Sons director and president of the forum A.D. Shroff. He was so impressed by Palkhivala's oratory that he recommended him to JRD as a replacement for the then legal head of the group, J.D. Choksi, who was old and and on his way out. Palkhivala went on to play an important role in the group, helping JRD navigate through difficult times. He was the most trusted advisor to JRD and his position in the group was similar to the other stalwarts of that time, namely, Russi Mody, Darbari Seth and Sumant Moolgaokar.

While the Tata group was struggling on many fronts, some groups like the Birlas were racing ahead—to the extent that once when *India Today* came out with an issue on India's progressive business leaders, JRD's name was conspicuous by its absence.

Birla group Chairman and patron Ghanshyam Das Birla's personality was quite different from JRD's. While JRD would keep politics at arm's length, Birla enjoyed mingling with politicians. He had also started a newspaper, the *Hindustan Times*, in 1924, which had been launched by none other than Mahatma Gandhi. G.D. Birla's son, Krishna Kumar Birla, was considered to be close to Indira Gandhi; it was believed that he donated large sums for her elections. While both JRD and G.D. Birla were almost of the same age, their style of business was very different, which reflected in the growth of the respective groups too. In the period from 1939 to 1969, the Tata group net worth increased from ₹62.42 crore to ₹503.36 crore while that of the Birla group grew from ₹4.85 crore to ₹456.4 crore. Thus, the Tatas' net worth grew by 709 per cent as compared to the Birlas' 9,310 per cent.

JRD had his hopes pinned on Sumant Moolgaokar's TELCO. The plant set up near Poona was yet to gather momentum. Investors too were unhappy about this. JRD believed that once the trucks manufactured at TELCO started plying the highways, things would change. But the change was happening slowly. TELCO was being compared with Ashok Leyland, the truck manufacturer of the Hinduja group, which was racing ahead. Many senior Tata executives were not happy about JRD's support to Moolgaokar. To top it, there was a persistent fear of irrational decisions by the Morarji Desai government.

GEORGE FERNANDES, AN UNEXPECTED ALLY

But there were some positive developments on that front. Unlike his bitter experience over Air India, JRD was pleasantly surprised with the way his application for expansion of capacity for ACC was treated. The Indira Gandhi government had sat on the files, but George Fernandes—industries minister in Desai's cabinet—not only approved it, but also opened up the sector, allowing many more companies to enter the business. From the Tata stable alone, Tata Chemicals and Tata Motors got permission to enter the cement business. In hindsight, such a foray may not make business sense but that was the case then.

Fernandes had another surprise up his sleeve. The Tatas had applied for capacity expansion of the Tata Electric Companies plant near Bombay in 1971. Indira Gandhi had, as before, overlooked the proposal. She had not forgotten the fact that Naval Tata had fought as a candidate against the Congress. She was quite upset with JRD on this issue. In her meetings with JRD, she would either look away or busy herself with papers in hand, trying to avoid direct eye contact. Thus, the application remained pending.

With the change of government and Fernandes holding the ministry, things should have been no different. After all, Naval had fought against him. But Viren Shah, then Chairman of Mukand Iron and Steel Works, advised Fernandes against holding back the application. Shah was close to the Rashtriya Swayamsevak Sangh (RSS) and was later Governor of West Bengal under the Bharatiya Janata Party (BJP) government at the Centre from 1999 to 2004. He was thus, in some sense, an advisor to the Janata government. I suggest you clear their proposal, he said, referring to the Tata Electric Companies expansion, as it would benefit the small and medium industries. Maharashtra was facing a huge crisis and the expansion was to benefit many.

Fernandes was convinced but wanted one of the government agencies to take up the task rather than handing it to a private enterprise. However, after Maharashtra Chief Minister Vasantdada Patil expressed regret that the state electricity corporation was not up to the job, Fernandes asked Naval Tata to send a representative to his office for a presentation. Naval decided to go personally.

When George insisted on knowing why the proposal had been pending for a long time, Naval reluctantly, after much cajoling, hinted at corruption. It was clear why the Tata proposals were getting stuck while other businesses were making merry. The Tata ethos prevented them from resorting to bribery. JRD was clear that he was willing to wait but not pay.

In another instance, George Fernandes invited JRD for a cup of tea. As he entered his official chambers, JRD was surprised to find Minister for Steel and Mines Biju Patnaik present. JRD smelt a rat. He knew that Fernandes wanted to set up a public sector unit each in areas like steel, car manufacturing, cement and so on, and realized that the discussion could lead to the nationalization of existing private companies. Fernandes had also wanted to merge all the private players in the auto business, including the two-wheeler manufacturer Bajaj Auto, and make it into a mega company owned by the government. Now, he told JRD he would like him to take charge of the company in the steel sector. JRD was stunned; it meant the government was proposing to nationalize Tata Steel. Patnaik clarified it in no uncertain terms.

Patnaik was no less adamant a man than Morarji Desai. The Orissa strongman was already miffed that nearby Bihar was enjoying prosperity thanks to Tata Steel. To add to the problem was the frosty relationship with the Tatas' Russi Mody, an equally adamant person. Patnaik had proposed expanding Tata Steel into Orissa but the proposal had been rejected by Mody. JRD sensed danger ahead. He had already lost two of his favourite businesses, Air India and New India Assurance, to the government's nationalization drive. The steel business was close to his heart but he knew that emotions would not play any role here. He left the meeting in a deeply troubled state of mind.

Luckily, the newspapers picked up the issue, criticizing the Desai government on the proposed nationalization drive. They questioned the government's intention in interfering in the working of companies which were profitable and doing well. Many raised the question as to whether there was really any difference in the working of the Nehru and Desai governments.

Rahul Bajaj led the revolt from the front. It was clear that the government had targeted his two-wheeler business. To add to Fernandes's discomfort, the workers' union at Tata Steel openly opposed the government's intentions. It was the first instance of the workers and management jointly standing for a cause against the government. The head of the workers' union wrote to Desai, expressing their resentment. The prime minister eventually called Fernandes and Patnaik and asked them to drop their plans for further nationalization.

15

A Question of Succession

Though the government's abandonment of plans for nationalization brought some relief to JRD, within the group there were murmurings because of JRD's advancing age. The question of succession had been playing on his mind.

THE BACKGROUND

Tata Sons had been formed with an initial share capital of ₹21,000 in 1868. It was made into a private limited company in 1917, with a share capital of ₹1.7 crore. A wholly owned subsidiary, Tata Industries, was formed in 1945. Tata Sons was renamed Tata Sons Limited, with a capital of ₹2.25 crore. The two holding companies, Tata Sons and Tata Industries, controlled the other businesses. 'Control' would be a wrong word as JRD believed in giving complete freedom and independence to his executives running the businesses.

JRD had stalwarts in his group: Darbari Seth of Tata Chemicals, Russi Mody of Tata Steel, Sumant Moolagaokar of Tata Motors, Tata Consultancy Services chief F.C. Kohli, and the chief of the hotels business Ajit Kerkar. Then there were figures like H.N. Sethna of Tata Electric Companies, N.A. Soonawala and S.A. Sabawala among others. They all were managing their businesses independently.

However, as per the MRTP Act, all the Tata businesses were listed companies, having raised money from the public. Tata Sons no longer had a controlling stake in any of them. The companies were at risk of being taken over through public markets. An insider revolt could also see the Tatas lose control of these companies.

In fact, at that time, the Birlas owned more shares in Tata Steel than the Tatas. JRD had invited G.D. Birla to be on the board of Tata Steel. If the Birlas had so decided, they could have staked their claim for Tata Steel! While the Birlas would not do that, the danger of a hostile takeover was real and not something JRD could turn a blind eye to. JRD's personality and his nature had prevented such an occurrence but he could not rule out something like that happening in the future.

There was an urgent need to reorganize the companies under the Tata group. There were more than fifty companies and JRD would need directors for each company. He could not have the same people being represented on various boards, as per the MRTP laws. JRD was able to find the right people with credentials for the board positions. It is admirable that he did not fill a single seat with family members.

Many companies like ACC and Tata Finlay (later, it was made into Tata Tea) were completely independent. In an interview, JRD had said with pride, 'These companies are independent entities. They are joined by a single thread; that is, the Tata name.' It was true to an extent. Later, the companies started competing amongst themselves. It was JRD's magnetic persona which bound them together but, with increasing age, the magnet was losing its power. Many like Tata Chemicals and Tata Steel wanted to enter into the cement business. Tata Steel also wanted to be in power generation. The companies were independent and there was not much JRD could do. The threat of a takeover still remained.

JRD: FLYING HIGH AT SEVENTY-EIGHT

JRD turned seventy-eight in 1982. While things on the ground were being tackled, JRD trained his sights on the skies. It was the fiftieth year of India's foray into aviation. The itch to fly again was strong. And the day 15 October 1982 arrived. A small but elite crowd of nearly a hundred gathered at Juhu airport. It included dignitaries like the governor and chief minister of Maharashtra, directors of the Tata group companies, and JRD's sister Rodabeh. While others were busy chatting, Rodabeh's eyes were scanning the horizon. She had lost her husband Leslie Sawhney, while her brother Jimmy had died in his youth in an air crash. And now Jeh had been adamant about piloting the Leopard Moth from Karachi to Bombay—at the ripe old age of seventy-eight. She was naturally worried.

Suddenly, amid cries of 'Here he comes', Rodabeh noticed a black spot in the skies, which soon turned into JRD's plane as he landed on the airstrip. As a mark of honour, two helicopters escorted the plane. The tears, held back for long, flowed down Rodabeh's cheeks. She could see age in JRD's posture, though he managed to step out with the same grace and dignity he had always shown.

Her brother stepped out of the plane like a warrior after a hard-won battle. He seemed lost, as if trying to collect his wits. But that was just for a few moments! He was soon himself again, and thunderous applause greeted him. It was JRD's turn to speak after the others had spoken. He said:

> I felt distressed that in recent times there was a growing sense of disenchantment in our land—there was a loss of morale, a loss of belief in ourselves ... So I thought that, perhaps, this flight would rekindle a spark of enthusiasm, a desire to do something for the country and for its good name ... And so, in a small way, this flight of mine today was intended to inspire a little hope and enthusiasm in the younger people of our country—they will feel like I do, that despite all difficulties, all the frustrations, there is a joy, not necessarily in actual achievement, for you can't always achieve great things, but in trying to achieve, in doing something as well as you can and better than others think you can...

Among those present to receive JRD were Nusli Wadia and his wife Maureen. About eleven years ago, Nusli had returned to India after having studied abroad. His father Neville Wadia was keen to sell Bombay Dyeing to the R.P. Goenka group. Nusli was against the sale but no one was supporting him. He was banking on JRD to back him. Thanks to JRD's request and influence, Neville Wadia agreed not to sell the company. Nusli, over the next ten years, took Bombay Dyeing to the heights of its glory. However, he had to ward off competition from Dhirubhai Ambani. It was not an easy fight but JRD's support was of immense help to him.

THE TAKEOVER THREAT AND INDIAN BUSINESS HOUSES

G.D. Birla's death in 1983 triggered succession drama within the Birla group. Talk naturally turned to the succession issue in the Tata group.

There were other concerns too that pushed the succession issue to the front of JRD's mind. H.P. Nanda, the promoter of the Escorts group, approached JRD for help because UK-based tycoon Swraj Paul had made a creeping acquisition into the Escorts group in 1983. Nanda, with less than 11 per cent of the shares, realized he was losing control of the group. JRD, along with Keshub Mahindra of the Mahindra group, met Finance Minister Pranab Mukherjee to emphasisize that simply having money to buy did not automatically give an individual a right to acquire anything. However, JRD also realized that his own position was no different from that of the Nandas.

The Tata group owned just about 4 per cent of Tata Steel; the Birlas owned more! While the Birlas were not Swraj Paul, another raider could potentially usurp their companies from the Tatas. It was a distinct possibility. JRD believed that Paul was close to Indira Gandhi and that he had political patronage. When Paul heard of this, he erupted with anger, saying that the Tata group did not hold the ethical standards for India.

JRD was sure of Paul's intentions now. In an interview to the *Sunday Observer*, when asked what he intended to buy next, Swraj Paul said that he was keen on TISCO, adding that the right time to buy was when the original promoter was old.

This rattled JRD. He knew Swraj Paul was upset with him for his support to H.P. Nanda. But Paul was now openly challenging the Tatas. Luckily, the Bombay High Court ruled in Nanda's favour and

Swraj Paul had to beat a retreat. The danger had, for the moment, subsided.

INDIRA ASSASSINATED, RAJIV GANDHI COMES TO POWER

On the political front, Indira Gandhi was brutally assassinated in 1984 and Rajiv Gandhi took over as the new prime minister. He was young and willing to experiment with new ideas.

One of the Tata companies under Ratan Tata was the National Radio and Electronics Company Ltd (NELCO). Electronics and computers were subjects close to Rajiv's heart and brought him closer to Ratan. In the meanwhile, the investments made during the Janata government's tenure in cement and power generation were showing results. The Tata group was once again growing rapidly and left the Birlas behind. 'For the first time, we get the feeling that the government needs us,' JRD said in one of his interviews.

The Tata group was on an expansion spree, investing nearly ₹210 crore in Tata Steel, while the capacity in TELCO was increased from 36,000 to 56,000 trucks. Tata Chemicals had invested in two fertilizer plants and Tata Power was focused on building a 500 MW plant at the cost of ₹180 crore. Tata Tea acquired a coffee company called Conscofe, also known as Consolidated Coffee.

Nearly fourteen Tata companies were born in this period, including Titan. The Tata group reported a net profit of ₹250 crore in 1985. Quite naturally, the shareholders reaped a large benefit. The Tata Steel share issued at ₹100 in 1971 was now worth ₹460, while that of TELCO was at ₹665.

Like all good times, these too were not to last forever. The Bofors scandal hit the Rajiv Gandhi government. Vishwanath Pratap Singh, the defence minister, resigned and formed his own party and projected himself as the sole campaigner against corruption. Singh's tenure as finance minister had been quite controversial, with many big businesses being raided. However, there were many who believed that the businesses needed to be raided and their owners and management taught a lesson. Encouraged by such public sentiment, Singh said in a speech in Allahabad on 12 May 1989, 'The Tata, Birla, Ambani, Thapar, DCM and such companies are running a parallel economy, selling our precious equity to foreign players. I have tried my best as a finance minister to stop them. They need to be taught a lesson—'

The speech made Singh popular. Ambani and Birla chose not to respond but JRD could not keep quiet. He was not sure of the others and their ethics but he was hurt that his name was taken in the same breath. After mulling over it for a few days, he wrote a personal note to V.P. Singh, saying that it was not right on his part to speak so poorly about a group which had been contributing to the building of the nation for the past hundred-odd years. He emphasized that the Tatas had never indulged in unfair trade practices or broken rules or asked for any favours; not a single government department had raised objections against any of the Tata businesses. On the question of foreign capital, he pointed out that their businesses were spread worldwide and they had formed subsidiaries as per the rules of the country and India—they had never violated any rules laid by the government or the Reserve Bank of India. 'You need to take your illogical and uncalled for views back,' he said.

The letter was expectedly emotional while being logical. JRD had shown the note to all his senior executives before sending it to V.P. Singh. Unfortunately, Singh decided not to reply. After waiting for a while, JRD decided to make the letter public and sent it to major newspapers. On 8 June, it was published by more than seventy newspapers.

Every newspaper on the flight which V.P. Singh took the next morning from Bombay to Delhi carried headlines to the effect: 'JRD's response to V.P. Singh.' While Singh was reading the papers, the person seated in the row behind him was Ratan Tata. He was keen to see Singh's reaction but did not get any. However, there could be no doubt about the media's full support for the Tatas. The common man believed in JRD and had great respect for him. Nevertheless, JRD was deeply hurt. At his age, it was becoming difficult for him to see the group being maligned this way.

Nusserwanji Tata in his twilight years. 'This boy is going to rule the world. He will be rich enough to build a seven-storey bungalow,' an astrologer had prophesied when Nusserwanji was born, and was, eventually, proven right.

A young Jamsetji Nusserwanji Tata, who would go on to become the grand old man, the 'Bhishma Pitamah', of Indian industry, laying the foundations of a global business empire.

Jamsetji in China, circa 1859–63. India was in turmoil in the years following the first battle of Independence in 1857, and it was against this backdrop that he set out to establish a business in Shanghai.

The main entrance of Empress Mills in Nagpur. The textile mill is considered to be Jamsetji's finest success story.

Jamsetji with his family: wife Hirabai, elder son Dorabji with his wife Meherbai, and younger son Ratanji with his wife Navajbai.

The setting up of Tata Iron and Steel Company (TISCO), now known as Tata Steel. It was the first time that the name 'Tata' was used for any of the group's businesses.

Indian Hotels Company Limited, which runs the Taj group of hotels, opened its first property, the Taj Mahal Palace, in Bombay in 1903.

The prestigious Indian Institute of Science in Bangalore, one of Jamsetji's dream projects, was established five years after his death, in 1909.

Dorabji and Meherbai at their wedding in 1897.

Dorabji, Jamsetji's elder son, who played a key role in the development of the Tata group.

Ratanji, Jamsetji's younger son. Among the Tatas, the idea of social welfare was most intensely present in him.

Meherbai and Dorabji with his uncle Ratanji Dadabhoy (RD) Tata and his wife Suzanne, who was of French origin.

Suzanne (Sooni) with her five children: Rodabeh, Jehangir, Jimmy, Sylla and Darab.

Jehangir Ratanji Dadabhoy (JRD) Tata, RD's and Suzanne's eldest son, was born in Paris on 29 July 1904, two months after the passing of Jamsetji Tata.

Bombay House, the Tata group's head office, located near Flora Fountain in Bombay's Fort area, was built in 1924 and designed by Scottish architect George Wittet, who also designed some of Bombay's other iconic structures, including the Gateway of India.

JRD with Jawaharlal Nehru. The two were
good friends but JRD often opposed
and criticized Nehru's policies.

JRD was like a foster
uncle to Indira Gandhi.

JRD with Sumant Moolgaokar at the Tata
Engineering and Locomotive Company (TELCO),
which later became Tata Motors. Moolgaokar is
known as the architect of Tata Motors.

JRD after the inaugural flight of Tata
Aviation Services from Karachi to
Juhu in Bombay on 15 October 1932.
JRD was passionate about flying and
had become the first licensed pilot
in India in 1929.

Sir Homi Mody, a noted Parsi lawyer and
businessman, guided JRD like an elder
brother after the reins of the Tata group
passed on to him.

Nani Palkhivala, the
Tata group's legal head,
was among JRD's most
trusted advisors.

JRD on 15 October 1982, the fiftieth anniversary of his inaugural Karachi–Bombay flight. At the age of seventy-eight, JRD was adamant about piloting the Leopard Moth on the same route once again to mark the occasion. 'This flight of mine today was intended to inspire a little hope and enthusiasm in the younger people of our country,' he said. 'They will feel like I do, that despite all difficulties, all the frustrations, there is a joy in trying to achieve, in doing something as well as you can and better than others think you can...'

The Indian postal department issued commemorative stamps and envelopes to mark fifty years of civil aviation in 1982.

Ratan Tata with the author.

THE SEARCH FOR A SUCCESSOR CONTINUES

JRD's search for a successor had begun apace but the question was: would he find someone with the right qualities to succeed him? He wanted a person who would not compromise on the values the Tata group stood for in the changing and difficult times ahead.

He considered Darbari Seth, but that might disappoint Sumant Moolgaokar. Russi Mody was tremendously capable, while Nani Palkhivala had the right credentials, though his earlier strong opposition of Indira Gandhi could be dangerous for the group. Would Naval's son Ratan be the right man for the job? And, of course, there was young Nusli Wadia.

JRD was so impressed with young Nusli that he wondered whether he might be the best possible successor. When JRD proposed the idea, Nusli declined politely, saying, 'I am a Wadia and will remain so. I could never become a Tata.'

About Ratan Tata, JRD felt he needed further exposure and experience. Ratan had been given charge of Tata Industries in 1981. While it was a much smaller role compared to the chairmanship of Tata Sons, there were rumours of the group breaking up. When asked, JRD had replied, 'It is for the board to decide the successor. There is no point in speculating who the candidate would be.'

JRD, while keen on exploring the possibility of Ratan taking over, was not willing to publicly state it. His silence was naturally creating confusion among the Tata stalwarts, who were trying to guess what JRD would decide. For instance, when Ratan Tata presented a blueprint for the group, saying, 'The Tata group, along with its traditional and manufacturing focus, should now enter into areas with more focus on modern industrial techniques. We need to look into the future, prepare for the same,' JRD did not comment, and his silence was taken by others to mean partial or complete disagreement with Ratan's views.

Later, Ratan Tata recalled in an interview that JRD had told at least two or three people that they were the likely successor. It was not that he was playing a game but he genuinely believed that the individual was capable of taking charge. Later, he would change his mind. Ratan said that in a way, in hindsight, it was good that he did not mention his name in the beginning. 'Who knows, he may have changed his mind later!'

Among those with whom JRD had been sharing his views about succession, there were some who felt they themselves should be considered.

Darbari Seth

The first move towards the top job was made by Darbari Seth of Tata Chemicals. Nani Palkhivala had announced a public issue of ₹26 crore for capital expenditure and expansion of ACC. The issue was to open on 11 March. Closer to the date of the closure of the issue, the realization dawned that the issue had not attracted people much.

By 11 April, the date the issue was to close, it was discovered that a large portion, totalling ₹10 crore, was being subscribed by Seth through various intermediaries. There were two others—Shapoorji Pallonji, who was bidding for nearly 6 lakh shares worth ₹7 crore, and Nusli Wadia bidding for another 5.6 lakh shares.

Seth, through Tata Chemicals, was thus clearly trying to grab a large slice of the ACC pie. The entire group was stunned. Palkhivala was quite upset. He declared the transactions 'benami'. The term used was naturally incorrect. One could not call applications made by Seth, Wadia and Shapoorji Pallonji as 'benami', or anonymous, and so they were now upset. But Palkhivala rejected the three applications as null and void. The matter did not end there.

Mahendra Swarup, promoter of Paharpur Cooling Towers, which had a substantial interest in selling its cooling towers to ACC, had a 7 per cent shareholding in the cement company. Swarup sold his stake to Seth, giving him a board position. What Palkhivala was trying to avoid happened without his knowledge. To add to his woes, Nusli Wadia filed a case against ACC for having rejected his share application.

They all had been friends till then—been on the boards of each other's companies. But the air was vitiated now, with allegations flying thick and fast. Palkhivala alleged that the Wadias were eyeing his company; Wadia retorted that he was merely a shareholder, that too because it had been Palkhivala's wish. Pallonji said JRD had requested him to step in and subscribe. Seth referred to JRD's assent on Tata Chemicals taking a stake in ACC, and Moolgaokar, managing TELCO in Poona, announced he was strongly opposed to Russi Mody of TISCO taking a stake in his company.

It was slowly becoming apparent that the only common thread holding all of them together was JRD, and he was weakening with age. Rumours of his ill health were exaggerated by the media. The drift of several media reports was that the Tata group was going to break up. Many firmly believed that all the stalwarts running their companies were itching to be on their own, and had been longing to get away for some time. When asked, JRD said they would all remain together due to their committent to the Tata values and ethics. No one was going anywhere.

While JRD was claiming all was well, he knew that that was far from the reality. The hold Tata Sons had on the group companies was gradually slackening. He knew he needed to do something. But what exactly was he to do? He did not have the answers. The stalwarts managing their individual companies were not getting any younger either, and JRD believed they were not the right candidates for facing the challenges of the future. But JRD could not simply ask them to step down—nor would they be willing to.

Russi Mody

Russi Mody was very different from all the other Tata group leaders— always enthusiastic and interested where the others were cautious and professional. They wouldn't like even a crease on their trousers, whereas Mody would talk to anyone and everyone and didn't mind having a meal sitting on the floor with his workers. He has a unique record to his name which still stands—he once finished a sixteen-egg omlette in one go.

He would wear colourful shirts, was talkative, an extrovert and hence everyone felt close to him. He was extremely versatile. He could play the piano very well—and, owing to his mastery, he was once invited to accompany the great scientist Albert Einstein, who played the violin, before a big gathering in New York. What a sight it must have been! Russi Mody lived life to the fullest. Very few directors in the Tata group were as multi-talented as him.

Because of all these qualities, JRD saw him as his potential successor. He often wondered how wonderful it would be if Mody, Palkhivala and Seth came together! Mody's directness and unique leadership style appealed to JRD. Hence, a lot of people thought that Mody would be the new chairman. In fact, there was a period when JRD had promoted his name openly. He was also the only Indian to feature in a BBC series showcasing the most illustrious industrialists of the time.

Some, though, considered Mody to be arrogant. They tell a story about how he was once entering Bombay House in a hurry, without parking his car properly. A policeman walked up to him and an argument ensued. The policeman asked him, 'Does this road belong to your father?' Mody pointed to a sign which read, 'Sir Homi Mody Road,' and said, 'Yes, that's my father. So the road belongs to him.'

Russi Mody's father, Sir Homi, had wielded a lot of power in the Tata group. But once JRD came to the helm, Sir Homi guided him like an elder brother and remained one of JRD's closest friends. Sir Homi's wife belonged to Bombay's famous Parsi Subash family. By the time JRD became Chairman, Sir Homi had established himself as a respected name in the Bombay business circles. He was elected as the head of the Mill Owners' Association five times. In those days, textile mills were the biggest industry in Bombay.

Russi was educated mostly in Bombay and then in the UK, at the Harrow School and Christ Church college, Oxford University. He joined the Tatas soon after his return. His career with the Tatas began when he joined the mining department in Calcutta and looked after coal trading. It so happened that JRD and Sir Ardeshir Dalal visited his office in February 1947. A few days before this visit, tension had built up between various employee unions. Each division had its own union, except the coal division headed by Mody. JRD noticed this and sent a messenger to invite Mody for a talk. Sir Ardeshir too was present.

How come your division is the only one which does not have a union, Sir Ardeshir is believed to have asked Mody. Mody replied that was because the employees of his department were a happy lot! JRD, who was listening quietly, asked, 'Then what are you doing here? Go to Jamshedpur. I will start a whole new department for you there.' By 17 March 1947, Russi Mody had shifted to Jamshedpur and it was to herald a long and sparkling career.

Mody was given the responsibility of all the workers of the coal division the day he joined Tata Steel in Jamshedpur. The mined coal had to be washed. In fact, the whole coal production process was very tedious. He was shocked at the working conditions of the workers. He also noticed that nobody was bothered about this division. The workers were living under hazardous conditions and, within a few days of his taking over, Mody had decided that he needed to do something for them.

He shot off a letter to JRD asking that ₹55 lakh be sanctioned for his division. He also detailed his plan for the use of the fund—₹12 lakh for roads, ₹23 lakh for the repair of workers' houses, and the remaining ₹20 lakh for providing electricity and water supply to all the workers' houses.

When the details of the letter became public, there was outrage at Mody's temerity. A young newbie had shown the guts to write a letter demanding funds straight to the chairman! A lot of senior people felt threatened. It was natural because till then the coal division had been suffering losses of around ₹50 lakh annually. The situation was so bad that it was next to impossible to turn things around. Despite that, Russi Mody had asked for ₹55 lakh!

But JRD did sanction the money. A lot of eyebrows were raised, but JRD felt there was substance in what Mody was saying. He sanctioned the funds; Mody provided all the necessary facilities for the workers, and slowly started building things afresh. Gradually, the situation changed. The strained relationship between the workers and the management started improving, and in time the division began making profits. From then on, Jamshedpur became synonymous with Russi Mody.

But the journey was a bumpy one. There was a spat once between Mody and the leader of the workers' union, Michael John. The situation got very heated, the seniors advised Mody to step aside for some time and he was transferred back to Calcutta. This was, in a way, a demotion for Mody, but he didn't take it personally and never changed his style of functioning. He continued to work the same way in Calcutta.

JRD assessed the situation after a while and transferred him again to Jamshedpur as the head of a new division. That division too was suffering losses. JRD said only one thing to him when he was being given his new role: 'You have to turn around this division and make it profitable.' Mody did exactly that; it started making profits.

By then, Mody knew the Jamshedpur project like the back of his hand. He was great at managing the workers. Tata Steel had a whopping 30,000 employees at that time, with different factions of workers and their leaders holding the company to ransom. But Mody ran a tight ship—sometimes reprimanding, sometimes cajoling and at times threatening. But to his credit, not once did he use police force. In a famous incident, close to 10,000 workers entered the factory and insisted that they be made permanent or they would resort to arson. The situation was serious and everyone thought the police ought to be called in. Mody put his foot down and refused. He went to the workers, sat among them, the tension slowly dissipated and the situation was brought under control.

Mody had a tremendous ability to understand politics and politicians. In 1973, the Bihar government took control of Jamshedpur, which meant that all the factories that the Tatas had established and all the settlements being run by the Tatas in Jamshedpur would be taken away. Mody, who didn't want to involve himself, accepted the staus quo and lost all hope. But he soon regrouped, took up the matter again and within no time freed the Tata group and the city from the control of the government. JRD was very impressed by Mody's leadership skills.

On 23 October 1984, Mody took over as Chairman and Managing Director of Tata Steel. JRD used to say that Mody had the capacity to connect with anyone and everyone. He built confidence in the people working under him and made them a part of his job. His immeasurable empathy for all their issues made him an unparalleled manager.

Sadly, the situation was about to take a very unpleasant turn soon.

Sumant Moolgaokar and Russi Mody: An Unexpected and Unpleasant End

JRD had been planning to eventually hand over the reins of another company to Russi Mody, and that was Tata Motors, headed by Sumant Moolgaokar, who was by then unwell and frail. It was his condition that had prompted JRD to decide that once he himself retired, he would hand over the charge of the company to Mody. Thus, the two precious jewels in the Tata crown—Tata Steel and Tata Motors, together worth ₹3,000 crore—would be in Mody's hands, setting the stage for the leadership of the group.

JRD started creating a conducive environment for the succession and started speaking about his desire to the seniors in the Tata group. These were very delicate times and the new person at the helm needed to handle people with care. At the same time, Moolgaokar's condition was grave and he needed to be kept away from stress. Everything had to be done with great sensitivity.

But Mody came short in this aspect. JRD had started indicating his intentions to the people around him and naturally word reached Mody too. The presumption that the control of the group was going to come to him led to a change in his behaviour and some thought that he had become high-handed. At the same time, in those days, Tata Motors had accrued a lot of losses and the newspapers reported that Mody would be able to turn around the company's fortunes, and so on. Some papers also stated that JRD and others were disgruntled with Moolgaokar, who became livid.

To hark back a bit, Darbari Seth, who had made a bid for the top post, was now out of contention. Nani Palkhivala had become active in politics and JRD was not too happy about it, so he was out too. That left Mody as the top contender for the job. But, unfortunately, Mody did not display the maturity and statesmanship needed in such delicate times. His impatience and the newspaper reports added fuel to the fire. Moolgaokar, who knew he was out of the running for the top job due to ill health, declared that he would not allow Mody into TELCO at any cost.

He instead proposed Ratan Tata's name for the job, suggesting that Ratan be given the post of caretaker chairman of Tata Motors while he, Moolgaokar, would take care of the company's day-to-day affairs. He felt that Ratan was young and had his own ambitions. The company would get a new direction if he took over instead of Mody.

JRD had wanted Mody to become Chairman of TELCO and Ratan the Vice-Chairman so that he could get Mody's guidance and be groomed for the future. But Moolgaokar's revolt threw a spanner in the works.

JRD was now compelled to choose a new successor. Naval Tata described the situation aptly when he said that there was a 'Mughal emperor' at the head of every Tata company. JRD wanted a person who could take the group forward with consensus and cooperation. JRD had to remove all the individual crowns and create a single one, and there was only one person whose name came forward: Ratan Naval Tata. And Russi Mody's last stand (discussed below), taken within months of JRD's announcement of Ratan as his successor in March 1991, just helped underscore the fact that JRD had chosen the right man.

Ratan Naval Tata

JRD was beginning to face niggling health issues and he didn't want to drag his feet on his decision any more. The year 1991 had dawned. He was now in his late eighties. Despite some chest pain and a back problem, he was avoiding a visit to the hospital as 3 March was celebrated in Jamshedpur as Foundation Day with great fanfare, and he had to go there. When he returned, it was clear the trip had taken a further toll on his health and he was rushed to Breach Candy hospital. He was discharged after a five-day stay. It was a Saturday, but he went directly to his office and spent a few hours there before going home.

On Monday, he was back in office. The news of his hospitalization had spread by then and many were surprised to see him at work. JRD called for Ratan and told him that he wanted him to take over Tata Sons and that he would be proposing his name at the next board meeting. JRD fixed an auspicious time on the advice of Ajit Kerkar and decided to hand over the reins to Ratan Tata.

On Monday, 25 March, a meeting was scheduled after lunch. Instead of the usual fare ordered from the nearby Taj Hotel, the spread for the lunch turned out to be one normally seen during Parsi festivals. Everyone was surprised. Lucas, the chef, was asked whether it was anyone's birthday. 'No,' he replied. 'JRD is announcing Ratan as his successor.' Those present were taken by surprise. Except for a few, no one was aware of JRD's plans.

JRD began his speech by talking of his sixty-year-long association with the group and the way things had moved. It was an emotional speech. He then said, 'I am now turning eighty-seven. I am tired. I propose that Ratan, sitting here to my right, should take over from me.'

Pallonji Mistry, sitting to his left, seconded his proposal. The matter was unanimously passed. Ratan had been chosen the head of Tata Sons. The group cheered. But despite fixing an auspicious hour, unfavourable events were bound to happen, and they did. Russi Mody boycotted the meeting and JRD was extremely hurt. Moolgaokar, sadly, hadn't lived to see the day, failing health leading to his demise two years previously.

Ratan, having worked with JRD for nearly twenty years, was ready to take on the responsibility. The Tata group had found an able successor. JRD was a relieved man, more so since Pallonji Mistry had personally assured him he would always stand by Ratan Tata, even if JRD was no more.

The Mistrys and Their History with the Tatas

The moment JRD had decided on Ratan as his successor, it was Pallonji Shapoorji Mistry's assurance that he would stand by Ratan Tata that had relieved JRD of a lot of anxiety.

The relationship between the Tatas and the Mistrys has always been an intriguing one. When the founder of the Tata empire, Jamsetji, was looking for different business opportunities, one Shapoorji Pallonji Mistry was trying to establish his construction business. In those days, the construction business was not as lucrative as it is today, and there were very few players who ran their businesses with honesty. They sincerely felt that their projects should stand for at least a few generations. Shapoorji Mistry felt that way too and aspired to build majestic buildings, but his company was not getting such projects at that time.

The Mistry family came from a very modest background and lived in a chawl on Grant Road in Bombay. Shapoorji was extremely self-assured and tenacious. He was certain that one day his family would be prosperous. His confidence was so high that, even in those trying circumstances, he registered a company in his name called Shapoorji Pallonji and Company. Gradually, this company started to get projects and soon gained a reputation for constructing prestigious buildings in Bombay.

The construction of two buildings in particular changed the fortunes of the Mistry family. One was Framroze Edulji Dinshaw's house and the other was Sorabji Pochkhanawala's house. Dinshaw was from one of the oldest and wealthiest families of Bombay and was also a lawyer and advisor to the royal family of Gwalior. At that time, the Dinshaw family owned 2,200 acres of land in Bombay. This gives us a fair idea of their wealth and prosperity. Having established themselves in Bombay, the Dinshaw family wanted a similar magnificent bungalow in Poona. They mentioned their desire to the famous architect George Wittet, who had built two of Bombay's iconic landmarks. One was the Victoria Terminus and the other the headquarters of the Tata group, Bombay House.

Dinshaw described his vision for his Poona house and Wittet returned with his drawings within a few days. Dinshaw was elated and he went to show the plans to his friend Pochkhanawala, who said, 'There is only one builder who has the capability to construct such a building—Shapoorji Pallonji. You give this contract to him.' Dinshaw accepted his suggestion and Dinshaw and Shapoorji became friends from that time on.

This was a tumultuous time for the Tatas. They were developing the country's first steel plant, the first hydroelectric project and several such massive projects, which were proving to be a boon for the country. But they were short of funds to complete their projects, and Dinshaw stepped in to provide the necessary capital.

Amidst such turbulent times, Jamsetji passed away in 1904 and the burden of completing all the projects fell on his two sons, Dorabji and Ratanji. They set out to work in earnest, and one more Tata stood with them to share the responsibility. That was Jamsetji's partner and cousin, R.D. Tata. He also had his own company and Jamsetji had his own. Ratanji and RD later decided to dissolve both these companies and establish a new entity called Tata Sons.

Just when things were looking up for the newly established Tata Sons, Ratanji passed away suddenly in his forties in 1918. Owing to Ratanji's death, Dorabji and R.D. Tata's responsibilities increased considerably. They were still establishing Tata Steel, and arranging funds was the biggest challenge. Many a time they had to put in capital from their personal wealth. Even that wouldn't prove enough and Dinshaw would then come to their rescue.

Dinshaw invested ₹1 crore in Tata Steel and, when the Tatas were setting up their power company, he invested another ₹1 crore in it. It was impossible for the Tatas to return such large sums, and hence they gave him shares of the company in return. Consequently, Dinshaw held a 25 per cent stake in Tata Steel, Tata Power and other Tata companies. At one point, he held more shares than the Tata family. But this did not cause concern because Dinshaw was like family to the Tatas.

In 1926, RD died, followed by Dorabji in 1932. After Dorabji's death, the reins went into the hands of Nowroji Saklatwala. When Dinshaw also died in 1936, it was a major setback for Saklatwala, to whom Dinshaw had been of huge support and guidance.

Dinshaw's assets were passed on to the Framroze Edulji Dinshaw estate (later transferred to Nusli Wadia). Dinshaw's bungalow in Poona, built by Pallonji, was converted into the office of the Tata

Administrative Services. Dinshaw's shareholding in the Tata group would have gone to a separate trust but somehow ended up with Shapoorji Mistry. How it happened was not clear because nobody ever spoke about it.

JRD was quite upset when he heard of this and he did not approve of Shapoorji meddling in the internal matters of the Tata family. He couldn't understand how Saklatwala, who was holding the reins of the Tata group and the family, could not see what was happening. Meanwhile, Shapoorji's relations with Saklatwala had strengthened and he was building a house for him.

Another shock awaited JRD. It turned out that at one point his younger brother Darab had, following a tiff with JRD, sold off his shares to Shapoorji. In 1938, it was ironic that when JRD took over the group, Shapoorji Pallonji Mistry was the largest shareholder in Tata Sons with 17.5 per cent shares.

Shapoorji, aware of his limitations, was sensible enough to allow JRD to run the business his way. As a board member, he never meddled in the affairs and remained behind the scenes, to the extent that his face was never seen in newspapers nor did he attend public events. This policy of non-interference proved eminently successful.

Shapoorji went on to build some of Bombay's most iconic landmarks like Brabourne Stadium, Bombay Central Railway Station, Breach Candy Hospital, SBI headquarters and the towering World Trade Centre at Cuffe Parade. He had expanded his business throughout West Asia, building bridges and other large projects for oil-producing nations.

After Shapoorji Pallonji Mistry's death in 1975, his son Pallonji Shapoorji Mistry was appointed director in the Tata group, but he too, like his father, was quiet and reticent. He kept busy managing his business interests and pursuing his love for horses. (As an interesting aside, the Mistrys continued to use the same names across three generations. Thus, Shapoorji Pallonji Mistry, Pallonji Shapoorji Mistry and Shapoor Mistry are three different people!)

Given that they were the major shareholders, JRD heaved a sigh of relief when Pallonji Mistry pledged complete support to Ratan Tata.

Freed of his anxiety about how Ratan would carry on after he, JRD, was no more, he was now able to follow his other pursuits, including his passion for poetry, in the time he had left. Among his favourite poems was one by Henry Shore which had a tragic touch, a strange sadness to it. It talked of the question troubling a man, of his destination, after having lived a full life. JRD would read it often:

> ...One day when I say goodbye
> To life and wife, and lie and fly
> Somewhere in the great flow
> I shall be free to roam again
> And will try to find but try in vain
> Where to go, where to go.

16

JRD: The Twilight Years

Things at home were far from fine. JRD's wife Thelma, or Thelly, was suffering from paralysis while his sister Rodabeh had dementia. Bombay House would be vacant by 5 p.m. but JRD would be found sitting late. Finally, his assistant would ask, 'Shall we?'

JRD would ask, tears in his eyes, 'What will I do after going home?' leaving his PA dumbfounded.

JRD, full of life, did not like birthdays, which reminded him of his getting older. He would recall the words of Sir William Mulock, a Canadian lawyer, businessman, educator, farmer, politician, judge and philanthropist: 'I'm still at work with my hand to the plough and my face to the future. The shadows of evening lengthen about me, but morning is in my heart.' JRD would always remind one of a pleasant morning. He was never seen tired or bored, but always fresh and full of energy. He loved his books, flowers, poems, paintings—the finer things in life. He had child-like curiosity.

He loved history, especially Greek, Roman and the French history around Napoleon. He had a good understanding of the future. He had predicted the fall of communists globally in a letter to Jayaprakash Narayan in 1955. He had repeated the same in his speech in 1979. It turned out true twelve years later. 'Private enterprise will flourish in the world. There is no option but to encourage it,' he had said. He was at ease on the international stage. The Chairman of Chase Manhattan Corporation, David Rockefeller, would organize a private discussion once every six months, inviting people from all fields from around the world. Only one Indian name would figure in this group: JRD.

Through such groups, JRD met many global personalities. He got along famously with someone like Henry Kissinger, exchanging letters with him regularly. Kissinger never visited India when JRD was alive. When he did, in 1995, JRD was no more. He said in his speech, remembering JRD, 'I met many people on the international stage but I cannot say that all were as respectable as JRD ... Jeh was different from others. I always believed I would meet him when I come to India but that was not to be.' French President Jacques Chirac was close to JRD and would often reach out for personal advice.

JRD believed in doing things with perfection. He hated a half-hearted attempt. 'Indians should learn to strive for excellence ... if we start with being good, then we will never produce the best,' he would say. He never hesitated to get into the details. 'I am the chairman and this is not my job' was a line you would never hear from him. He was approachable to anyone. Even a janitor had access to him. A janitor is an employee of the Tata group and has the same rights as any other employee; this was his opinion. His memory was elephantine. He would remember the minutest details, making it embarrassing and difficult for his managers many times. They could not get away with saying something not grounded in fact as they knew he would remember.

Ratan Tata too shares this attribute. 'Ratan is in many respects like me. His memory is impressive. His passion for values is as strong,' JRD had said in one of his interviews.

But JRD's health issues were increasing by the day. He said he would like to die abroad—while flying, in a plane crash, vanishing into the sea below. When asked, 'Why abroad?' his reply was that if he died in India, a lot of people would stop working to attend the funeral, which would be a waste of time and something he could not appreciate. If he died in France, however, very few people would attend. Secondly, all the heads of the Tata group before him had died abroad, so he too wished to die outside India.

He had no regrets in life. He did not have a child of his own. When asked if he had ever wanted an heir who could have taken over from him, he replied that while he loved children, he would have never looked at a son or daughter as a successor. He said he would have played with them but never searched for a successor in them, which is why he never adopted a child.

He did not believe in god or a supreme power. Not that he was an atheist. He never had anything against folding his hands in prayer. But he did not reach out to god for help. 'He has so much to do. Why trouble him?' JRD would say, when asked why he did not pray for help. When asked if he prayed to god in his youth, while flying a plane without any help, all alone in the skies, he replied once that being alone in the air, like a tiny speck in the sky, made one humble and realize the position one held in the vast universe. He would have an inner dialogue with himself, which would then engage him with the world around him, with nature and with the emptiness around. He would see god in that nature. To him, the endless, indestructible force around him was god.

Was his god guiding him in the last leg of his life?

Within three months of his stepping down from the chairmanship of Tata Sons, JRD's health started deteriorating. The new year of 1991 had begun with him losing his voice on 4 January. His regular physician, Dr Gul Contractor, came in, followed by Dr Farokh Udwadia. JRD was unwilling to get admitted and wanted to rest at home. Dr Contractor was angry but JRD was insistent on attending a function at the Taj the next day. Within two days, JRD was to inaugurate the Tata Central Archives.

On the domestic front, Rodabeh, in an advanced stage of Alzheimer's, was refusing to allow a full-time nurse to stay with her.

She was happy with her seven dogs. JRD had requested her, to no avail, to shift to the Taj but finally managed to admit her to Breach Candy Hospital. After a couple of months at the hospital, JRD shifted her to the Taj.

After her husband's death, Rodabeh used to stay with her younger brother Darab, and her condition had worsened after his death. She would often resort to shouting and screaming at the Taj staff and JRD had to rush to pacify her.

'Who else does she have other than me?' JRD would ask, when people suggested he avoid going there. At home, JRD's wife Thelly too was confined to a wheelchair. His own heart condition was getting worse and he would often complain of chest pain. He would doze off in office and in his car while commuting. Both Dr Contractor and Dr Udwadia decided he needed to be taken to the US for an angioplasty. When JRD heard the cost, $35,000, he declared he would have the procedure done in Bombay itself. But the doctors had their way and JRD had his angioplasty done in the US. He felt much better and was back to his normal routine of work and travel.

Soon after, on a visit to London to attend a board meeting, he again complained of chest pain. Dr Contractor rushed to London and one more angioplasty was carried out, followed by two more procedures. He returned to India after recuperating there for a month.

A close confidant of his, R.M. Lala, was then writing his biography, and JRD decided to spend some time on it. Lala himself was suffering from cancer and would write whenever he found time from his treatment. 'Don't worry; we both are not going to leave this place till we finish the book,' JRD would joke with Lala, trying to boost his morale. JRD's health was improving but the doctors were keeping a close watch and had suggested a bypass surgery. But JRD wanted to avoid it.

The year 1992 passed but not before India had witnessed the distressing demolition of the Babri Masjid in Ayodhya. The riots that followed shook Bombay, and JRD called for a meeting of the executives of various Tata trusts to discuss how they could help the victims. The Tata Institute of Social Sciences (TISS) alone donated

₹50 lakh. Someone who had refused angioplasty in the US as it was to cost $35,000 was willing to donate ₹50 lakh without batting an eyelid.

JRD lived a multifaceted life. He had varied interests and he never denied himself the opportunity to indulge in the things that gave him joy. He was fond of wine but would hardly have any in India. He would say, 'They are too expensive here.' He smoked once in a while. 'I used to enjoy smoking a pipe when I was in England,' he said.

JRD had a magnetic personality. When asked if that meant a lot of women, he replied that he used to enjoy conversing with women more than men at social functions. The reason was that the moment men met him, they would start off discussing the economy, business or such issues, but the women were different.

JRD had a simple philosophy; he was involved in all but not attached to any. He never pursued greatness. He was clear that greatness surely did not mean accumulating wealth. The Tata name had given him a kind of regal aloofness. His simplicity was legendary. Often, while en route to his office, he would spot one of the employees standing at a bus stop and ask him to get into his car, much to the embarrassment of the employee! In his earlier days, he would often stop at a bus stop and ask anyone there whether they wanted to be dropped off further ahead. He was not well known then.

Once, while returning from the airport, JRD's car was held up at a traffic signal for a long time. JRD called the deputy commissioner of the city's traffic police, P.S. Pasricha, who had a PhD in traffic management, to inform him why it was wrong for a traffic signal to stay red for more than a minute. When reminded of this incident many years later, JRD replied, 'I may have sounded or seemed uncomfortable waiting for something, whether the event was small or big. But my inner core was never rattled. I never get impatient.'

This was true, but he was about to be rattled soon. On 13 August 1993, Dr Contractor was hit by a truck while getting down from her car to meet JRD. The accident was near fatal and her chances of survival were bleak. Ratan Tata rushed to JRD's house not knowing how to break the news. JRD had seen many of his close family members die but he had really been shaken when his sister Rodabeh's husband Leslie Sawhney died, saying, 'Why did he die? What should I do now?'

Dr Contractor's death was going to be a rude shock for JRD. He had always felt that, after him, she, considered a family member, would take care of Rodabeh and Thelly. He had said that often. But now she was fighting for her life. Ratan managed to convey the message in bits and pieces, trying to prepare JRD for the eventuality. But when JRD asked him outright, Ratan could not lie and had to tell the truth: Dr Contractor was not going to survive.

After a month, a memorial service was held, attended by a select few including JRD. He was looking frail and weak but Ratan did not have the heart to ask him not to come. JRD said in his speech:

> When someone so close to us leaves us, a part of us goes away with her. We too start dying, bit by bit. I have never prayed, but ever since I heard of Dr Gul's accident, I have been in constant prayers, asking for her to be saved. The Lord has to take care of more than 80 crore people, so asking Him to help me alone was not my intention. I pray for Dr Gul's soul to rest in peace...

Like the faint glow of an oil lamp burning in the evening hours, JRD's speech too cast a sad shadow over those present. There were tears in the eyes of most. While the homage was being paid to Dr Contractor, they were acutely aware that the lamp called JRD too was running out of its oil. But it nevertheless continued to burn brightly.

On 30 September 1993, Latur in Maharashtra was rocked by a severe earthquake, with Killari in the district being the epicentre. JRD called a meeting of all senior executives of the Tata group on 1 October to work out a relief plan. JRD was personally involved in the strategy for relief operations and wanted security measures to be put in place to protect the remaining homes and property. However, given the scale of the destruction, security concerns appeared to be the least of the police's problems. But the very next day, the *Times of India* reported widespread looting in Latur, and JRD's plan to provide security measures was immediately implemented.

He left for Geneva on 9 October. R.M. Lala, who wrote his biography, had once asked him: Which country would you like to be born in, if you had a choice? JRD had replied, 'USA is ruled out ... so is China. Russia is not what it used to be ... I would prefer Switzerland or Germany. Well, the Swiss are a bit boring!'

JRD checked into a clinic in Geneva to get a health check-up done but was constantly monitoring developments in Latur. He was pleasantly surprised to hear that the employees of Tata Steel had each donated a day's pay for the relief work. He was doubly happy as he had not instructed the employees to do so, and the fact that they had done it of their own volition meant they truly believed in the Tata values of helping others in times of need.

JRD wanted to write a personal note to the leader of the employees' union, V. Gopal, congratulating him and the entire workforce. He was denied that joy when Gopal was brutally murdered on 14 October. It was rumoured to be a political murder. Gopal and his driver Madan Prasad had been killed in broad daylight when he was coming out of the union office at Bistupur in Jamshedpur. The matter was handed over by the Bihar police to the Central Bureau of Investigation but the two main accused were not apprehended.

The brutal killing affected JRD deeply and his will to live decreased further. His appetite had diminished considerably and, after a while, he stopped eating completely. The doctors were at a loss. There was no Dr Contractor to reprimand JRD now. She was the one person who could scold him.

When Dr Udwadia met him on 24 November, he asked, 'Jeh, what exactly is your problem?' JRD replied, 'Farokh, it is just my old age. I am now eighty-nine. What can trouble me?' Later, when a French friend came visiting, JRD said, 'Death must be a pleasurable experience, isn't it?' leaving the friend speechless.

That day, Simone Tata came visiting and spent a lot of time with JRD. She could sense JRD moving from consciousness to semi-consciousness and back. At one point, JRD said, 'I am about to discover a new world. It is going to be very interesting. Very interesting.'

He stopped mid-sentence and looked at her, his eyes glowing with a strange light. He was possibly seeing the 'new world' he was about to enter. Simone looked at him while JRD fell silent after having spoken his last words. He lapsed into a coma and his soul left his body on 29 November 1993.

Jehangir Ratanji Dadabhoy Tata was no more.

17

Ratan Tata: New Directions, New Challenges

The group's transition from JRD's leadership to that of Ratan Tata was certainly not going to be easy. Many people had the secret ambition of occupying JRD's chair. Their journey had run parallel to JRD's, and they too, like him, had given their sweat and blood to the Tata group, helping it grow to dizzying heights.

When JRD had decided to hand over the reins of the Tata group to Ratan, it had eighty-four companies, of which thirty-nine were listed on the stock market. This meant that ordinary people had made huge investments in the group. When JRD stepped down, the group's turnover was ₹24,000 crore and the pre-tax profit was ₹2,100 crore. That year, different Tata companies had paid taxes to the tune of ₹3,500 crore to the government. The Tata group companies had a whopping 26 lakh shareholders that year. This meant that the Tata group alone held 16 per cent of the total number of shareholders in the market. The backbone of this massive turnover were its 2,70,000 employees. Considering an average family size of five members, this meant that the Tata group was taking care of 13,70,000 households. The heads of the Tata group companies thus wielded enormous power and mostly ran little fiefdoms they considered their own empires.

Having been made chairman of Tata Sons, Ratan Tata now faced the difficult task of dethroning them—a job both immediate and delicate. These were men of power, prestige and social status who were seen as bigger than the companies they ran.

UNSEATING THE MUGHALS

Russi Mody would often jokingly say, 'The school where I studied in England has had only three great men so far—Winston Churchill, Jawaharlal Nehru and me!' Having immense confidence in his own qualities, he was confident that the reins of the group would be handed over to him. But that had not happened and Mody had abstained from the board meeting on 25 March 1991 where JRD had handed over charge to Ratan Tata.

He nevertheless intended to challenge Ratan and he did so through newspaper interviews. He spoke to the *Hindu*. He alleged that Ratan Tata and the General Manager and President of Tata Steel, J.J. Irani, were causing serious depreciation to shareholder value. Russi Mody's media interactions were causing a lot of embarrassment to the Tatas and action needed to be taken.

Ratan Tata, in his composed manner, made his first comment: 'The managing director either agrees with the views of the board or resigns.' Russi Mody did not want to do either.

On 26 November, he sent out a note demoting Irani, a Joint Managing Director, to an Additional Managing Director and promoting Executive Director (Marketing) Aditya Kashyap and Executive Director (Finance) Ishaat Hussain to Joint Managing Director. This effectively was a snub to Irani.

Ratan, upset that a large organization like Tata Steel had been put through such unnecessary turmoil, simply asked how Mody could go ahead and make these changes without the approval of the board. The first person to raise an objection to Mody's orders was Palkhivala. Then

Nusli Wadia joined the fray, criticizing Mody's orders. Ratan, after consulting all legal options, decided that the decisions taken by Mody were outside his purview; Palkhivala provided all the necessary legal expertise. Mody, then in London, must have got an inkling of trouble and flew to Delhi to meet the prime minister, hoping he would put his weight behind him. But Narasimha Rao refused to intervene.

Mody then approached Finance Minister Manmohan Singh, who too declined politely. Mody realized that he had no option but to call a truce. He reached Bombay House on 1 January 1992 to reconcile with Ratan Tata. The final ruling was that Ratan Tata would take over as Chairman of Tata Steel. J.J. Irani and Mody were made Managing Directors. Kashyap was reverted to his earlier role. Ratan's final touch was the announcement of a retirement policy that forced Mody to hang up his boots.

At a board meeting in 1992, Ratan announced he had fixed a retirement age of sixty-five for managing directors and seventy-five for chairmen. Anyone older but still holding those posts would be requested to retire with immediate effect, as per the new rules.

As expected, there was a lot of resistance. He was criticized for coming up with what they saw as a 'devious' plan to remove the top bosses. Russi Mody compared Ratan to a circus performer and predicted doomsday for the group. To his credit, Ratan Tata chose not to respond to such criticism. In a rare interview, he wondered what was wrong in bringing out a retirement policy which would allow young blood to rise to the top. He said it was natural for anyone to lose their vigour and energy after crossing a certain age. He emphasized that he only wanted to ensure that no one, including he himself, believed the company to be their private property.

Ratan Tata's announcement brought the curtains down on the Mody era for good. It was a shock to all. If he could force Mody's hand, what would be the fate of others? People like Darbari Seth and Voltas Chairman A.H. Tobaccowala also eventually decided to take a step back. In an interview with the *Financial Times* of London, Ratan once said, when asked about his peaceful demeanour, 'I am in no hurry. I am sure the times are with me.'

The times were truly in his favour. He had ended the practice of allowing complete freedom and unrestrained powers to the chieftains that had led to arrogance. He was ready to face many more brickbats. In the coming decades, the newly appointed successor to JRD was to take the Tata group to even further heights.

RATAN NAVAL TATA: THE MAN BEHIND THE NAME

In 1992, Indian Airlines staff held a poll amongst themselves. The idea was to choose their most loved passenger, the one who travelled the Delhi–Bombay route most frequently, did not throw his/her weight around and did not trouble the staff unnecessarily. The idea behind choosing the Delhi–Bombay route was that top politicians, industrialists or anyone of importance travelled between these two cities the most. The winner, unsurprisingly, was Ratan Tata.

He was a VIP who travelled alone and never had an assistant to carry his files, bags or anything else. He had a habit of quietly working while in flight. He would ask for a black coffee with very little sugar. He had never berated a flight attendant for not making coffee to his liking.

His simplicity had not changed even after being made Chairman of Tata Sons. He did not move to JRD's room but got a simple cabin made for himself. He continued to issue instructions in person to his staff. He did not appoint a lackey who would pass on his orders. He did not believe in creating power centres. He would often make a senior executive wait if he was in conversation with some junior executive. 'I don't like celebrations during festivals and formal meetings. I would rather just spend time doing my job,' he would say.

He has two German Shepherds, Tito and Tango, whom he loves dearly. Such is his love for dogs that whenever he arrived at Bombay House, the dogs nearby would crowd around his car and accompany him to the elevators. The company bore the cost of feeding and taking care of them.

Like JRD, Ratan Tata was known for his punctuality. He would leave the office at half past six. He would get irritated if someone disturbed him with office-related work once he was home. He could be reached only if it was an emergency. He would read his files and other papers in the quiet solitude of his house. He would spend the weekends, if in Bombay, at his farmhouse in Alibagh all by himself. Of course, the dogs would accompany him. He was not interested in sightseeing or giving lectures all over.

While growing up, Ratan had been greatly influenced by his grandmother, Lady Navajbai, who had brought up him and his brother Jimmy. He was only ten and Jimmy eight when their parents separated. Lady Navajbai had been a strict disciplinarian, having spent her childhood in England and later in France. She set high standards at her residence, Tata Palace. The household employed nearly fifty domestic helpers, and there were strict rules about dealing with them. No one behaved rudely. Lady Navajbai also believed in never breaking her promises and never losing her cool, no matter how obnoxiously the other person behaved.

Ratan has the same traits and never uses foul language or loses his temper. 'I can never forget the values my grandmother instilled in me,' he says. He comes across as a genuine and magnetic personality. Whosoever meets him finds him to be dependable. When asked, Ratan has a simple answer: my grandmother was this way. He dislikes showing off and, even as a child, felt uncomfortable being dropped to school in the family's Rolls-Royce.

Ratan was eighteen when his father got married again—to Simone. The couple have one son, Noel, who has been responsible for the Tata group's foray into various sectors, opening businesses like Westside, Star Bazaar and so on. Simone herself, of course, was the power behind Lakmé.

Ratan's mother, Soonoo, married Sir Jamsetji Jejeebhoy after her separation from Naval. This marriage took place much before Noel's birth. She went on to have three daughters, Shireen, Diana and Geeta, with whom Ratan has good relations.

Ratan had returned to India at the behest of his mother, grandmother and JRD. He had been quite happily settled in the US, having studied architecture at Cornell University in New York state and found a nice house in a gated community. But, on receiving

JRD's letter asking him to return and join the group, he left his job and packed his bags for India. He replied to JRD's invitation by saying that he did not have the words to convey his happiness and gratitude on being asked to come to India and join the Tata group. He said he would express that through his work and JRD would never regret his decision.

He returned to India with his American girlfriend but she soon left, not being able to adjust to the lifestyle in a vastly different country. Ratan remained a bachelor thereafter.

He joined Tata Steel at Jamshedpur in 1962, where he worked for nearly six years, initially as an apprentice wearing blue overalls like a shopfloor worker before being promoted as a project officer and then working as an Executive Assistant to S.K. Nanavati, the Managing Director. Ratan was recognized for his diligent and hard-working attitude, a trait which the Tatas were proud of. The news of his dedication reached Bombay House and JRD called him to Bombay, another promotion of sorts.

Upon his return to Bombay, he stayed at the Tata Palace for a while before shifting to a small but independent flat in Colaba, where he invited his mother and three stepsisters to join him, which they did for some time. Thereafter, he worked in Australia for a year and, on returning, was given the charge of turning around the sick Empress Mills, also called Central India Mills.

Textile mills were becoming sick because consumers were turning to nylon and synthetic fabric instead of cotton, and also because the workers' unions and their unreasonable demands were scuttling numerous efforts by mill owners to modernize. Many mill owners preferred to shut down rather than run into losses. Ratan ensured that Central India Mills eliminated all its carried forward losses and made money.

At that time, the textile industry was dominated by Bombay Dyeing, run by Nusli Wadia. A new challenger had also emerged on the scene—Dhirubhai Ambani. Union leader Datta Samant was rising to the peak of his popularity while the Shiv Sena was spreading its wings slowly. George Fernandes was shining on the political horizon. A seasoned group like the Tatas had given the charge to Ratan to change the dynamics.

TURNING AROUND NELCO

Another company in the Tata group facing losses was NELCO, which manufactured radio sets, televisions and other such electronic items. When Ratan Tata took over NELCO in 1971, it had a measly market share of 2 per cent and its turnover was ₹3 crore.

NELCO's competitor, the R.P. Goenka-led Murphy, was doing well in comparison. To make things worse, three other companies had entered the electronics market; Venugopal Dhoot's Videocon, Gulu Mirchandani's Onida and T.P.G. Nambiar's BPL. The three were doing well, having got the latest technologies and designs. Comparatively, NELCO's products looked staid. It was not a company the Tata group had focused on.

In the period from 1972 to 1975, the company was able to tide over its accumulated losses and managed to show a small profit. Over twenty years, Ratan Tata increased the turnover to nearly ₹200 crore. The company faced many problems, including a drastic decrease in demand during the Emergency period. The workers' union and its demands only added to the problems.

Once, during a board meeting, all the directors were hell-bent on attacking NELCO. The only one who stood by Ratan's side was JRD. Seeing the way Ratan was handling NELCO gave JRD tremendous confidence that he was a chip off the old block. He noted that whatever Ratan did and how much profit he made was not relevant. For JRD, it was important to know that Ratan was on the right path and would not do wrong things just to make profits.

'My foundation was laid thanks to my experience with NELCO,' Ratan said once. It was a time when he did not even know where his next pay would come from. He honed his leadership skills there.

TATA INDUSTRIES AND MOTHER'S PASSING

In 1981, JRD gave Ratan charge of Tata Industries. It was insignificant compared to Tata Sons, with a turnover of merely ₹60 lakh, but the fact that the company, so far managed by JRD directly, was being handed over to Ratan created a stir. The press was keen to understand whether it meant Ratan would eventually take over from JRD. But Ratan avoided facing the press and answering any questions. He knew that it was not a big deal for him to be taking over Tata Industries, which had neither the capital nor the required turnover to make an impact.

Ratan was also facing the toughest time of his life personally. His mother was suffering from an advanced stage of cancer, and in 1982 he flew her to the Sloan Kettering Cancer Center in New York and stayed on till she breathed her last. In his free time at the hospital, he dreamt of expanding the Tata business. It was a typical Tata trait that even in times of personal crises, he was thinking of his business responsibilities.

In his younger days, when JRD had fallen ill rather frequently soon after his father's death, he would lie in bed thinking mostly about how he could expand the Tata business—much to Rodabeh's exasperation, who was looking after him and wanted him to rest. Now his successor was doing the same. The group in itself was doing well but complacency had set in, Ratan felt. Not that it was visible to those running the business, but someone like him, standing on the threshold, could sense it well. Nothing new was being achieved. He realized that the group lacked a sense of the future.

He was also acutely aware, in a larger sense, that changes in the Tata group would be representative of the changes India would make. He was worried India would remain just a big market for the naysayers, known not as a producing country but as a consumer. He believed that the Tata group, as India's largest business house, should take the initiative for change.

He could clearly see the road ahead. The West Asia oil crisis had hit the world in 1973 and given the world a wake-up call. Oil exploration and refining was a capital- and technology-intensive area that Ratan believed the Tata group should be involved in. But none of the Tata companies were in that field. The computer had been invented quite some time back and the world was now witnessing the birth of the microprocessor. IBM had already created a super-computer. Artificial Intelligence or AI was becoming popular. The Tatas had a company,

Tata Consultancy Services (TCS), which could work in the field of computers and computing. Ratan decided to focus his energies there.

'I had only one wish—' he says, 'you may call it my inspiration—that I do something for the country, that we start the process of creating something really unique and great for India.'

Tata Sons, he felt, was the right vehicle to initiate the change. Unfortunately, its directors were no longer visionaries. Jamsetji Tata had created things that were beyond the imagination of most people. In fact, he was ahead of his times. If Ratan Tata was to even hope to replicate what Jamsetji had done, he had to think of the future.

Using his time in New York, he framed a grand vision for the group.

Once his mother Soonoo breathed her last, Ratan was not keen to stay on in New York. He returned to India and presented his vision to JRD, who was highly impressed. JRD agreed that the group needed to get into areas of high technology and automation. But, though he endorsed Ratan's views, he did not really do anything to make it happen. It is quite likely that most of the stalwarts of the group then did not appreciate Ratan's approach.

FUTURE STRATEGY FOR THE TATA GROUP

Ratan suggested two primary ways in which future growth should be driven:

(1) Demarcate growth sectors: This would involve dividing the group into sections: (i) steel, mining and minerals with S.A. Sabawala; (ii) TELCO with J.E. Talaulicar; (iii) chemicals and fertilizers with Darbari Seth; (iv) other manufacturing with K.M. Chinnappa; (v) domestic appliances with Minoo Mody; (vi) social services with Freddie Mehta; and (vii) Ratan Tata himself looking after high technology and international businesses.

(2) Increase Tata family shareholding across all group companies: Ratan had also suggested increasing the Tata shareholding in each of the companies. Other than JRD, none of the stalwarts encouraged the idea. Quite obviously, it was not in their favour. Naturally, Ratan's proposal did not see the light of day.

GIVEN CHARGE OF TELCO

By the time Ratan Tata took over TELCO on 7 April 1988, it was already being termed a white elephant. Performance had slipped almost a decade ago—in 1979, Tata Motors had reported a net profit of just ₹2.3 crore and a turnover of ₹1,200 crore—and there was no sign of a major upturn yet. Nevertheless, employee strength had increased considerably in the ensuing years.

TELCO's legendary head Sumant Moolgaokar was now a frail eighty-two-year-old whose health was deteriorating rapidly. It was a tricky situation. Ratan decided to put his weight behind Moolgaokar and promised him his complete support.

However, Ratan had been given charge of the company at a time when the global economy was showing a major slowdown. The markets collapsed in 1989; the Dow Jones Index declined by 22.6 per cent on a single day.

Union boss Krishnan Pushparajan Nair, or Rajan Nair, was to become the first problem Ratan had to tackle on joining TELCO in April 1988. A month earlier, in March, Nair had had a tiff with one of the security personnel. No one knows what exactly happened, but Nair threatened to kill him.

When Ratan Tata took over, he investigated the matter and found Nair guilty. He was asked to apologize but he refused. The company had no option but to initiate action against him and Nair's services were terminated. As he left the premises, he vowed revenge.

Nair had joined Tata Motors in 1976 and worked his way up. The son of a union leader, he had formed a workers' union of his own at Tata Motors and had risen to the post of treasurer. Union leaders enjoyed huge clout at that time—they could transfer anyone to any department; many union leaders had a say in the company's affairs.

In September 1988, a near lockout scenario seemed to be developing over wages, and the management expressed its interest in meeting to resolve the issue. Nair demanded to be part of the discussion, something which Ratan Tata made clear would not happen as he was no longer part of the organization. The talks did not make much progress and Ratan Tata decided to visit the plant on 31 January 1989.

The situation on the ground was volatile, and the police had already nabbed Nair to ensure he did not create trouble. However, the police's initiative had stirred up a hornet's nest. Ratan Tata reached to find workers protesting at the plant and, as the day wore on, thousands of more workers headed for the court where the police were to produce Nair. The city administration had its hands full. Ratan Tata calmly met with the workers' representatives, but refused again to meet Nair, and returned to Bombay.

Maharashtra Chief Minister Sharad Pawar, who took special interest in Poona, kept a close watch on the situation as well, and Nair was told to be patient. But violence did erupt at the plant in March, when around twenty senior executives were physically attacked along with the leaders of the opposing union. The Tatas, who had played an important role in developing the entire Poona-Chinchwad region, took the unusual step of drumming up support by getting their PR team to place newspaper advertisements to publicize all the work they had done for the people and the region—TELCO had been the first major company to enter the area.

Eventually, an agreement was signed by Ratan Tata and the workers' union on 19 September, according to which the workers would receive a sum of ₹485 per month with retrospective effect for the past three years, plus a bonus of ₹7,000. The step was a welcome relief to the workers and they were naturally happy. The general feeling was that the issue would be resolved.

Ratan emphasized one thing: that if such union activities continued, it would deter the management from investing further in the company. This had a direct impact on future employment and growth prospects. The workers agreed. Many felt that Nair had been unnecessarily harsh and demanding, but none voiced their opinion, fearing a backlash. It was clear that the union led by Nair was getting weaker by the day.

The agreement was not only a snub but a serious threat to Nair's identity. He declared a fast unto death in front of the famous Shaniwarwada in Poona. Nearly 3,000 workers joined him in support.

The fight had moved from the workers' union against TELCO to Nair against the Tatas.

Nair had managed to garner support from a lot of workers in the Pimpri-Chinchwad region. In his support, the unions declared a day-long strike in many factories. Datta Samant from Bombay joined in, pledging his support. Samant's approach had always been violent and Nair found a natural ally in him. Sambhajirao Kakade of the Janata Dal proclaimed his support, while George Fernandes, who had himself been a union leader once, initiated talks with Nair along with another senior politician, Madhu Dandawate. In other words, Nair was becoming a star.

Within three days of his declaration of fasting unto death, Nair's image became larger than life. With general elections just a couple of months away, he became a political tool to be exploited. Sharad Pawar was a worried man; any further lockouts would have repercussions and he was worried about losing the election. He was unwilling to allow the factories to shut shop. He thus started pressuring both the Tatas and Nair to find a solution through discussions.

Ratan Tata agreed. On 27 November, a meeting was organized at the Chief Minister's residence, Varsha. Ratan Tata and Pawar spent more than an hour waiting but Nair failed to show up. Meanwhile, Datta Samant led a demonstration to Bombay House and made speeches against Ratan Tata. The whole idea was to delay the meeting as much as possible.

Nair became an embarrassment for Pawar and news reached the party headquarters in Delhi. Pawar had to take action. That night, nearly eight police vans reached Shaniwarwada and rounded up all the people demonstrating there. Nair, on his way from Bombay to Poona, was arrested midway and taken to Ratnagiri prison, where he was charged with attempted suicide and disturbing the peace. Now that the police had swung into action, most of Nair's sympathizers in Poona were a worried lot. The strike ended without any further ado and the workers' union agreed to the conditions put forth by Ratan Tata. 'It was a very important battle for me personally,' he later confessed.

Ratan had won the battle convincingly. To add to it, Tata Motors' profits increased despite the strike—so much so that Tata Motors overtook Tata Steel. In 1991, the year Ratan Tata was voted in as Chairman of Tata Sons, Tata Motors showed sales of ₹2,600 crore with a profit of ₹235 crore, while Tata Steel had sales of ₹2,300 crore. The Tata Motors plant had sold 81,931 vehicles in that year.

As far as Ratan Tata was concerned, he had embarked on a new journey and it was expected that he would face new challenges.

Settling Down as Chairman of Tata Sons

A lot of people mistook Ratan Tata's simplicity for weakness. Many of his decisions were initially opposed. One such decision was to increase Tata family shareholding in all the group companies.

INCREASING TATA SHAREHOLDING IN GROUP COMPANIES

Most of the companies, despite carrying the Tata name, had other majority shareholders, the Tatas being in a minority. In Tata Steel, for example, the family's shares amounted to a mere 2.4 per cent. Pilani Investment, the family investment arm of the Birla family, owned nearly 6 per cent of Tata Steel. In Tata Motors, Tata family shares were just 3 per cent, in Indian Hotels 12 per cent, in Voltas 18 per cent, in Tata Oil and in Tata Chemicals 19 per cent each.

All the companies were controlled by Tata Sons, but 81 per cent of the shares of Tata Sons were held by various trusts. The Pallonjis held the largest individual share at 17.5 per cent. The Tatas held a mere 1.5

per cent. Government-owned companies like LIC, UTI, IDBI bank, etc. held more shares than the Tatas in the group companies. This had happened when money was raised at various points in time, diluting the Tatas' share and increasing the share of the new investors and lenders. Many debt-to-equity swaps had led to another increase. While the Tatas were able to raise capital at a low price, they had paid heavily by giving away ownership.

Potentially, government-owned banks and finance companies could create a problem for the Tatas. There was a theoretical danger of them selling their shares to a third party. There was a risk of an aggressive takeover. Swraj Paul had nearly managed to take over Escorts. It was clear that such a situation was possible within the Tata group companies too.

Till the time JRD was around, there was no question of anyone attempting that. But Ratan Tata realized it was a dangerous situation to allow a company's future to depend on a single individual. He believed that processes and policies and not individuals should run a business. He thus decided to embark on a project to increase shareholding across all companies. This quite naturally met with opposition. Many of the stalwarts running the businesses were considered bigger than the companies they ran.

The opening up of the economy in 1991 had paved the way for more capital to be available. The threat of a hostile takeover was thus even more pronounced. It was way back in 1983 that Ratan had proposed his plan for an increased stake in the companies and ways to prevent a hostile takeover. No one had taken him seriously then. Now, with him at the helm, he was in a position to implement his plans.

He came up with a plan to have a ₹22 crore rights issue, which was open only to existing shareholders. The Tata trusts and the Pallonji family would not participate, nor would the other companies, allowing Tata Sons to pick up the stake.

The other directors on the board were stumped. They had never seen a situation where someone had borrowed money from the market to increase his own shareholding in the companies he managed. No one was willing to oppose Ratan Tata openly but they managed to leak the information to the press. One business daily, in a scathing editorial, wrote in May 1992: 'The total value of the Tata Sons' holding is currently pegged at Rs 1,500 crore. To subscribe to the rights issue, Tata Sons would have to put in Rs 500 crore. To merely strengthen Ratan Tata's hands, is this justifiable? The money could have been used to expand and modernize many plants. The money would come into Tata Sons. It is not clear what Tata Sons intends to do with the amount. Is it justifiable to do this just to reduce the total shareholding percentage of the Mistry family? The Tatas have been exemplary in their behaviour but the current proposal does not surely create a good example of governance.'

The piece disturbed Ratan Tata. He had earlier been targeted for the removal of Russi Mody, and many had found reasons to criticize him for his role in NELCO and Central Mills, both of which had not been great successes. He sent a stinging reply to the newspaper, saying that the Tatas had always believed in giving value to their shareholders and had never misused share capital. He objected to the allegation that the company was being turned into a family-run business and emphasized that the Tata group was a business entity, would always operate on the basis of economic principles, and would always remain true to its values when it came to running a business or acquiring wealth.

Against much opposition, he managed to get the preferential issue of TISCO to the market. It led to the Tatas owning 16 per cent of TISCO. Riding on the success of TISCO, he came out with a similar issue for Tata Sons. There were crossholdings amongst Tata Tea, TISCO, TELCO, etc. and the rights issue ensured that the companies gave up their options, allowing Tata Sons to increase their stake.

Jamsetji had laid the foundation of the Tata group while JRD had given it wings. It was Ratan Tata's job now to take it on a new path. He focused his attention on TELCO. The company had grown in size and become unmanageable with its large number of employees. There was no clear direction to its progress. TELCO also had more than 1,200 vendors supplying different parts for its automobile business. Ratan Tata managed to reduce the vendors to 600 while creating a competitive spirit amongst them to supply the best parts at the lowest possible price.

The vendors, used to an easy life, were now asked to pull up their socks and find the best way to reduce price and increase quality. Ratan Tata managed to reduce the cost of manufacturing considerably.

He liquidated TELCO's investment from Daimler Chrysler, thus freeing capital. In order to reduce manpower, he introduced a voluntary retirement scheme. Knowing that such a scheme in isolation would generate a lot of dissent, he targeted those who were nearing retirement, offering them the balance of the pay for their remaining years in service. For those who opted for the scheme, he also mitigated their fears of medical costs by offering them the same facilities which were available to those in employment. Quite obviously, no one objected to such a scheme and, in one stroke, Ratan Tata managed to reduce the manpower in TELCO by 40 per cent to 22,000. He used the capital thus freed to reduce TELCO's debt burden.

During Moolgaokar's time, TELCO had been a single product company, making just one model of a truck. This had created a sort of lethargy in the company. It was only during the monsoon season, when more trucks were bought, that the company saw a spurt in sales. Else, it was routine, predictable growth. Ratan decided to focus on new models to be introduced soon.

After taking charge of TELCO, he introduced two new models, the Tata Sierra and Tata Estate, a sports utility vehicle and a station wagon respectively. It prompted TELCO to think of manufacturing cars. Finally, in 1992, he laid down his plans for making a car. The idea was to make India's first fully indigenous car. The capital requirement was expected to be to the tune of a few thousand crores. Premier, Ambassador and Maruti Suzuki were already dominating the market.

Ratan Tata faced a lot of flak for what critics saw as a waste of precious capital for a pipe dream. As before, he decided to ignore the critics and focused on the task at hand. He was not in a hurry. He had to get other things right. The increased shareholding in Tata Sons had given him a lot of confidence and he was ready to announce his next big idea.

He proposed a royalty to be charged from all group companies for the use of the Tata name, either directly in the company's name or indirectly. After the initial shock, there was a wave of unrest and opposition. No one wanted to pay royalty to Tata Sons for using the Tata name. The refrain was that all the companies were set up by the Tatas and were part of the group. Why should they pay any money to Tata Sons?

It was on 26 September 1996 that the issue came into the public domain. It was an important day as the annual general body meeting of the shareholders of Indian Hotels Company (IHC) was to take place the next day. It was even more pertinent as IHC was not even using the Tata name, but many promoters were trying to increase their stake in the companies, though behind the scenes. Ratan Tata received a lot of flak in the meeting despite not being present there. Questions such as 'Why should we pay Tata Sons?', 'What benefit would the company receive?' were thrown up. Ratan decided to go ahead with his plan, nevertheless.

The proposal was simple: all companies within the Tata group were to pay 0.25 per cent of their turnover as royalty to Tata Sons. The upper cap was 5 per cent of the company's profits. The companies were classified into different categories. The A list was for blue-chip companies. The B list companies were asked to pay 0.15 per cent, while the figure was 0.10 per cent for those that sat in the bottom category.

Ratan Tata knew that, despite opposition, the companies would fall in line and start paying. He was not gathering the cash for profits but to ensure that the group companies were safe from a predatory takeover. It was also a clear message to the stalwarts and self-proclaimed lords of the companies that the final authority lay with the chairman of Tata Sons. While most companies agreed, there was one which continued to strongly oppose the idea: IHC.

THE FRACAS WITH IHC'S AJIT KERKAR

Ajit Baburao Kerkar was the Chairman and Managing Director of Indian Hotels Company Ltd, which ran the Taj group of hotels and did not use the Tata name anywhere. Logically, he was right in opposing to pay any royalties to Tata Sons. But Ratan's argument was that without the Tata backing, Taj could hardly be the brand it became. When a

Titan watch does not work or a person gets bad service at a Taj hotel, his first comment is that he did not expect it from the Tatas—this was his reasoning. Ratan was clear that the Tata name meant a lot and the companies had to pay their share for associating with it.

But Kerkar was not willing to buy the argument and was ready for a fight. On 12 June 1997, Kerkar turned sixty-five and, as per the Tata policy, was forced to retire as Managing Director. However, the board secured his retirement from the post of Chairman as well. But Kerkar was not going to give in so easily. After all, he was the one who created the entire Taj chain of hotels.

His growth had been meteoric. Having joined the group in 1961 in the canteen department, he began his career at the age of twenty-eight in the Taj Palace Hotel opposite the Gateway of India. But Kerkar, originally from Goa, was a diligent and hard-working man who rose through the ranks steadily. He was keen to have a Taj hotel in Goa and is often credited with improving Goa's status as a tourist destination. Building hotels was not a priority for the Taj group and Kerkar would often be faced with a cash crunch when he came up with a new project. His proposed hotel project in Goa too faced the same problem.

Kerkar did what he had done earlier; he started planting the idea of the Goa project in the minds of visitors to the Taj in Bombay. Knowing Kerkar's capabilities, most agreed to invest into the new project. The Taj Fort Aguada Resort was thus born in 1974. He became a name to reckon with when it came to setting up iconic hotels.

But Kerkar did something which was not expected of a senior executive of the Tata group. A letter written on 26 August, jointly by Ratan Tata, legal advisor Nani Palkhivala and other seniors, accused him of wrongdoing.

According to them, IHC had set up a lot of subsidiaries abroad, unknown to the Tata group. Kerkar had committed to invest a huge sum of ₹1,000 crore in the proposed Bandra-Kurla Complex without the knowledge of the Tata Sons board. He had also signed agreements with foreign airlines for the use of Taj Hotels in two locations, the money for which was being remitted abroad in a clear violation of the Foreign Exchange Regulation Act (FERA).

Kerkar's son Peter was a senior executive in a travel agency. He had been given a huge commission on behalf of someone who had invested in IHC. In fact, the travel agency had invested in IHC and vice versa through crossholdings and in non-transparent ways. The end result was a monetary loss to the Tata group while Kerkar personally benefited.

The travel agency in question was originally a British company which had decided in 1971 to reduce its shareholding in its Indian subsidiary. Kerkar took advantage of the opportunity and bought shares with money that belonged to Taj, but since Taj and Kerkar were considered synonymous then, no one raised an eyebrow. It was assumed that Kerkar had implicit approval from the Tata group. Kerkar had shareholding in the parent British company through another company he had set up in London. He had been careful in his financial dealings and did not have a single share in his name. All the shares were held by the company Kerkar had floated. It was a complicated structure and it was not easy to point fingers at Kerkar unless a thorough investigation was carried out. But Ratan Tata and Nani Palkhivala were determined to unravel the complex web of companies and crossholdings. Palkhivala found FERA violations which could draw punitive action. Kerkar, however, believed that his investments were safe and did not amount to FERA violations.

In 1996, he had signed a twenty-five-year agreement with the travel agency on behalf of the Tata group through IHC. The agreement had a clause whereby it could be extended by another seventy-five years. As per the agreement, all bookings and reservations for Taj properties around the world were to be managed by the travel agency. Now, not only was he enjoying all the benefits as the head of IHC, but was also benfiting from the added commission being paid to the travel agency, which was indirectly his own business.

Kerkar had plans to come out with a public issue for the travel agency. He was also mulling over plans to launch a bank, for which he had taken on board some of the top names in the business like retired Supreme Court Chief Justice M.H. Kania, retired Foreign Secretary J.N. Dixit and retired State Bank of India Managing Director

V.S. Natarajan. Kerkar had visions of setting up his own empire post retirement.

Ratan Tata was deeply hurt. He may have tolerated the investments made by Kerkar in various entities but he could not tolerate unethical practices. Kerkar had probably guessed the outcome of the board meeting to be held on 28 August and absented himself, stating he was suffering from high blood pressure. But he was still deeply involved and was keen to have his nominee as the next CMD of IHC. He had proposed the name of Lenny Menezes, chief of Taj's international operations, but Ratan Tata did not agree to his proposal. It was clear that Kerkar had lost the confidence of the board members.

A telegram was sent to Kerkar asking him to attend the next meeting. If Kerkar abstained from the meeting, the board was entitled to select a successor. Palkhivala had created a watertight proposal which would stand legal scrutiny if the need arose. As soon as the meeting began, a proposal to remove Kerkar was put up. Kerkar had made sure he was present at the meeting; he knew he had influence over the eleven board members. But Ratan Tata had added two more directors on the board—R.K. Krishna Kumar of Tata Tea and S. Ramakrishnan.

The new retirement policy mooted by Ratan Tata in 1991 allowed a chairman to continue till the age of seventy-five, but Kerkar's activities were seen as unpardonable by the board. He tried to win the board over, but no one agreed. Ratan Tata proposed R.K. Krishna Kumar as the next MD of IHC while he himself would take on the role of Chairman.

That afternoon, the news spread like wildfire—Kerkar, an integral part of the Tata group for decades, had been summarily dismissed. An affronted Kerkar was seen walking out of his office for the last time.

Soft-spoken Ratan Tata had shown that he was a man of steel and could take tough decisions. He had emerged from his battles victorious. As planned, the fiefdoms had been disbanded and the task of increasing the Tata family shares in the group companies was well under way. Now he needed to focus on the third and last element of his plan—providing all the companies across Tata Sons with a new, modern outlook as envisioned in the strategy paper he had prepared in 1982 by his dying mother's bedside.

19

The Birth of a Motor Car

Once, countries used to be identified with the cars they built. England had its Rolls-Royce and Jaguar, Germany its Mercedes-Benz, the Americans their Ford, Japan had Toyota, Suzuki and others. Even a small country like Sweden could boast of a Volvo. But India had nothing.

Sanjay Gandhi had got Maruti Suzuki to India but it was never considered a truly Indian car. The Ambassador was built in India but no one considered it an Indian car. It was considered a car meant for politicians, and the common man was not keen to adopt it as his own.

TELCO was then known for manufacturing trucks. Ratan Tata had started introducing newer models in TELCO. With the Tata Estate and the Tata Sierra, he had shown it was possible to make a passenger vehicle. The models were the favourite of the rich and famous. Balasaheb Thackeray was among their first customers. The three-door Sierra was very popular. In its advertisement, it was seen going through jungles and crossing small streams. It appealed to the nouveau riche. The stage for a small car was being set with the introduction of these two models.

Riding on the success of these cars, Ratan Tata decided to come up with a fully indigenous family car. No one had thought of that earlier. JRD had dreamt of it but government policies did not allow him to turn it into reality. Ratan was to fulfil JRD's dream.

He made his plans public in 1993 at an exhibition of automobile component manufacturers, urging motor parts and spare parts manufacturers to come together to create India's first indigenous car. He believed that with the opening up of the economy, the time was ripe for such a venture. Capital was easily available and there was little risk in trying out such a thing.

He did not stop at just making speeches. The project was to cost ₹1,700 crore. He created a separate engineering group in TELCO whose job was to get the entire design in place. Critics argued that either he was being foolhardy or that he was not looking at the reality. 'Even if the Tatas were to create such a car, there would be no market for it,' was their refrain. The costs were expected to be astronomical and would leave TELCO debt-ridden.

There had been no instance of a car being made from scratch in India. Ratan had in mind a car which was as elegant as the Maruti Zen, as spacious as the Ambassador, and with a cost comparable to that of the Maruti 800. It had to be a family car, which meant it could seat five people. Knowing the Indian family's way of travel, it had to have sufficient boot space for luggage. In order to survive the treacherous Indian roads, the car had to be tough. Plus, for foreign markets, the car not only had to fulfil utility and aesthetic criteria but also ensure that safety features were up to the mark. Ratan Tata got personally involved in the project.

He picked the best design engineers and put them on the job at TELCO's Engineering Research Centre to work out the design plans. Computer Aided Design or CAD had not become popular, but Ratan, knowing its potential, invested in a facility, spending ₹120 crore. It had 225 computers and nearly 350 engineers working to create a world-class design.

Ratan managed to get the best brains, including young IIT graduates, and some engineers who had worked on the Tata 709 and the Tata

Safari, to work on the new project. He planned to send the design to a famous design centre in Turin, Italy, for its design engineers to improve on the basic concept developed by the Indian team. Not everyone appreciated the idea. And some of them decided to confront Ratan directly, expressing their displeasure at his lack of faith in the Indian team.

He replied that he did not doubt their capabilities, but said that the kind of products being sold in Europe, Japan and the US often surprised and amazed customers. He noted that design played a crucial role there. He told them that the institute in Turin led in design, and while India might be very good at manufacturing techniques, it might not be the best in design. Therefore, there was nothing wrong in learning from the world's best.

The design engineers were convinced of Ratan's logic when they heard of the kind of manufacturers the institute in Turin had worked with—Fiat, Lancia and Alfa Romeo, among others. When some of the engineers visited the centre, they fell in love with it. Nestled amidst the Alps, it was in the midst of greenery. Without a doubt, nature played an important role in the inspiration for world-class design!

In the meanwhile, another set of engineers was working on accessories and small parts. In total, there were to be 3,800 small parts. There was need for 700 dies and the car would have 4,000 joints. Nearly 600 vendors were identified to manufacture the parts. Quality control, right manufacturing techniques and ensuring the training of vendors were crucial parts of the process.

Another set of engineers was working on the main engine. Ratan had taken the help of engineers from France's Le Moteur Moderne. The engine parts were to be made in India but the testing of the engine was to be done by the French company.

Finally, a prototype was ready in Turin. To inaugurate and test it, a group of Indian engineers was in Turin. After a lot of searching, they finally managed to find a coconut they could break before the launch! They had to forego the other items needed for a pooja and make do with a solitary coconut! The car was carefully packed in a container and sent to Poona. Then followed an anxious and eager wait of two weeks until the container reached the Poona factory. Everyone had heard of the work done in Turin and now eagerly awaited the result.

No one had a clue about the final product. It had been a heavily guarded secret. The container was opened in a remote location, a little away from the factory.

The crowd exclaimed in delight as the light purple car was unveiled. No one could believe that it was going to be a domestic product. Except for a few, others had not been privy to the final design. The engineers working on the project were doubly excited at the prospect of rolling out such a car from the manufacturing assembly line. On opening the door, they noticed the half-broken coconut. Everyone was convinced that the car was truly Indian now!

The bigger challenge was to get all the parts right. Most of the vendors and the assembly line workers were used to assembling trucks, in the case of which precision was not tested to the extent it was in car manufacturing.

In order to ensure quality control, Ratan Tata appointed A.J. Agnew, who was earlier the director of supplier quality at Cummis Engineering. His forte was training vendors to deliver quality. Many of the suppliers were taken aback that someone would help them improve quality. After a little initial hesitation and objection, they all agreed. After all, if the Tatas felt they needed the training, there must be some merit in it, they decided. The vendors were not told of the final product, though.

For the seating systems, an agreement was signed with Johnson Controls, while the mirrors were to be supplied by a Spanish company. The Japanese company, Toyo Engineering, was to supply radiators. Ratan Tata personally worked with nearly 300 small-scale manufacturers in and around Poona. He wanted to ensure that nearly 98 per cent of the parts were indigenously made. It is important to note that this initiative alone generated nearly 12,000 new jobs.

When most of the parts and other engineering systems were in place, the next challenge was to set up a completely independent and fully functional assembly and manufacturing line. Ratan Tata selected a space inside the TELCO factory for setting up the new line, an area covering nearly 6 acres. Seeing the scale, people were convinced that

Ratan Tata was thinking big. Many before that assumed that it would be small line, making a few cars to prove a point. The facility Ratan Tata had in mind would produce a few thousand cars a day. He was clearly thinking big and thinking ahead.

Now the time had come to set up the plant. The design, suppliers, space and everything else was falling in place. Ratan Tata had budgeted ₹1,700 crore for the project. Incidentally, he heard of a completely built but unused plant made by Nissan in Australia which was available for purchase. Just to keep the machinery in shape, the plant was being run for fifteen minutes a day. It was an opportunity for Nissan to recover part of its investment, and Ratan managed to get the plant for just ₹100 crore. The next challenge was how to transport the plant and reinstall it in India.

Teams were deployed by TELCO in Australia to study the entire plant. They pored over the design, layouts and architectural drawings before dismantling the assembly line and other machines. After careful numbering and marking of the parts, the entire line was shipped to India. It was a massive 14,800 tonnes of load, which filled nearly 650 containers. It was a challenging task involving sixteen container ships and requiring enormous coordination, but the TELCO engineers managed the feat well. The whole exercise was completed in just six months.

The entire plant was reassembled at the designated place in the TELCO factory. While many car parts were to be assembled manually, there were a large number of robotic applications, especially for delicate and precision parts. The assembly line had nearly 450 such robots, which were part of Ratan Tata's vision for the new plant. In one of his visits, he realized that the worker would have to bend twice to assemble a particular part. If the plant were to manufacture 300 cars a day, it meant bending 600 times. This was unacceptable to him. He felt the worker would be unduly stressed. 'Get a robot here,' he said. 'We cannot allow such back-breaking work to be done by our people.'

The line was 500 metres long and Ratan realized that some workers would have to go up and down at least fifteen or twenty times in a day. So, he ordered swanky bicycles for the workers to traverse the line without getting tired! The robots, the cycles—they charged the atmosphere, impressing any lay observer with the investment in technology and modernization. It was history in the making.

Meanwhile, bookings for the new car had created a record of sorts, with more than 1.25 lakh people vying for it. When the first car was finally assembled, no one could believe it. It looked like an imported car! The first one took eight days to assemble but the next one took a day. Finally, the line picked up speed, producing a car every fifty-six seconds! This was in 1999.

Just a little earlier, on 28 December 1998, the bi-annual car exhibition at Pragati Maidan in New Delhi had attracted a whole host of manufacturers. Cars were being displayed on rotating platforms, with beautiful women posing as models for added attraction. But one stall was different. The models wore sarees, while the men sported turbans. School children waved the Indian flag when the car arrived, driven by Ratan Tata himself. Murasoli Maran, the Union industries minister, exclaimed, 'Wow! This is Kohinoor on wheels.'

His comment was apt. The government of the day was fighting a legal battle with Suzuki over the ownership of Maruti Suzuki. The company's products were very popular and the well-to-do middle class considered the Maruti 800 a necessity. The Tatas had given Indians an alternative. It was a matter of pride for the country.

Ratan Tata announced the name: Indica!

It was a name that spelt history. Not only did it represent India, it had a connection with the ancient and prosperous period of its civilization. Megasthenes, writing about India more than 2,000 years ago, had referred to India as Indica. The Greeks could not capture India, and Indica remained invincible to them. Now, Indica was being reborn in the form of a car brought to the world by the Tatas.

Ratan Tata knew that the group was not particularly known for its marketing flair and he did not want to miss cashing in on the buzz the preview of the car had created. A company known for its heavy and sturdy trucks had created a good-looking and functional car. It was like a daughter being born in a family crowded with boys! The spirit of celebration was of the same kind. There was also the pride of the first indigenously built car.

Ratan Tata ensured that the Indica was displayed at prominent places in all major towns. He wanted people to touch, feel, sit inside and get familiar with the Indica. People from all over the country came in droves to check out the new car.

Once, a Tata executive was driving home in an Indica when he was chased by a motorcyclist. Fearing that he was about to get mugged, he increased his speed, and the motorcyclist did the same. The Pune-Chinchwad road, which they were on, was deserted at night and the executive was now a worried man. The motorcyclist managed to halt the car by stopping his bike in front of it. When he got down, the executive realized that he had a small boy sitting pillion. He gathered that the man was not a mugger but a fan of the Indica and was keen to have his son take a close look at it. They both touched the car gently and thanked the executive for giving them the chance!

Indica bookings were being managed by a Tata Motors dealer called Concorde Motors. A network of sales offices and spare parts and service centres was being set up across the country. Rajiv Dube, a Tata Administrative Services graduate, was given charge of setting up the network. Rajiv had worked in Ratan Tata's office and was familiar with his style of working. The contract for advertising was given to FCB Ulka. 'India's most awaited car' was launched by the advertising agency with the slogan 'More car per car'. The campaign proved successful, with more than 1.25 lakh bookings at full price, giving the Tatas ample working capital. It also showed that the bookings were genuine. The customer had, after all, paid the full price.

Within the first month of its launch, Indica captured 14 per cent of the market share. It was now giving the Maruti 800 tough competition.

Maruti, reacting to the wave of Indica's popularity, dropped its prices by ₹25,000. The timing was deliberate. Ratan Tata was to give away the first few cars to the buyers at a programme organized at the Mahalaxmi Racecourse in Mumbai. The Maruti announcement was meant to disrupt, but Ratan Tata was unfazed. While addressing the buyers, he said, 'Thanks to the Tatas, now whichever car you choose to buy … you will get more!'

Unfortunately, the initial lot of cars turned out to be problematic with lots of glitches. The Indica, which was a darling of the customers a few months back, soon became the subject of controversy and was facing customers' ire. It cost Tata Motors a whopping ₹500 crore in the year 2000–01 to fix the issue. Quite naturally, the competition took advantage of the situation.

There were reports of how the basic design had a flaw and that the Tatas did not know how to manufacture a passenger car. The financial dailies too took Ratan Tata to task. Editorials vied with each other to lambast Tata Motors. The sad part was that the blame focused on the indigenization of the Indica. Ratan Tata was upset at the overwhelming lack of faith displayed by Indians in the ability of Indians to manufacture a fully indigenous car.

He called for a meeting of the senior executives of Tata Motors. It was held at the Taj President in Mumbai's Cuffe Parade. He allowed each one to speak. He wanted candid feedback on the problems. The executives, aware of Ratan Tata's appreciation of honest feedback, were relieved to be able to speak freely.

After hearing them out, he took charge of the meeting, asking for solutions to the problems placed before the group. It was decided to hold customer camps across the country and replace the defective parts free of cost. In many cases, entire engines were replaced. Ratan Tata announced, 'We shall do whatever it takes to make Indica trouble-free and make you a satisfied customer.'

The wave of resentment against Tata Motors subsided. Customers were pacified. The Tata company had wholeheartedly accepted its mistake and was willing to make amends. Ratan Tata ordered his executives to come out with a new model as soon as possible. The first model had been advertised as 'More car per car'. The next one said: 'Even more car per car.'

The second model was launched with an attractive television campaign. In the commercial, the Indica V2 is shown being revered by what appears to be a Japanese technical team (Japan still being considered the Mecca of automobiles in terms of technical expertise) after the vehicle is taken through a gruelling test drive. The new model turned out to be even more successful than the previous one.

The Indica V2 changed the fortunes of Tata Motors. It was far superior to the earlier model and became an instant hit. It got the best car award in the BBC motor show in the category of models priced ₹3-5 lakh. A magazine dedicated to cars did its own independent survey and concluded that the Indica V2 was indeed the most popular choice amongst customers. The V2 had won the J.D. Power survey. Tata Motors was now flying high on its success.

How did this happen? Ratan Tata had, after all, dug a deep hole worth ₹1,700 crore. To add to it, there was a lot of effort put in but no success had been in sight. No one had really believed him. The common refrain was that the burden of debt was going to be the proverbial last straw on the camel's back.

Ratan Tata credited all his success to one factor: belief in oneself. He said that despite all the cynicism and opposition, he was clear that the car had to be fully indigenous. He wanted his engineers to believe that they could make something truly remarkable—he could not tolerate engineers with no vision, no dreams in their eyes. He needed them to have a grand vision, and the Indica turned out to be such.

How did Ratan Tata manage to create that grand vision?

He said, 'I asked the engineers a simple question: Would you love to do something which has never been attempted before in India? If the answer is yes, here is what we would do—'

Ratan Tata managed to inspire the young engineers to believe in themselves and their capabilities. The rest is history.

20

Tata Finance Ltd and the Dilip Pendse Case

Many people in the Tata group still remember the day. It was 12 April 2001 when many senior Tata executives, a few officials in the Securities and Exchange Board of India (SEBI) and some journalists received a letter. No one to date has been able to find out who the sender was. Receiving letters of complaint was not uncommon. In an atmosphere of internal politics and increased competition, it was routine to see a letter trying to sabotage the progress of an organization. The whole idea behind such letters was to cast aspersions on someone or some organization. Most letters would be trashed without any further action. But this one was different. It prompted a serious investigation.

The letter was related to Tata Finance Limited (TFL) and its Managing Director, Dilip Pendse. There were serious allegations of fraud. The company had recently come out with a rights issue. By the time the letter arrived, the issue was already in the market. It was a legal requirement that all declarations be made before that stage. Such declarations were to be made in a public advertisement which clearly stated the risk factors so that the investor could take an informed decision.

The letter questioned the lack of transparency in the prospectus of the issue. It stated that, contrary to the claims made in it, the company's financial health was seriously damaged. No one could verify the authenticity of the sender but the allegations were serious enough to be examined.

Such a thing had never happened in the Tata group. TFL was one of the newer Tata companies, set up in 1990 with great hopes and expectations. It lent money to retail customers for the purchase of commercial vehicles, cars, domestic appliances and such products. The source of funds was fixed-term deposits from retail investors. TFL was paying a reasonable return on the deposits and hence managed to garner large deposits. The Tata name added to its 'safety' tag. The company had plans to enter into the banking and investment banking space. Its swanky office in the Fort area was quite different from the offices of other Tata companies, with its modern furniture, display screens, stylish cabins, etc. The whole idea was to impress the customer and any visitor to the company.

The company was rapidly growing and another subsidiary, Tata Home Finance, was carved out. The company also launched a credit card in association with American Express. It had a grand launch on the terrace of the Taj Mahal Hotel. In other words, the company was soon a star. Amongst its siblings, the other Tata companies, it stood out as an outstanding performer. Dilip Pendse was a rising star in the group, and was considered Ratan Tata's favourite.

Now, the letter had created a storm. Reporters flocked to the TFL office and many questions were being raised in the media coupled with gossip, rumours and speculations. But TFL was confident that none of the allegations were true. All the senior executives believed that none of the companies in the Tata group would cheat or fool investors and prospective shareholders. None took the media seriously. On the contrary, they issued a public statement against such allegations. The message was meant to pacify the shareholders and investors that none of the allegations had any substance and they were meant to spoil the name of the company and its group.

But soon, realization dawned that there was some merit in the allegations. There were doubts raised about some of TFL's executives as well as the international audit firm A.F. Ferguson. Before the letter had reached TFL, the Enron scandal had already shown how internal auditors, hand-in-glove with the company, could wreak havoc. There were doubts that AFF had played a similar role, and that Pendse had invested large amounts of company reserves into the public market without the knowledge of the board. It was not illegal to do so but there were questions about personal integrity being raised.

AFF was given the task of carrying out the internal audit. The idea was to investigate the period between 1999 and 2001. AFF charged a hefty fee of ₹95 lakh to carry out the exercise. It carried such clout that it could charge such high fees. The job was personally handled by one of its senior partners, Y.M. Kale.

Kale was asked to inquire into the affairs at TFL and its subsidiaries between 1999 and 2001. He commenced his work in June 2001 and submitted an interim report to the Tatas within a month. The final version was submitted in April 2002. By July, extracts of the report appeared in the media, but the controversy exploded when AFF announced that it was withdrawing the report and returning the audit fees. In its press release issued on 8 August, AFF expressed reservations about Kale's 'past conduct' and stated that its partners had 'lost faith' in Kale, who had joined AFF three decades ago.

In a dramatic development on 19 August, officials of the Registrar of Companies (RoC) in Mumbai, acting on behalf of the Department of Company Affairs (DCA), commenced search and seizure operations at AFF premises in the city. The operation was conducted after invoking rarely used provisions under Section 234-A of the Companies Act. The legal clause is specifically meant to enable the RoC to act if, in his perception, there is a fear that documents may be 'destroyed, mutilated, altered, falsified or secreted'. The allegation of AFF and TFL acting hand-in-glove was a damning one. The DCA wanted to raid TFL offices.

Ratan Tata publicly acknowledged that there had been some misappropriation in TFL. He assured the shareholders and investors that they need not be worried and that the group would look into the matter. It was a question of prestige that the Tata name carried. 'We will ensure none of the investors and their money is put to risk,' he said.

As of 30 June 2001, the total losses in TFL amounted to ₹500 crore. It was not about the losses, but the manner in which the matters had been conducted was to pose a question mark on the integrity of the Tatas. It was a black mark for the entire group.

At the core of all this was a small investment company called Nishkalp Investment and Trading Company. It was one of the subsidiaries created by Tata Finance. Nishkalp was responsible for raising inter-corporate deposits to take care of the capital requirement of the subsidiary companies. Prima facie there was nothing illegal about the activities of Nishkalp.

Nishkalp had been indulging in trading in the stock markets and had raked in substantial profits before the crash of 2000. Before the bubble burst, it had invested more than ₹500 crore between March 2000 and March 2001. In order to garner such an amount, TFL had openly flouted Reserve Bank of India (RBI) norms, which required a non-banking finance company (NBFC) to maintain certain capital adequacy. The market crash had reduced the investments to zero.

In order to show that Nishkalp was not part of TFL, the company started the procedure to separate it from the parent company. By then it was clear that Pendse had been involved deeply in all the matters. The total amount received from investors was ₹2,700 crore, out of which ₹875 crore came from nearly 4 lakh small investors. A lot of them were retired people who had poured their life savings into TFL. They had put their faith behind the Tata name. Apparently, Dilip Pendse had acted in ths manner to 'create more profits for Tata Finance'.

This, of course, was not true. A large part of the speculative investment was for personal profit. The three companies where most of the money was invested were Global Telesystems, DSQ and Vakrangee Software. Since Nishkalp was controlled by Pendse, most of the profits accrued from the market transactions were to his benefit. He had used the deposits collected by Tata Finance for personal gain.

Ratan Tata realized that he needed some immediate corrective action. There was no question of allowing TFL to go bankrupt. The Tata group would lose the faith of lakhs of depositors. There was a fear of its backlash on other Tata companies. The immediate task at hand was to raise ₹875 crore to cover the losses. The message to the depositors was clear: 'You can withdraw your deposits at any point in time.'

Tata Sons and Tata Industries put ₹700 crore together. What Ratan Tata did was not required by law. But he could not afford to allow one of the group companies to fail during his watch. His main objective was to not allow the faith in the Tata group to diminish in any manner. He had kept two helicopters on standby in case there was a need to deposit cash in any TFL branch. He did not want an impression in the market that the Tata group was cash-strapped.

Pendse was terminated and a case filed against him by the Tata group. His misdemeanours were many—cheating, forgery, criminal conspiracy and misappropriation of funds were the stated charges, along with criminal breach of trust, falsification of accounts—but it was the alleged misuse of his position to dupe small investors and the resulting loss of faith in NBFCs that was said to be his biggest crime.

It was important for Ratan to take the step as there had never been a case of a financial fraud of such magnitude. The investors had never faced such a situation. It was necessary that the guilty were punished. Not only would it send out a clear message to the investors who had reposed their faith in the Tata name but it would also set the tone for the future and deter any such frauds in the group. It was crucial for Ratan Tata to get to the root of the problem. He personally got involved in the investigations.

All records were investigated, whether letters, emails, bank transactions, property purchase and any such documents which would lead to further information. After collecting the necessary information, a case was lodged in the local police station against Pendse and other senior executives. Nothing much emerged as the police did not have the necessary expertise to look into a matter of financial fraud. For reasons not fully known, the police did not pursue the matter. Surprised at the stance taken by the police, the Tatas filed a petition in the Supreme Court requesting that the CBI take up the case.

Pendse, in the meanwhile, issued his reply. He claimed that he had kept former TFL Chairman Freddie Mehta informed of Nishkalp's investments on a daily basis. 'All transactions had the consent of the TFL board. They are now trying to make me a scapegoat,' he alleged. He claimed that Bombay House was very much aware of his dealings and now he was being targeted for the losses. Not that anyone believed his claims.

He further alleged that Ratan Tata was in the know regarding his dealings. At the same time, AFF came out with a public notice alleging fraudulent practices by Kale and the police arrested him.

There were various complaints from SEBI and RBI against Pendse. Ratan made some significant changes in the corporate governance structure of the group companies. Earlier, the finance head of a company reported to its managing director. With the new change, the finance head was to report to Bombay House too. The finance head was also told that he should report any wrongdoings to Bombay House directly. A whistleblower policy was put in place. TFL thus became a case study for the group's governance practices.

Later, TFL was merged with Tata Motors in 2004. It was a logical merger, as TFL's main job was to provide loans for commercial vehicles and cars being sold by Tata Motors. The new entity was called Tata Motors Finance or TMF. In 2007, another company, Tata Capital, was formed to look into capital markets and other investments. Tata Capital made rapid strides and proved to be successful. Soon, people forgot the omissions and commissions of TFL, and Tata Capital became a name to reckon with.

Dilip Pendse committed suicide in July 2017 by hanging at his Mumbai office, leaving behind a note that said he was frustrated because of the legal cases going on against him and had therefore decided to end his life.

21

Building Tata Consultancy Services

Tata Consultancy Services (TCS) is now the most admired company of the group and the largest in the information technology space in India. It is also among the largest private employers in India, with more than 2.5 lakh staff, second only to the Indian Railways. To understand its genesis, we need to go back in time—to the 1960s, in fact.

THE BIRTH OF TCS

It was a decade of turbulence. There had been two wars in a short span of three years, leaving the economy in tatters, with a mere 3 per cent growth in the gross domestic product (GDP). The socialist and controlled economy approach demoralized anyone who wanted to set up a business. The licence raj was at its peak. The core areas of the Tata group were iron and steel, automobiles, chemicals, etc. But the government was eyeing these for nationalization. The Tatas were exploring an area which was not in the government's sphere of interest. It was JRD's brother-in-law, Leslie Sawhney, who came up with the proposal. 'Let us get into data processing,' he suggested.

The various companies under the Tata group needed to have a centralized database, where records and other information could be stored. There were records related to employees, their salaries, gratuity and pension plans. It was a cumbersome task to store the data in physical files and it was almost impossible to retrieve information from such files as and when required. Sawhney had proposed storing all such information in computerized form. But those were the days when computerization was looked upon as an evil that took away jobs. JRD was aware of the possibilities of the computer and how it could help the group in the long run. He had seen how computers were being put to use in other countries. TISCO and TELCO were huge and maintaining their records about production and other details was a good starting point.

JRD immediately agreed to Sawhney's idea and decided to implement it. He selected a few people from the Tata Administrative Services for training in computers. He knew these candidates would be more open to such new learning. There were only two computer manufacturers then: IBM and Burroughs. These companies did not sell computers but would give them on rental basis. JRD decided to form a new company to undertake the task. A space was carved out in Bombay House for the new division, which was christened as Tata Computing Centre. Later, the centre was moved to a larger space in the Army and Navy Building and then to a bigger place at Ballard Pier.

Not many were in favour of the new initiative as they saw it as a 'waste of money'. JRD had spent nearly ₹50 lakh on the new entity. The opposition also came from those heading the various businesses. They were reluctant to share their information with the centre. At most they would send across bare minimum information just to pacify JRD. But there was one more individual in the group who knew the value of computerization and its long-term advantages. The man was in Tata Electric Companies, which later became Tata Power.

FAQIR CHAND KOHLI: FATHER OF THE INDIAN SOFTWARE INDUSTRY

He had studied computer science at the prestigious Massachusetts Institute of Technology in the US. He decided to put computers to use in Tata Electric Companies to manage power supply in Bombay. The fact that the city rarely sees power cuts even today is thanks in large part to the vision of this young man named Faqir Chand Kohli. Decades later, F.C. Kohli was honoured as the Father of the Indian Software Industry.

The young team selected by JRD christened the division as Tata Consultancy Services. It was thus in 1968 that TCS was formed. Within a year, Kohli was moved from Tata Electric Companies to TCS. He took six months to understand the workings and what they were expected to deliver. He had a young team at TCS and the atmosphere in the office was fun-filled. IT was yet in in its infancy and miles away from manufacturing.

Kohli used to teach at the Indian Institute of Technology in Bombay. None of the colleges in India even had a department of computers or information technology at the time. One had to go abroad to study, so there was no question of the industries having this know-how.

The first institution to start the department was IIT Kanpur. When Kohli came to know of it, he recruited all its graduates into TCS! It was thanks to his far-sightedness that the students he selected laid the foundation of the IT industry in India. But this was all to happen much later. When TCS began operations, they would hardly get any projects in the IT space. Yet, they had to survive and the company decided to offer 'administrative services' to earn some revenue. Some of their clients then were the Nuclear Power Corporation of India, Delhi Development Authority, and Hindustan Aeronautics Limited.

Kohli decided to overhaul the image of TCS completely when he was given independent charge of it in 1974. Just a couple of years before this, he had been lucky to find an IT expert who would later on earn a lot of accolades. The young man was a Tamilian born in Nagpur. After his engineering degree in India, he had earned his master's in computer science from the University of California, Los Angeles in the US. It was the dawn of the IT age in the US and he was enjoying his job and a good pay there. But two phone calls from India were to change his life forever. The first was from his father telling him about the bride they had selected for him. The would-be wife, Mahalakshmi, had a condition: she would not leave India. The message from his father was: 'Enough of America; please return to India.' The second phone call was from Kohli inviting him to join TCS.

The job opportunity along with the condition put forth by his future wife was a golden combination and he returned to India to join TCS as an Assistant Systems Programmer and Analyst. Compared to his salary of $12,000 per month in the US, he was offered a monthly remuneration of just ₹1,000 in India! Yet, he decided to join!

He was to lead the company two decades later. The young man's name: Subramaniam Ramadorai. Alongside offering administrative services, Kohli had started many divisions, such as data centre management, software, hardware, marketing, and so on, which gave an impetus for TCS to grow. Those were the times of socialist policies, the Emergency and licence raj. It was difficult for industries to grow in such conditions.

To add to the woes, the imposition of FERA was another blow to the industry. There was huge demand for the import of computers but the high duty of 135 per cent was a deterrent. There was a further duty of 100 per cent on software imports. Buying computers was an impossible task. The government was not even willing to label computers as a machine. The logic was that it had no moving parts, hence did not qualify as a machine! TCS had, in fact, taken legal recourse to solve this problem.

At the time, three ministries—defence, commerce and finance—were required to give their consent before a computer could be imported into India. Each ministry had to be sent eleven copies of the request form. One could imagine the time taken to push all this through the bureaucratic red tape. The application required details of all spare parts and, if there were any discrepancies in the actual consignment, it would be confiscated by customs!

Moreover, the government did not recognize software as an industry, making it impossible to get loans from banks. Foreign companies were not allowed to open offices in India. They could open a subsidiary with 40 per cent equity participation. That was the time when companies like IBM and Coca-Cola withdrew from India. The withdrawal of the former turned out to be an opportunity for TCS, in a way. Burroughs approached TCS to form a joint venture to take care of the business left behind by IBM. But the rules and regulations were stifling, making it impossible to grow.

So, TCS invested $300,000 and an equivalent amount in duties to import a mainframe computer. It had to agree to purchase a software equivalent of the duties before it was allowed to get the computer into India. It was an investment ahead of its times as TCS did not have the necessary workload to keep the mainframe busy. But the company used the time available to send its engineers abroad to learn on mainframe systems.

Gradually, work started coming TCS's way and, apart from foreign companies, Indian organizations too started approaching it for help. It worked on varied projects—from conducting board examinations to helping telcom divisions create telephone directories, setting up billing processes for electricity distribution companies and municipal corporations, and so on. The engineers trained at the Burroughs facility turned out to be extremely useful when the business opportunities arose. They were familiar with both the hardware and software aspects of the business. Realizing that there were savings in terms of foreign currency, a lot of business turned the TCS way.

The belief that computers would take away jobs was still strong. One of the victims of such a mindset was the Life Insurance Corporation of India (LIC). Having bought a mainframe computer at its Calcutta office, the corporation was not allowed to use it thanks to an agitation by its employees' union. Realizing that the sale was of no use, TCS offered to take the mainframe back at the price at which it had sold it to LIC.

Kohli and his team were keen to get into the manufacture of mainframes but the Tata group was not willing to invest the kind of capital required for such a venture. Finally, TCS and Burroughs started another joint venture named Tata Burroughs. But soon Kohli realized that Burroughs, riding on the Tata name and connections, would be the larger beneficiary of the two partners. In fact, Tata Burroughs was now competing with TCS in the market.

Finding that there was no reconciliation between the two organizations, it was finally decided that TCS would focus on the software business while Burroughs would address the hardware side of it. It was in some sense a challenge for TCS as many of the TCS employees had moved to Burroughs. Now, with the focus on software alone, TCS was required to build the entire marketing and sales capabilities. The future did not look bright and there was a lot of stress all around. It was a question of survival.

SUBRAMANIAM RAMADORAI: TAKING TCS TO THE AMERICAN MARKET

Kohli took a bold yet visionary decision. He realized that if the company were to focus on software, the Indian market was too small and he needed to look outside of India. The biggest market was the US. He decided to open a branch in New York and named Ramadorai as the head. Sales was not his forte, yet Kohli felt he was the right man for the job. 'You know the American market; you have worked there. I am sure you will learn sales too.' This was in 1979. Ramadorai was literally working with a door-to-door approach, asking prospective clients whether they needed any software. A lot of doors were shut in his face!

He had to face challenges on two fronts. The fact that he was an Indian reduced his credibility considerably. No one wanted to buy software from an Indian. The other objection was from Naval Mody, who was the head of Tata Sons in the US and was not well disposed to Ramadorai's appointment there. He was strict about sanctioning official expenses for Ramadorai. In fact, Ramadorai did all sorts of odd jobs in his office, from typing out letters to acting as a software expert, in the initial days.

But soon Mody realized Ramadorai's potential and calibre and was convinced that he had not come to the US to splurge the company's money. It so happened that on the day Mody had called for a review meeting, the New York metro workers went on strike. Ramadorai could not afford to spend cab fare as he was conscious of Kohli's maxim of 'earn first, spend later'. That day, Ramadorai walked for nearly an hour and a half from his home to the office and reached in time for the meeting. When Mody heard of this, his opinion of Ramadorai began to change. Later, he invited him for a lunch meeting when JRD came visiting. It was the first opportunity for Ramadorai to spend time with JRD. Naturally, he was overwhelmed. The chance to meet JRD convinced him that he was on the right track and that his efforts would produce results.

Within a year, that happened. The Institutional Group Information Corporation, IGIC, a subsidiary of the Union Dime Savings Bank, was likely to use the services of TCS. IGIC needed a lot of programmers which TCS was capable of providing. TCS was willing to sign an informal agreement to get the contract going. The contract meant that in case IGIC did not like the services of TCS, it could terminate the contract. For the first six months, TCS was to provide two programmers. This was increased to three and then to six. They liked the work and, within two years, TCS had thirty-six programmers working for IGIC. Finally, the number rose to 300.

It was a historic moment for TCS. It was the origin of Business Process Outsourcing, BPO, as we know it today. It set up a new paradigm of doing business, taking advantage of time zone difference. More than fifty engineers were working for IGIC round the clock. This was long before the advent of the internet. Such was Kohli's vision! The business, which started with Ramadorai being alone in the US, was now worth $700,000. TCS bagged prestigious accounts of the likes of Young & Rubicam, the advertising agency, and Smith & Wesson, a manufacturer of firearms and ammunition, among others.

THE NATIONAL STOCK EXCHANGE CHALLENGE

After stabilizing the business abroad, Ramadorai returned to India in 1981. The American software business was booming but there was hardly any software business in India. It was logical that TCS would want to spread to other countries. It signed agreements with several Swiss banks. The modus operandi was the same: it would get the work done in India for customers outside the country. TCS was now growing at a rapid pace.

There were changes happening in India in the meanwhile. Rajiv Gandhi was made Prime Minister in 1984 and Ratan Tata was becoming more visible in the group. Both Rajiv and Ratan were fond of computers and believed in their potential to transform businesses.

As mentioned earlier, Ratan, while spending time with his convalescing mother in New York, had made a detailed proposal on what the Tata group's future plans and way forward should look like. JRD, fully supporting his views, had said that the group was already strong in the steel and automobile sectors and needed to focus on software services. He saw an IT wave coming and the group needed to be well prepared to take advantage of it.

While the predictions were turning out to be true, TCS had taken its baby steps and was ready to fly. It had branches in the US, Switzerland, Argentina, England and many European nations. In the early 1990s, its services were in great demand. Manmohan Singh had opened up the economy and the stock market crash, thanks to Harshad Mehta, had made people acutely aware of the need for controls in place. Computerization was to play a major part in it.

On the basis of the recommendation of a high-powered committee, a new exchange, the National Stock Exchange (NSE) was created in 1992. Till then, the Bombay Stock Exchange (BSE), started in 1875, was the only national exchange. NSE was the first in the country to provide a modern, fully automated, screen-based electronic trading system to investors spread across the length and breadth of the country.

TCS had done work for stock exchanges in Hong Kong and Taiwan and was well positioned to bid for the work at NSE. But the task at NSE was mammoth and involved setting up the entire infrastructure from hardware to networking across 500 branches. We must remember the telecom system of the time to understand the magnitude of the challenge.

The crucial point to keep in mind is that the system was being developed for the retail investor and any error would have an impact across the nation and on the market. TCS had never undertaken a task so huge and was competing with IBM, Wipro and other such companies. Ramadorai was personally involved in the proposal with sixty of his top executives. Finally, they bagged the contract. The team worked day and night and completed the task before the deadline. Most of the members had toiled hard, leaving office not before midnight every day. The new exchange was inaugurated in June 1994 by Finance Minister Manmohan Singh.

Today, the NSE is counted amongst the top three exchanges in the world in terms of volume of trade, and is one of the most modern. It handles more than 70 lakh trades daily and is connected to twenty-three exchanges. The work done by TCS laid the foundation for its ability to handle such high volumes.

Creating a stock exchange was one part. The other challenge was to dematerialize the share certificates. The paper share certificates had posed several challenges, with frauds, errors and reversals in transactions leading to innumerable problems. Not to talk of delays for months in finalizing the transactions.

The formation of the National Securities and Depository Services (NSDL) was to eliminate the problems of paper trading. NSDL was headed by Chandrasekhar Bhave. TCS bagged the contract of NSDL and managed to successfully deliver it. Many other huge contracts, like the one from Standard Chartered Bank, were bagged by TCS, catapulting it to number one position in India. The year 1996 was a significant one for TCS. Kohli retired, handing over the reins to Ramadorai, who had joined TCS as a trainee in 1972. It was a milestone event for both TCS and Ramadorai.

RAMADORAI TAKES CHARGE: Y2K, INCREASED COMPETITION AND THE TCS IPO

Ramadorai's style of working was very different from that of Kohli. Kohli could be described as a 'benevolent dictator', who would ensure that each employee contributed to the best of his abilities. His project managers would keep an eagle eye on each of the team members. If anyone was found lacking, Kohli would call him and ask whether there was a problem. He would thus make everyone feel that they were being observed. He was the only one who would speak in meetings. The others would follow his instructions.

Ramadorai was the exact opposite. He was friendly and open to ideas and suggestions from anyone. More importantly, he had been with TCS right since its inception. There was no job he had not done—from assembling a computer with a screwdriver to making a sales pitch to big multinational companies. Now, having taken charge of the company, he had the opportunity to build on the solid foundation laid by Kohli.

Ratan Tata had said, talking of the change in TCS, that the organization was once a data entry operator, a card-punching company, but Kohli had created the grand vision and the ability to think big while Ramadorai had turned the vision into reality. Within six years of Ramadorai's taking charge, by 2002, TCS revenues had more than doubled. It was the first for any Indian IT company. The company had its operations in thirty-four countries, with an employee strength of 28,000. Six of the top ten organizations in the world were using services provided by TCS. It was truly a multinational company now. One of the reasons for the transformation was the turn of the century from 1999 to 2000.

The problem, commonly known as Y2K, was a boon for TCS. On 1 January 2000, computers would read only the last two digits of the date as '00', taking the year back to 1900. While on the face of it this did not look like a daunting problem, in reality it would have created chaos, especially in banks and other important systems. The challenge was to rectify the problem before 31 December 1999. But it was also a massive opportunity that was seized very well by Indian IT companies. TCS bagged major contracts.

It was becoming evident to Ratan Tata that TCS could not remain under the shadow of Tata Sons. By then, Infosys had already entered the market with an initial public offering (IPO) and had debuted on the New York Stock Exchange too. Many felt that TCS had missed the boat.

The idea was mooted by Ishaat Hussain after he took charge as the finance director of Tata Sons. But it was not a proposal which would be immediately approved by Bombay House. After all, TCS was generating record profits, of which 50 per cent would accrue to Tata Sons after ploughing back the rest into the company. Ratan Tata was clear that he needed to take TCS public and set up a high-powered committee of twenty-five people to propose the way forward. The biggest challenge was legal: Tata Sons' ownership was with different trusts. It was necessary to change the laws if these trusts were to participate in the TCS IPO.

It was the first-of-its-kind exercise in India wherein a company was being separated from its parent, and it was necessary to study all legal loopholes. The committee recommended approaching the courts and SEBI to clarify their position. It took nearly two years to get things sorted out. Investment bankers were eagerly waiting for the IPO, which was expected in 2004. Many bankers were vying for the issue, which was finally awarded to Morgan Stanley, DSP Merrill Lynch and J.P. Morgan India. The issue price was fixed in the band of ₹775 to ₹900, with nearly 5.5 crore shares on offer. It was the biggest IPO Indian markets had ever seen.

The IPO was slated for May 2004, and the change in the political climate proved to be the decisive factor. The Atal Bihari Vajpayee-led National Democratic Alliance (NDA) faced a shock defeat. The Congress emerged as the single largest party and entered into an alliance with the communists. The result was a stock market crash. The alliance with the Left signalled a reversal of the NDA's pro-market policies. A.B. Bardhan of the Communist Party of India (CPI) had famously remarked, 'Let the stock markets go to hell.' His words proved true, with the BSE Sensex falling by nearly 710 points on a single day. Investors had lost lakhs of crores of their wealth.

It would have been suicidal to launch the IPO in such a situation. The Tata group decided to delay the IPO till the markets improved. By July, the markets were stable and the TCS IPO was finally launched. It received an unprecedented response. The situation was similar to when Dorabji Tata had reached out to individual investors. People stood in queues to fill up forms for investing into the IPO. More than 25 per cent of the issue was subscribed by the common man, reposing his trust in the Tata name. The issue, launched at a price of ₹850, opened in the market with a jump of ₹300.

Most of the people in the Tata group at the time remember the day of the listing. Employees came with cameras to capture the moment when, on 25 August 2004, Ratan Tata, Ramadorai and the person who would later become TCS CEO and eventually Chairman of Tata Sons, Natarajan Chandrasekaran, hit the gong at the BSE. The stock opened at ₹1,150, much to the cheer of investors. After thirty-six years of the existence of TCS, the retail investor was getting a chance to participate in its equity offering. Interestingly, the stock exchanges on which the TCS stock was listed were running on the infrastructure and platform created by TCS itself!

It was in 1984 that Ratan Tata had said that the future belonged to IT and the Tata group must be prepared to take advantage of it. Twenty years after that, his words were being proven true by the faith reposed by investors in TCS. Ratan Tata had toiled day in and day out for the IPO. He had travelled extensively across the globe making presentations to international investors. It was a physically demanding exercise. He would fly overnight on little sleep, land in a city, make presentations the whole day and then fly out to the next destination. The routine was exhausting and continued for nearly two months.

A lesser industrialist would have put his feet up after the success of the IPO. But not Ratan Tata, who was already dreaming up his next project. One of the peculiarities of the Tata group leaders is that no sooner had they captured one peak than they would start thinking of ascending the next. The Tata name meant taking up multiple challenges at the same time. Ratan Tata was to live up to it in both spirit and action.

22

Small Car, Big Trouble

'How many trucks do you need to move all this?'

Ramesh Vishwakarma was taken aback by the question. It was 17 October 2008—the date most people in Tata Motors would remember. Vishwakarma, the head of manufacturing at the Nano factory in Singur, West Bengal, had not anticipated such a question and was not sure what his answer should be. He was not even sure why he was being asked such a question. The question was posed by his boss, Ravi Kant, the Managing Director of Tata Motors.

The Singur project had been Ratan Tata's dream. But the conditions were not conducive for it to be fulfilled. In fact, many people had tried to ensure the project never took off. Ravi Kant's question to Vishwakarma was thus not out of context. After a quick back-of-the-envelope calculation, Vishwakarma said, 'We would need at least 3,000 trucks, give or take a few hundred.'

After a few deliberations, it was decided to carry out an enormous logistical exercise—that of moving an entire plant from one place to another! There are not many examples of a task of such magnitude being carried out in the world. The plant was to be moved to a location thousands of kilometres away: from Singur in West Bengal to Sanand in Gujarat. The entire logistical nightmare involved 3,340 trucks and 495 containers and took nearly seven months to complete. Sanand was about 2,000 km from Singur. The operation would cost a few hundred crores. Why was this exercise carried out in the first place?

THE ₹1 LAKH CAR

It was Ratan Tata's dream to produce a ₹1 lakh car. He wanted to help the middle class population graduate from two-wheelers to four-wheelers. He wanted to give them an indigenously produced car which would not only be affordable but which the owner would also feel proud of driving.

The seeds of the idea were sown in his mind many years back. He would see the common man pulling a hand-rickshaw in Calcutta, or his factory worker carrying goods on his shoulders while walking for miles, and wonder if he could create a common man's car. He would cringe seeing a family of four going on a scooter, the lady riding pillion with a child in one hand while the other hand held on to her husband, the second child standing in the front between his legs. To such families, he wanted to offer a car which would be affordable and comfortable.

While he mulled over these thoughts, he once happened to see a three-wheeler car displayed by BMW at an international car exhibition. It had two large rubber bumpers on the sides, which were meant to protect the car if it toppled. Unfortunately, the response to the car was quite poor. Ratan realized that even a giant like BMW was not successful in launching a small car. He was reminded of another instance of such failure. Chrysler, the American car giant, had launched a car for Asia. The car's body was made from a single mould. While the material was plastic, it was as strong as steel. Despite its low price, the car hardly sold.

People wanted a car which was affordable. Yet, a car with a low price did not garner sales. Ratan was keen to understand buyer behaviour and the psychology behind it. He discovered that in the case of both Chrysler and BMW, while the car was priced low, it was not a car in the true sense of the word. The customer was not going to buy a car just because it was low priced. The discerning buyer wanted all the features which a regular car would offer and would not settle for anything less.

Many American homes proudly displayed a small car standing between luxury cars like a Mercedes or a BMW. The customer had bought the small car for a specific reason, whether for local commute or for travel over small distances. Companies like Chrysler or BMW had not been able to identify such a need. All they did was produce a low-priced car which expectedly failed. Ratan realized he had to produce an inexpensive car which had all the minimum essential features of a regular car. A year before the highly successful IPO launch of TCS, he called some of his engineers in TELCO and asked them to work on a car design which 'would be affordable for the common man'.

He also added that an affordable car did not mean a compromise on safety or engine performance. It was a challenging mandate as each feature would increase the cost. But Ratan was clear about his end objective, and he was sure his engineers would be able to come up with a solution. One of the engineers in the group selected for the project was a thirty-two-year-old, Girish Wagh. It was coincidental that his father had been part of the Indica project. Now, the next generation was to work on another of Ratan's dreams.

The group began in right earnest. Ratan Tata himself was closely involved in the design from day one. The group knew that while other features were being considered, they could not afford to neglect the aesthetics of the car. It could not be a shoddy job. The group started working on removing all the inessential features of the cars in use at the time and then focused on the main body. Many of the solid parts were to be replaced with hollow tubings to reduce weight. The engine had to be small and compact, yet powerful. They wanted to contract Bosch, as it was a global leader in engine injection systems and management.

But Bosch was not willing to come on board. Other spare parts manufacturers also showed disinterest. It was not new for Ratan Tata. Even while conceptualizing the Indica, he had faced similar resistance from the Automotive Component Manufacturers Association. Several industrialists had questioned the need for and the financial risk involved in it.

The response this time too was no different. Ratan Tata was not discouraged and started a dialogue with a few small parts manufacturers. Some of them agreed. His challenge was to convince the manufacturers that it was possible to produce such a car. Winning them over was crucial. They had never thought on these lines. But that was the Tata philosophy: if you don't dream big, you can never make something happen. It took a while for Ratan Tata to convince his stakeholders that it was possible to create a small, yet powerful, and cheap car. He had had tested the waters with the Indica and he knew that convincing the people involved was an important first step.

The tie-rods connecting the steering to the wheels are quite heavy. Their weight was to be reduced. The engine design underwent three changes. There was a debate on the engine capacity—whether it should be 540 cc or 550 cc. The unique combination of a smaller capacity delivering higher power was a challenge. Finally, an engine capacity of 624 cc was finalized. It was also decided that only two wheels, either the front or the back ones, would be powered by the engine. It was to be a two-wheel drive.

The tie-rod design was changed thirty-two times before the final one was approved. This was done with the help of French and Italian auto experts. Another challenge was to reduce the size of the clutch pedal. At the same time, Ratan Tata was clear that the car should have space for a six-foot man to sit comfortably. The design engineers were losing sleep trying to arrive at a solution. Ratan had clearly stated that he was going to drive the car. He himself was 5'10" tall, and the engineers tried out multiple versions to get the design right. The initial one looked like two two-wheelers put together, while a few of them looked like a mechanized rickshaw. Quite obviously, they were rejected.

It took nearly two years to get the design and technical specifications in place. Many small manufacturers had, in the meanwhile, agreed to come on board. A number of MNCs, which were earlier sceptical of Ratan Tata's plan to make a car costing less than $2,500, came forward to help.

BATTLEGROUND WEST BENGAL

The next question was the site for manufacturing the car. The logical choice was Poona, which was home to Tata Motors. Indica was born there and it was quite natural that its younger sister too should be delivered there. But TELCO's business had expanded and there was hardly any room for the new assembly line. There was no space to expand in the Pimpri-Chinchwad area. Even if it were available, the cost was prohibitively high. Ratan scouted for a state which would not just be willing but would also see the huge potential in having a TELCO plant set up there.

The West Bengal government came forward. For years, the state had suffered on the industrialization front, thanks to the policies of successive Left governments. The agriculture scene too was not encouraging, leading to high unemployment. A large industrial project was a golden opportunity for the state. Chief Minister Buddhadeb Bhattacharjee took the lead in inviting the Tatas for a discussion. He had succeeded Jyoti Basu, who had ruled West Bengal for decades and had a commanding persona. Buddhadeb was keen to get large industrial houses to invest in West Bengal and create employment. Being part of a Left party, he knew there would be resistance to any foreign investment. Creating special economic zones was clearly ruled out. The only thing possible was to encourage domestic investment.

The Tatas presented an opportunity which was unlikely to be objected by anyone. The labour unions too would welcome such a move. Buddhadeb met Ratan Tata and proposed a place for the upcoming project, which would draw an investment of more than ₹1,000 crore into the state. A lot of small manufacturers would also get an opportunity to support the plant, adding to investment and employment. Buddhadeb was thus keen to see the project come to fruition.

A few other states too had shown interest, but Ratan was keen on West Bengal as it would offer the additional convenience of a port facility for exports. The land required for the project was around 1,000 acres and the West Bengal government proposed six places, of which

Singur was finally chosen. The responsibility of getting the land was that of the government. The land was primarily rice fields but the Tatas were clear that they did not want to get involved in acquisition. Only recently have some changes been made to ease the process, but until 2013 it was governed by the Land Acquisition Act of 1894.

The Act allowed a government to acquire land for public use like roads, dams, airports, railways, etc. Using the powers under the Act, the West Bengal government started acquiring land for the project. At that time, with state elections around the corner, Mamata Banerjee was looking for an issue over which to bring down the Left government. The Congress was a nonentity in West Bengal, while the BJP had not gained any foothold. Singur provided her an opportunity. She began accusing the Left government of supporting industrialists at the cost of farmers. She did not buy the argument that the project would help the state's economy by providing employment to thousands of locals.

Well-known personalities like Aparna Sen, Arundhati Roy, Kaushik Sen and others extended their support to her. Social activist Medha Patkar also joined in. The whole objective was to stall the project. While the immediate target was the Left government, the real loser was going to be the Tatas. Mamata argued that the project was a classic example of capitalists exploiting the poor.

It became a prestige issue for the Left government, while Mamata made it her personal goal to scuttle it. The matter reached the courts, which ruled in favour of the government, stating that it had the right to acquire land. The Tatas heaved a sigh of relief, hoping that the matter would end. But, on the contrary, the issue escalated further. Mamata and her party members appealed to the people to go on strike. The call for 'Save Singur' was further fuelled by Naxalites, who gave their support for the 'Remove Tata' campaign.

The work to erect a fence around the designated land was to start on 1 December 2006. In order to prevent Mamata and her supporters from creating trouble, the state government issued orders to stop them from entering Singur. Mamata started a hunger strike and appealed to the farmers in Singur to give in writing that their land was being taken away forcefully by the government. The fence was erected and the work for the construction of the factory started. Little did they anticipate that a huge problem was on its way.

While the supporters of the Left government were guarding the project site, news of their excesses against the protesters started spreading. A sixteen-year-old girl, one of the youngest and most dedicated protesters in Singur, was raped and burnt alive. It was believed that supporters of the ruling party had a hand in it but the government refused to accept the charge, vitiating the atmosphere further. The matter was handed over to the CBI and the perpetrators were booked. By 2007, the factory was taking shape, but the situation was going from bad to worse.

The Tatas had, in the meanwhile, set up another project at Pantnagar in Uttarakhand, which was to supply some components to Singur. Also, Ratan Tata had showcased the new car at an exhibition. He had announced that it would be available for sale from 2008 onwards. By then, nearly 4,000 workers were employed in Singur. Graduates from the local industrial technical institutes were being trained for the new project. As promised, the Tatas had ensured that jobs were being offered to the locals. A total of 997 acres of land had been acquired and the project was in full swing despite the problems outside.

The project was on schedule to produce the first car by 2008. But the optimism turned out to be short-lived. Mamata's Trinamool Congress upped its ante. Buses carrying workers from Kolkata were regularly stopped, leading to delays. On 28 August, Trinamool Congress supporters gheraoed the plant. Work came to a standstill. The police had to intervene to allow workers to go home. Discussions with Mamata failed to make any headway; she was adamant that the land had to be returned to the farmers. It was becoming increasingly apparent that the Tatas could not carry on in such a situation.

Girish Wagh made a detailed presentation to senior Tata executives. The situation was becoming tense and they could not afford to have their employees' lives at stake. Ravi Kant listened to him patiently and promised to ensure that the situation would be taken care of. He asked Wagh to focus on the task at hand. While Ravi Kant pacified Wagh, it was becoming clear to him that the project at Singur would not take off. Realizing that there was no point wasting further resources, energy and money, they decided to bite the bullet and take a tough call. The writing on the wall was clear: the plant had to be wound up and established elsewhere.

NANO PROJECT LEAVES BENGAL

But Ratan Tata was worried about the 3,000-odd men who had been given employment at the plant. The workers were shifted to the Ramakrishna Mission for training. At least, they would remain gainfully employed without any fear for their lives.

He met Buddhadeb Bhattacharjee and then, on 3 October, announced, 'We are shifting the plant from Singur.' In a departure from his usual self, he strongly criticized Mamata Banerjee for causing enormous financial loss to the government. He decided to move out of Singur at the earliest.

Where would the plant be shifted to? It was a question to which Ratan Tata did not have an immediate answer. What would happen to the investment made in Singur? There was also the question of the equipment getting spoiled in the humid climate if it was not put to use immediately. In such a situation, Ratan Tata's mobile beeped one day. He was not a very socially active man and not many people had access to his personal mobile number. Who would contact him directly? He looked at the message. It said: 'Suswagatam.' Welcome!

NARENDRA MODI WELCOMES TATAS TO GUJARAT

It was a direct invitation from Gujarat Chief Minister Narendra Modi. Ratan Tata swung into action immediately. He conferred with Ravi Kant and a few senior executives and soon a team of top officials was sent to Gujarat for further discussions. It was decided that the plant would be set up in Sanand, 22 km from Gandhinagar. Four days after his announcement of closing down the Singur plant, he declared, 'The plant will be shifted to Sanand, Gujarat.' He also said that the new car would roll out in March 2009.

Three different plants—the ones in Pantnagar, Pune and Sanand—had to work in tandem to produce the car. With just fourteen months on hand, Vishwakarma began the work of dismantling the Singur plant. He ensured that each and every part and machine was marked. It was crucial as the plant was to be reassembled in Sanand. Workers were trained in a week to ensure they understood the importance of this exercise.

There was a choice between two routes from Singur to Sanand: one was via Agra and Jaipur, with a distance of 2,163 km, while the other was via Raipur and Nagpur, with a total distance of 1,843 km. The latter was shorter and seemed like the logical choice. But Vishwakarma wanted to determine which would be the better route and asked a few of his men to travel both. The conclusion after the actual journey was different. The former route, while longer, had a narrow stretch of only 390 km. The latter, on the other hand, had a narrow stretch of 1,633 km. To add to it, there were a lot of bridges which seemed unstable or not strong enough for the heavy containers.

The longer route was selected. It would take ten days more but it was better than struggling on narrow roads and risking the unsafe bridges. The contract for the transport was finalized. Vishwakarma also nominated a few people to escort the caravan. Each truck driver was given a mobile phone and clear instructions for stops and so on. It was a perfectly coordinated exercise. While the machinery was dismantled at Singur, work for the foundation began at Sanand. The assembly line was laid first at Sanand; the compound wall could come up later. The idea was to get the machines unloaded directly at the assembly line and save time.

On 23 March 2009, Ratan Tata launched the Nano at a function in Mumbai. He had taken it upon himself to produce an indigenously made car at a price which seemed impossible to foreign companies. A lot of water had flown under the bridge between Singur and Sanand. Sceptics had concluded that the car could no longer be priced at ₹1 lakh.

It was in such a charged atmosphere that Ratan Tata arrived at the scene driving the car himself. Necks were craned and cameras were ready to capture the moment. 'Ladies and gentlemen,' he began in his sombre and steady voice. There was pin-drop silence in the audience. He described the entire project in brief and praised Girish Wagh and his team of 500 engineers. He then said there had been no compromise on any key features.

He went on to explain how in the meantime the prices of raw material had increased. The tax structure too had changed. Everyone present thought he was building a case for a higher-priced car. But he surprised them by announcing, 'Yet, the car will be priced at ₹1 lakh. I had given my word. After all, a promise is a promise…'

23

The Tata Culture

TATAS DROP LUCRATIVE PROJECT TO SAVE FLAMINGOS

On the face of it, it was an ordinary incident which happened in Tanzania in 2012. It was discovered that Lake Natron in Tanzania carried a large amount of soda ash. Natron is an important lake in the country and the discovery was of immense economic importance to the nation. A factory to produce soda ash from the waters of the lake would provide a boost to the economy. The government thus started looking for a strategic partner. The soda ash deposits were estimated to be to the tune of 4.68 billion cubic meters while the investment to set up the plant would cost nearly $500 million. The government was keen to find a partner who would not only get the money but the right technology as well. There are not too many manufacturers of soda ash in the world and they shortlisted Tata Chemicals and invited them for a discussion.

The Tata group was excited. It had business interests in the African continent and such a project in Tanzania would boost their presence significantly. But a long, red-legged bird got in the way. The flamingos! Flamingos in Tanzania are a protected species, with more than 25 lakh found in East Africa. Lake Natron was a breeding ground for the birds. It was a birdwatcher's paradise.

The moment news of the proposed project was made public, there were objections raised by organizations like BirdLife International and Wildlife Conservation Society, India. The fear was that the manufacturing plant and its associated activities would disrupt the natural habitat of the birds. A developing nation like Tanzania had to make a tough choice between environment protection and a project that would boost the economy, and the government eventually decided to go ahead with it. It wasn't the primary responsibility of the Tatas to look into Tanzania's environmental issues. Yet, the group took a bold decision and withdrew from the project.

BirdLife International publicly acknowledged the decision of the Tata group and asked other organizations to follow their example.

THE JAGUAR LAND ROVER ACQUISITION

In January 2014, the Lord Mayor of the City of London, Fiona Woolf, visited Mumbai. The purpose of her visit was to invite Indian companies to invest in Britain. She mentioned, while meeting reporters, 'We want industrialists like the Tatas to invest in England. Our Jaguar Land Rover was in a shambles but the Tatas turned it around. Our workers are happy with them—to the extent that we have started considering the Tatas a British group!'

The Tata group had bought Jaguar and Land Rover (JLR) from Ford Motors in June 2008 in an all-cash transaction of $2.3 billion—just half of what Ford had paid to acquire both brands. At that time, JLR's retro designs were becoming outdated, and competing with new efficient diesel engines was proving to be difficult for the British car-maker. The American company Ford too had tried a turnaround but had not met with any success in making an impact in the luxury car market. But Ratan Tata was convinced that the acquisition would work out well. Tata Motors focused on three areas: improving liquidity, cost control and new products. And over the next ten years, it reinvigorated JLR from its depreciating value and dwindling sales figures to one of the biggest and most successful automotive brands in the UK—from losses of £400 million in 2008 to profits of £2.6 billion in 2015.

From the start, Tata Motors saw JLR as an opportunity to leap into the big league of global automakers. It recognized that both brands carried a strong emotional connect with their target audience, the European and the US markets. But at the time of the acquisition, it found itself in a debt of ₹21,900 crore. The acquisition also came at a time when the Tata group had recently acquired the steel company Corus and Tetley Tea, and the Nano was struggling in posting its estimated targets. Moreover, Tata Motors and JLR catered to two very different segments of the car market. With the JLR bailout, Tata Motors' market value plunged and its stock crashed.

But the Tatas set up a proper cash management system in the company and pumped in around ₹1 billion, even raising money by selling some of the stocks in Tata Steel and other group companies. In two years, sales rose sharply on the back of new product launches and improved market sentiment. JLR accounted for more than half of Tata Motors' business in 2010 and recorded profit that year for the first time after the acquisition.

At the level of the ordinary workers, when it was announced that JLR was to be sold off to the Tatas, they were relieved as they believed the Tatas would look after their interests better than anyone else. It was a throwback to the time when TELCO had announced a voluntary retirement scheme and not one employee had protested.

THE TATA CULTURE

In the aftermath of the terrorist attack on the Taj Mahal Hotel opposite the Gateway of India in Mumbai on 26 November 2008, the Tatas not only compensated the families of the employees who had lost their lives, but also ensured that the families of the vendors selling their wares outside the hotel were adequately compensated too.

What made the Tatas act so in such situations—be it in Tanzania, the JLR case or the Taj attack? The answer lies in the Tata culture, the values which are embedded in the DNA of the group.

Let us go back in time to see some more examples of this culture of goodwill.

It was only in 1892 that the British government allowed Indians to appear for the Indian Civil Service exam. Jamsetji had taken a lot of efforts to encourage Indians to take the exam. He also sponsored several Indian doctors to enable them to pursue higher studies in England.

The first two Indian women doctors to study in England were aided by Jamsetji. He had said, 'I can easily afford to sponsor their expenses but I am not going to do so. I am going to give them a loan. They can repay me at their convenience. The idea behind the loan is that the amount can then be used to sponsor more people who need the money.' Over the next hundred-odd years, the J.N. Tata Endowment for the Higher Education of Indians had sponsored more than 5,000 such deserving candidates to go abroad for further studies. To date, people consider it a matter of great pride to be known as J.N. Tata scholars.

This is an amazing example of the Tata culture. But what exactly is this culture? How does one define it? Is it about using the group's profits for various social and religious causes? Many business houses are doing that. Now, under corporate social responsibility, it is mandatory for companies to spend 2.5 per cent of their net profits on social causes. How are the Tatas different then? There are a number of multinational organizations which donate millions for charitable purposes. Why should the Tatas be singled out for praise for what they do?

There are many facets to the Tata culture. One is that the group's ambition has never been to capture the world or to be the biggest or richest business conglomerate. It believes in giving back to the people. It is a common thread which binds all of its businesses.

The Tatas have never claimed that they set up businesses for the purpose of social welfare or charity. It is quite natural that a business should make profits. But the objective is not profits and profits alone.

The Tata philosophy states that if a part of the profits is invested back into society, not only does it help the business but also helps others. Such thoughts have been instilled into the group since its inception.

While establishing Empress Mills in Nagpur, Jamsetji put in place practices which were then unknown in the West. At a time when the world was yet to witness funds for future protection, he set up pension plans for his employees. He was criticized when he thought of the workers' health. But he simply said that their welfare was linked to his own—that it was in his own interest to ensure they remained healthy.

Jamsetji was not just known for his enterprising ability. His decision to set up a steel plant was not driven as much by a desire to reduce India's dependence on imports as by his entrepreneurial ambitions. He showed the world that one could create an artificial lake to generate hydroelectric power. If profits were his sole motive, he could have started many businesses. But he realized that when India became independent, there would be a need for such projects. Scientists and engineers would be in demand and so he decided to set up a science institute with his own funds, even if that meant selling his properties to generate the resources. In 1896, he sold seventeen buildings in Bombay and four parcels of land to generate the required funds. The result was the Indian Institute of Science in Bangalore.

There are a number of industrialists around the world who are known for their charity. But there are fundamental differences between them and the Tatas. John D. Rockefeller, Henry Ford, Andrew Carnegie, Warren Buffet and Bill Gates made a fortune beyond our imagination. They set aside large parts of their wealth for philanthropy. Most of them formed trusts in the names of their family members or themselves to act as vehicles for their charity. These charities contributed substantially in confronting and solving problems which had troubled humanity for ages. The world is grateful to these individuals. But the difference between them and the Tatas is that the individuals are known the world over for their generosity and not for creating social wealth. They did not use their enterprising ability to create social wealth. They first did what they wanted to do and then used the money so generated for charitable purposes.

It is pertinent to note that charity is different from creating social wealth. Each business or enterprise in the Tata group was set up to fulfil the needs of society—be it steel manufacturing, chemicals, engineering, passenger cars, TIFR, or the cancer hospital. The Tatas recognize the need to fill a gap in the society and their enterprising ability is then put to use to that end. Thus, creating wealth and solving social problems happen in tandem and profits are a secondary outcome.

In a country like India, such an approach is of huge significance. And it has been sustained over generations. Many of the organizations in western countries known for their contributions to charitable causes have not been able to do so. They had successors who did better than the founders in terms of growing the organizations, but without carrying forward the same social zeal of the early leaders.

It is not so with the Tata group. Each of its leaders was grounded in reality and was aware and alive to the responsibility of social welfare. Sir Dorab and Sir Ratan took forward the agenda set by Jamsetji with the same missionary zeal. Sir Dorab set up the Tata Memorial Hospital for cancer treatment while archaeological excavations that led to significant discoveries took place thanks to the grants given by Sir Ratan. Sir Dorab donated all his wealth to the trusts he formed for various social causes. Sir Ratan contributed to Gopal Krishna Gokhale's Bharat Sevak Samaj and was a benefactor to Mohandas Karamchand Gandhi's efforts in South Africa.

JRD raised the flag much higher. He wasn't a direct descendant of the elder Tata. His father RD was Jamsetji's cousin, yet the fire in him to work for social causes was equally strong. TIFR and Air India flourished under his leadership and vision. He roped in Homi Bhabha to run TIFR, arranged for the required funds from the Tata trusts and got the institute in shape. The institute has since done phenomenal work and when, a decade after Independence, the first atomic energy plant was being set up in Trombay, Homi Bhabha had forty-six engineers to help him. All of them had been trained in TIFR.

Ratan Naval Tata, who took over the reins from JRD and took the group to commanding heights, was the son of an adopted child. He was not related to his predecessor the way Jamsetji and JRD were. But he too carried forward the Tata values. It was these values which made him dream of a car for a family of four struggling to reach their destination on a two-wheeler. While another industrialist was building a skyscraper for himself in densely populated Mumbai, Ratan Tata was staying in an ordinary flat. It is an example of the Tata culture in action.

Ratan Tata has not been known to throw his weight around. At Bombay House, he stands in queue for the elevators along with the other employees, without demanding any special treatment. He is friendly even to the mongrels on the street outside his office. There is no arrogance in his behaviour. It is this simplicity of nature that binds the Tatas and is embedded in the Tata culture.

Amongst the business families of the world, it would be difficult to find members of a family bearing the same last name who would be in line with each other in how they view their social responsibilities. But the Tatas' objective has always been clear: to build businesses, grow them and create social wealth. They have always been an example of capitalism with a heart.

Another valuable contribution of the Tatas is that of encouraging and building local talent. Most businesses do not hesitate to get talent from wherever they can at the lowest prices. There is nothing wrong with it, but it hasn't been so with the Tatas. They have made the effort to build the local talent pool and develop it.

An example of this can be seen in Hosur, Tamil Nadu, very close to Bengaluru. The people of Hosur, living in poverty, depended on subsistence agriculture. When the Tatas set up a plant there in 1987, it would have been a logical choice for them to get trained engineers from Bengaluru. But they instead selected nearly 400 local students who had completed class 12 and got them trained in Bengaluru. For many of them, it was their first visit to a city. After getting them adequately trained, they were inducted into the factory. They had no clue what job they were to do and who the Tatas were. But the factory went on to produce a world-class brand of watches. The brand is Titan.

The factory was later expanded to include three more plants and more than a thousand people—all of them locals! They too were trained the same way as the earlier batch. The workers were now manufacturing the slimmest watches in the country, even diversifying into exquisite jewellery. How did the Tatas manage to create such world-class products using local talent? What led them to have faith in it? The answer is that it is yet another aspect of the Tata culture.

THE TATA BRAND

The Tata name is also a brand unto itself. More than 60 per cent of the group's revenues are from countries outside of India. Yet, Indians claim it to be their own while the mayor of London feels that Tata is a British company. It is not just money power or size which gives a company such a position in the minds of people.

During JRD's time, there was a period when many businesses were bigger than the Tata group. One of them was the Birla group. Yet, no one got the kind of international recognition which the Tatas did. As far back as 1969, JRD was on the world advisory board of the Nobel Foundation. He was in the elite company of people like the writer Arthur Koestler, poet W.H. Auden and two-time Nobel winner Dr Linus Pauling. One can imagine the kind of reputation JRD had. In 1970, Esquire magazine published a list of 300 most influential people. The two from India were JRD and Prime Minister Indira Gandhi. In 1994, the only Indian to be named in the International Encyclopaedia of Business and Management was JRD. He was the business face of India on the international stage. To pay homage to him on his death, Henry Kissinger, a much bigger personality and advisor to international companies, especially came to Mumbai.

Ratan Tata, his successor, shows the same quality of being grounded and yet being able to leave a mark on the international stage. There is only one Indian industrial house whose name is taken with respect in the top business schools of the world like Kellogg, Harvard or Stanford. It is nothing short of a miracle for a business to keep up such an influence for nearly 150 years—to be true to its calling and to continue to generate wealth for the company and others at the same time. It is even more surprising that such a group exists in India, which does not set much store by wealth creation.

It is important to note that the Tata group is rarely marketed as a brand. One can see the group advertising while paying homage to Jamsetji or JRD. But the tone is gentle and not in-your-face. Yet it is able to resonate with the common man. Be it someone in his fifties or sixties, or someone who has just joined the corporate world—people across the board feel a sense of affiliation with the Tatas.

The understatedness, which is a hallmark of the Tatas, is reflected in its advertising campaigns too. Take the Tata Tea campaign, for example, which with its famous 'Jaago Re' slogan exhorted people to be mindful of their social responsibilities. Not many were aware that Tata Tea had become the world's largest tea company after buying out the British firm Tetley. But rather than boasting about its accomplishment, it pitched itself as a wake-up call for the nation. In 2007, 'Jaago Re' launched its first campaign, with an aim to awaken the people to the fact that they should demand accountability from the government and participate in politics by voting for candidates with the right credentials. It even facilitated voter registrations on its website. The next year, the campaign was against corruption, with the slogan 'Khilana Bandh, Pilana Shuru'. The advertisement called upon citizens to discourage bribery. Through a website, users were encouraged to share anti-corruption messages, take pledges against giving or receiving bribes, and confess if they had paid a bribe.

TCS is an inspiring success story. It is considered amongst the world's biggest IT companies. With its 2.5 lakh employees, it is the second largest employer in India after the Indian Railways. It is also the group's most profitable company, which has left Tata Motors and Tata Steel behind. But unlike other businesses which bombard consumers with continuous advertising, the Tata group has never boasted of the success of TCS or that of any other company in the group. The Tata values are clearly visible in each of its businesses even though brands like Taj, Titan or Jaguar Land Rover do not wear the Tata tag on their sleeves.

Brand science tells us that often the absence of the brand name leads to better recognition and in fact makes the brand more effective. The Tatas have used this logic well. Overexposure can reduce brand value. Titan and JLR are thus able to maintain their own identity while being part of the Tata stable. The strength of the Tatas cannot be quantified, but it is very much in action nonetheless.

24

The Search for a Successor

The Tata group chairmen have been distinct personalities. Jamsetji was a typical Parsi in his looks and behaviour. He dressed like one and sported a beard like most Parsis of that time. JRD was quite the opposite. He was part Indian and part foreigner to look at. He was always seen sporting a suit and was clean-shaven. In his youth, he sported a pointed moustache, which added to his sharp and incisive persona. Later, the moustache vanished, giving a soft and caring touch to his appearance. Ratan Tata has been similar to but also different from both—mild-mannered and humble to a fault, and a little introverted.

Their styles were very different. Jamsetji was born more than a hundred years before India became independent. He had a grand vision whose scope only he could see, but unfortunately he did not live to see it turn into reality in his lifetime. JRD believed in getting people together, involving everyone and working with consensus. If he found a deserving person, he would trust him completely and encourage him all the way. Ratan Tata was extremely methodical. He was able to get the widely spread and diversified group companies bound by the thread of the Tata name. He believed in creating systems and following the processes laid down.

He showed the same diligence in selecting the next head of Tata Sons. There had been a lot of confusion when Ratan Tata was named JRD's successor. Many names like Russi Mody, Darbari Seth, Nani Palkhivala and Nusli Wadia were proposed and speculated upon. He was fifty-four years old when he took over the group in 1991. He was young then but he had often mentioned that one's risk-taking ability goes down with age and one tends to stick to the comfort zone. He therefore came up with a retirement policy which forced many of the stalwarts to resign. There was speculation that when his own turn came, Ratan Tata would not stand by the retirement rule himself. But he was to prove his detractors wrong.

'I don't intend to come to the company's headquarters on a wheelchair,' he said famously when discussing his succession plan. He started the process much before his retirement age. The rule was clear; no one should be heading a business after the age of seventy-five. He began the task of finding a suitable successor for himself when he was seventy-three.

He constituted a committee of five senior members. Quite naturally, rumours regarding the probable candidates were flying thick and fast as people speculated who the successor would be. Reporters hounded Ratan Tata for the names. His answer was simple, 'Whosoever the committee selects.'

The committee members were: R.K. Krishna Kumar, who had headed Tata Tea, Indian Hotels and Croma; N.A. Soonawala, a close confidant and legal advisor to Ratan Tata; Shirin Bharucha, whose association with the group went back to the 1960s and someone who had advised almost eighty companies of the group; and Lord Sushant Kumar Bhattacharya, a seventy-three-year-old engineer, educator, government advisor, founder of the Warwick Manufacturing Group, a member of the House of Lords and a close friend of Ratan Tata's. The fifth member of the committee was much younger, a director in the group and someone who was known as a reticent man who rarely hogged the limelight.

All the members of the committee were publicity shy. Ratan Tata disliked people who talked loosely at parties or social functions. He himself never did that. He wanted the committee members to also be so.

Names started appearing in the media once the committee was formed. One of them was Indra Nooyi, the global head of Pepsico. Another name was that of Arun Sarin, the global head of Vodafone. Citibank's Vikram Pandit was speculated as one of the candidates while Vindi Banga of Lever too was talked of. The real serious contender who emerged, as per speculation, was Noel Tata.

Other than Ratan, Noel was the only Tata in the group. He is Ratan's stepbrother, born to Ratan's father Naval and Simone. He was similar to Ratan in being extremely shy. He displayed the Tata values in his work and behaviour. He headed the retail company Trent, set up by Simone. Later, Trent was made into Westside. Businesses like Star Bazaar were added to it. An important point to note is that Noel is married to Pallonji Mistry's daughter. Pallonji Mistry holds nearly 18 per cent of Tata Sons. Noel had been given charge of the Tatas' international business. It was quite evident to most that Noel was the most likely candidate to succeed Ratan Tata.

But Ratan Tata himself clarified that Noel did not have the necessary experience to run such a large and diversified conglomerate. He was clear that the successor had to be a visionary, and someone young enough to lead the business for the next twenty or thirty years. He was also clear that the successor had to be one with no ego. He did not want an arrogant person leading the Tata group. The committee dropped the idea of looking for a name from outside India. They wanted someone who knew the Indian ethos. While the group's business was international, the ethos and identity were clearly Indian. The committee realized that they had such a person in the committee itself! He was the reticent fifth member: Cyrus Pallonji Mistry.

When the committee started considering Cyrus, he resigned from it as he was now a contender himself. The papers had not discussed his candidature much, unlike many other names. But the committee and Ratan had been keen on him from the start. Cyrus had been part of key decisions taken by Ratan. He had played a vital role in the acquisition of the steel company Corus and Jaguar Land Rover. Ratan had taken a liking to him since then. He was young with a great future, a mild-mannered disposition, shy, and not one to spend his evenings socializing in parties. All these were in favour of Cyrus.

The committee announced in September 2011, 'When Ratan Tata retires next December, forty-three-year-old Cyrus Mistry would be made the next Chairman.'

There had been only five heads in the nearly 150-year history of the group. Cyrus was the sixth, after Jamsetji Nusserwanji Tata, Sir Dorabji Tata, Sir Nowroji Saklatwala, J.R.D. Tata and Ratan Tata. And he was only the second to not have the Tata name. With an 18 per cent stake, the Shapoorji Pallonji Group was the largest shareholder in Tata Sons and he thus also represented the largest shareholder of the group.

Cyrus was born into a Parsi family in Bombay, the younger son of Indian billionaire and construction magnate Pallonji Mistry by his wife Patsy Perin Dubash. Both his parents belonged to the Zoroastrian faith and had roots in India. However, Mistry's mother was born in Ireland, and his father chose to take up Irish citizenship.

Mistry has an elder brother, Shapoorji Mistry, who is also an Irish citizen and is married to Behroze Sethna, the daughter of Parsi lawyer Rusi Sethna. Mistry has two sisters, Laila and Aloo. Laila is married to Rustom Jehangir, a London-based portfolio fund manager. Aloo is married to Noel Tata. Cyrus is married to Rohiqa Chagla, daughter of lawyer Iqbal Chagla and granddaughter of jurist M.C. Chagla.

The speculation regarding Ratan Tata's succession ended with the announcement. This was followed by a debate whether Cyrus was the right candidate with the credentials to hold the post. No one in the group, especially Ratan, wanted to participate in the debate. They were used to such questions. When Ratan Tata was given charge in 1991, similar doubts had been raised. He knew that some questions were best left unanswered. Time would tell.

The group had stood the test of time. When Ratan Tata retired in 2012, he had just one wish: that the Tata story would continue to inspire and shine.

25

The Storm and a New Beginning

Cyrus Mistry began in style. He was as reticent as Ratan and someone who consciously stayed away from the limelight. In fact, he was conspicuous by his absence at social events. He was never attracted by the world of glitz and glamour.

When the family-loving Cyrus took over, it was expected that the group would get a breath of fresh air, though with a sense of continuity. After all, he belonged to the Mistry family, which had been part of the Tata group for more than a century and held 18.5 per cent of the shares. Moreover, his sister Aloo was married to Noel. It was Cyrus's father who had supported JRD when the group was going through a crisis precipitated by Russi Mody. It was thanks to his support that JRD had been able to get Ratan to take charge. In some sense, Ratan was paying off the debt by handing over the post to Cyrus.

Cyrus began in right earnest from day one. Each chairman had given his own vision and direction to the group after taking over. When JRD was made Chairman, his personality was such that he allowed the big honchos to create their own empires. There was growth, but a lot of it in different directions. The group was not tightly controlled.

When Ratan Tata took over, the style of management changed. And the change was visible. He put in place a new professionalism, giving weight to the Tata name and ensuring that the brand represented the right businesses and philosophy.

Cyrus's entry naturally marked a new beginning for the Tata group. The first thing he did after taking over in 2012 was to dismantle two important committees set up by Ratan Tata—the Group Executive Office (GEO) and the Group Corporate Centre (GCC)—and made up of the top executives of the group companies. He created a Group Executive Council (GEC) instead, which he himself led. The other members of the council were: N.S. Rajan, a partner in Ernst & Young; Madhu Kannan, the CEO of BSE; Professor Nirmalya Kumar of the London Business School; Mukund Govind Rajan, Chief Ethics Officer; and Harish Bhat, the CEO of Tata Global Beverages.

Many of the CEOs of the group had retired, so it was easy for Cyrus to replace them. Some of them were J.J. Irani, N.A. Soonawala and R.K. Krishna Kumar. In 2013, Arun Kumar Gandhi too retired. He had been instrumental in the Jaguar Land Rover deal. The others reaching superannuation were Kishor Chaukar, R. Gopalakrishnan, Ishaat Hussain, Ravi Kant of Tata Motors, B. Muthuraman of Tata Steel and S. Ramadorai of TCS. Raymond Bickson of IHC, who was considered close to Ratan, quit. Each had different reasons to leave the group. But the end result was the same—they all had ended their formal ties with the group.

Each chairman of the Tata group has left his mark on the group, based on personal likes and dislikes. JRD's contribution was Air India, while Ratan's were notably the Indica, Nano and getting the Jaguar Land Rover deal. He gave the group a truly global standing. Getting a steel company like Corus merged into Tata Steel was a major achievement. Tata was earlier known as an Indian company, but during Ratan's time more than 60 per cent of the group's turnover came from businesses abroad. Ratan Tata's rapid expansion into diversified areas had had a strong impact on its revenues. But, of the nearly 100-odd businesses with a workforce of more than 7 lakh, only two companies were formidable performers. One was Jaguar Land Rover and the other TCS.

The Tata group was known for thinking long-term and building businesses accordingly. It did not take decisions based on performance in a particular year. Integrity was the foundation on which the businesses were built. It did not try and influence government policies to help build its business. But some of the policies of the group had diluted its focus on revenue growth.

Cyrus was not comfortable with that approach. He was of a new generation and that too from outside the Tata family. He was most keenly interested in the numbers. He measured everything in terms of profit and loss. It was not a wrong approach in many ways as, when he took over, global conditions were not exactly favourable and the steel industry around the world was in trouble. And steel was the foundation on which the group was built. One of his first steps as chairman was to start identifying businesses that were not making profits and ordering their closure. He decided to sell off the steel business in England. He cancelled the deal which was meant to take over Orient Express, a hotel giant in the Bermudas, which had properties in forty-five locations in twenty-two countries. He closed down the urea importing division of Tata Chemicals as it was not generating any profits.

At the same time, he started investing and getting into new areas. He bought the power generation business of Welspun and merged it into Tata Power. The Singapore Airlines and Air Asia deals happened under his leadership. The Tata group was planning to enter the banking sector but Mistry was opposed to it from the start. He wanted to focus on the retail sector, financial services, leisure and tourism, and the defence sector. He believed that instead of being spread thin, the group should be focused, nimble and revenue generating. He would attend the annual general body meetings of all group companies to get a sense of their performance and future plans. He would answer questions raised by investors, giving everyone the confidence that he was firmly in charge.

But the board meeting of Tata Sons on 24 October 2016 changed all that. Cyrus was busy getting ready for it as chairman of the board.

He had just finished a round of talks with prospective investors and had visited China and Singapore. The agenda for the meeting had been circulated in advance. Cyrus had heard that some of the board members had an unscheduled informal meeting earlier that morning. But what they had discussed was unknown; he did not give it much further thought. To his surprise, though, two unexpected visitors arrived at his office just before the planned board meeting was to begin.

One was Nitin Nohria, Dean of Harvard Business School and a member of the Tata board of directors, and the other was Ratan Tata. Cyrus was surprised as Ratan normally did not attend the meetings. He had, in fact, been consciously staying away ever since handing over charge to Cyrus. It was a Tata tradition not to interfere in or influence matters once the reins had been handed over. JRD too had done the same, taking a back seat once Ratan had taken charge. Cyrus wondered why Ratan Tata had made an unannounced arrival.

'Please sit,' Cyrus said, but the two remained standing.

Nohria cleared his throat and began, 'Cyrus, it is unfortunate that the relations between you and Ratan are not exactly wonderful. The board, in fact, feels that you must resign. The meeting today is being held to remove you from the post of Chairman. Do you have anything to say?'

Ratan interjected before Cyrus could reply. 'Sorry, Cyrus ... things should not have reached this stage.'

Nohria further asked, 'Cyrus, are you going to resign or should we place the agenda of termination before the board?'

Cyrus recovered from the initial shock and retorted, 'Gentlemen, you are free to propose whatever you wish to; I am free to decide what I should do.' He knew he could not do much. He sent a message to his wife: 'I am being sacked.'

By then, Ratan Tata and Nitin Nohria had come out of his office on the fourth floor of Bombay House. Cyrus did not waste a minute. He asked his secretary to collect his personal stuff and, putting on a coat, left for the board meeting at the other end of the floor.

The meeting began. Nohria proposed a motion requesting Cyrus to step down and the members agreed. It was said the board had lost confidence in him for a variety of reasons. The reasons were not clearly spelt out, though. Cyrus objected, saying that as per the Articles of Association, the board had to be given fifteen days' prior notice before such an item could be taken up for consideration. This had not been adhered to and hence the decision was illegal. Amit Chandra responded that the board had taken legal opinion and no such notice was required.

It was the first time in the 148-year history of the Tata group that a chairman had been removed by the board. The group did not have a tradition of changing its chairman every few years. When Cyrus had been given charge in 2012, he was just forty-six years old and it was expected that he would continue to lead the group for the next twenty or thirty years. But he had been at the helm for just four years when the board lost confidence in him. The initial contract under which he was serving as the chairman had been passed via a shareholder resolution of Tata Sons, due to expire on 31 March 2017. But instead of waiting for it to end, he was asked to step down in October 2016.

It was a shock for everyone. Reporters from the financial dailies were waiting outside for news from the board meeting. But none had expected this bolt from the blue. Within half an hour of the meeting at Bombay House, the news spread like wildfire. No one believed it at first. This had never happened before. The Tata group was now part of a controversy and at the centre of a storm. Everyone tried to guess the reasons behind the decision. No one believed that it was a sudden one and they all assumed that this must have been a premeditated move. The Tata board had ensured that they had the best legal minds supporting them. They feared Cyrus would fight the battle and wanted to be prepared for it.

The board was also conscious of the fact that the termination of the chairman, the very representative of the group, was a serious public relations issue and had to be tackled with care. It was expected that the press and public at large would have sympathy for the one sacked. He would be seen as the victim even though no one was aware of the real reasons. Sympathy for Cyrus would make Ratan Tata seem like the villain who had orchestrated the whole thing. The board feared such a negative backlash. Ratan Tata was prepared for it and had hired six public relations firms to ensure that the group's name would not be tarnished. Along with the PR firms, there was one more name being spoken of—that of a PR advisor who was close to Ratan Tata.

Her name was Niira Radia. The group vehemently denied any contract with her. But the common perception from Delhi to Mumbai was that Radia worked for the Tatas. Her name had earlier been linked with Ratan Tata during the 2G scandal. The Radia tapes had created quite a sensation then.

A. Raja, the Telecom Minister in the Manmohan Singh government, was alleged to have allocated spectrum on a first come, first served basis instead of following the traditional approach of issuing tenders. There was talk of deep-rooted corruption and allegations that the manner in which spectrum was allocated had caused a loss of thousands of crores of rupees to the exchequer. It is a different matter that the allegations did not stand in court eventually.

At the time, Radia was accused of lobbying to ensure that Raja continued in his portfolio. It was alleged that she had been supported by a few journalists, editors and businessmen. The tapes, in which she is heard having conversations along these lines with them, created a controversy.

Radia ran a PR firm called Vaishnavi Communications and was handling the Tata and Reliance accounts for their telecom businesses. It was said that everyone wanted Raja to continue holding the telecom ministry as it would be beneficial to those in the business. One commonly encounters lobbyists and middlemen in Delhi's political circles, but the Tata group was known to stay away from such practices. While talking to some journalists, Radia reportedly said that successive governments had been unfair to the Tata group in the allocation of licences and contracts in the field of natural resources. There was nothing wrong prima facie in her statements but the question was whether the Tatas had appointed a controversial figure like Radia to lobby on their behalf. The CBI was asked to investigate the issue and, in 2017, it gave a clean chit to Raja.

It was rumoured that Ratan Tata had asked Radia to handle communication over the Cyrus Mistry matter now. Many newspapers reported so but Ratan firmly denied it. There was also speculation that two of the directors, N.A. Soonawala and R.K. Krishna Kumar, were firmly behind Radia. The conclusion was that if they were supporting her, Ratan Tata would be the man behind it all. But the real question was not whether Radia was working for Ratan Tata but about the differences between him and Cyrus Mistry.

The day Cyrus was removed, Ratan Tata took charge on a temporary basis till the new chairman was selected. The question which bothered everyone was why the differences between the two had reached such a stage.

One of the reasons stated was the way Cyrus handled some of the businesses. The Tata group chairman is first the chairman of Tata Sons. Tata Sons is the holding company for most of the businesses. The chairman of Tata Sons is automatically the chairman for the group. But Tata Sons is not a listed entity. It provides capital to most businesses. Cyrus was said to be reluctant to fund businesses which were not profitable. Many were forced to look for other funding options. This was either through an expensive market route or by liquidating some assets.

Another reason was related to the various trusts which worked for social causes. Two of them, the Jamsetji Tata Trust and Navajbai Ratan Tata Trust, were headed by Ratan Tata. Cyrus was apparently ignoring these important trusts. It is said that a few months before Cyrus was removed, Ratan Tata had managed to take back the investments made by the trusts in Tata Sons. He reportedly withdrew nearly ₹3,941 crore ten years prematurely. This was said to be an example of mutual distrust, given that Cyrus was the head of Tata Sons while Ratan Tata was heading the trusts. Of course, Ratan Tata never commented on the issue or criticized Cyrus publicly.

Cyrus, though, was not going to take the matter of his termination lying down. He challenged the group on various grounds. He had the support of Nusli Wadia, Chairman of the Wadia Group that runs Bombay Dyeing. Wadia was the godson of JRD and had, in fact, named one of his sons Jehangir. The brother of his maternal grandmother Rattanbai was married to JRD's sister Sylla. At one time, JRD was keen to hand over the reins of the group to Nusli. The Wadias and the Tatas had excellent relations. Ratan Tata too had taken his help when he wanted to implement his retirement policy in the group. The Tatas had stood behind the Wadias and helped them sort out various family issues.

When Nusli returned to India in 1971 after studying abroad, his father had wanted to sell the business to the R.P. Goenka group. But Shapoorji Pallonji had stepped in to save the company. He had a whopping 40 per cent stake in the Wadia group and held 7 per cent shares of Bombay Dyeing. JRD intervened to ensure that the company was not sold to the RPG group.

It was a surprise to the Tata group that Nusli had put his weight behind Cyrus Mistry in the matter of his termination. Nusli was, after all, on the board of several Tata companies. On 10 November, a few weeks after Cyrus Mistry was removed, the board of Tata Chemicals voted in favour of Cyrus Mistry. This was in a way a challenge to Tata Sons by Wadia, who was then the director of Tata Chemicals. From 5 November onwards, most of the listed Tata companies had removed Cyrus as chairman of the respective companies. Some of the independent directors in a few companies had refused to take sides and stayed away from the decision. In other words, they were against his removal. Nusli Wadia even filed a criminal defamation case against the Tata group, Ratan Tata and some directors after a resolution was moved seeking his removal from three Tata group firms. He also shot off a letter to SEBI, alleging that many laws were violated while removing Cyrus.

In the meantime, Ratan Tata personally met Prime Minister Narendra Modi. Many government-owned companies like LIC had a substantial stake in Tata companies and he wanted to ensure that the government was in favour of his decision. Finally, in December 2016, Cyrus resigned from all the Tata companies.

But it wasn't the end of the saga as he had filed a complaint with the National Company Law Tribunal, accusing the Tata group of treating minority shareholders unfairly. He filed one more complaint showing technical irregularities in the way he was removed. But the government of the day, SEBI and the Company Law Board refused to enter into the debate. Their view was that it was an internal matter of the Tata group.

Slowly, from the matter of Cyrus Mistry's sacking, focus shifted to who the next chairman of the group would be. While selecting Cyrus, the group had formed a high-level committee. Many names had been discussed publicly then. The Tata group was careful not to allow such a thing to happen again. But speed was of the essence as they did not want the Cyrus Mistry episode to remain in public memory for long.

They did not have to look around too much. They felt that it was better to zero in on someone who had been working in the group for a long time. Quite obviously, the new chairman had to display the same qualities which were the hallmark of the group. They did not want someone who would hog the headlines. They found their candidate well within the group: Natarajan Chandrasekaran.

He was the CEO of TCS, the most profitable company in the group. Like his predecessor S. Ramadorai, Chandrasekaran had grown with the organization. He was a graduate of the National Institute of Technology, Trichy, and had done his master's from Coimbatore. He was well-versed in classical music, painting and fine arts. A sober, soft-spoken and quiet personality, Chandrasekaran was also a marathon runner. He had participated in a number of marathons across the globe, earning a name for himself when he completed the New York Marathon in five hours and fifty-two seconds. This was a trait which suited the Tatas very well—they preferred a marathon runner to a sprinter! Chandrasekaran too was looking for a new challenge. He had been with TCS from the start of his career and had headed the company since 2009.

On 12 January 2017, the Tata group announced his name as the new chairman. He followed one rule without fail—that of not speaking about the earlier tussle. On 6 February, Cyrus was removed from the board of Tata Sons while Chandrasekaran took charge as Chairman on 21 February.

There were many challenges for the new leader. The biggest of them was to resolve an ongoing dispute between the Japanese telcom giant DoCoMo and the Tatas. As per a contract signed by Ratan Tata with DoCoMo in 2009, the Tatas were to buy back the Japanese firm's shares in Tata Teleservices at half the acquisition price in five years. But when DoCoMo expressed its intention to withdraw from the Indian market in 2014, Tata Teleservices offered a lower exit price than the prefixed one.

The Tatas countered by saying that RBI rules had changed in the interim, prohibiting the buying of shares of a foreign partner at a predetermined price. The new rate was naturally not agreeable to the Japanese giant as it was far lower than what had earlier been agreed upon. The Tatas had approached the RBI to allow them to fulfil their agreement but they were denied. Finally, the Japanese company filed a case against the Tatas demanding adequate compensation.

The matter had erupted during Mistry's tenure, but he did not manage to mitigate it. It was alleged that he allowed it to fester, leading to a loss of face and reputation for the Tata group. The general feeling was that the Tatas had reneged on their word.

The first thing Chandrasekaran did was to close the issue. The Tatas paid DoCoMo $1.18 billion and the Japanese company took its lawsuit back. In any case, the telecom business was turning out to be unprofitable, with losses mounting by the day, and the Tatas were far behind in the game.

The European steel business was also in losses thanks to a global slowdown in the steel sector. And so Chandrasekaran merged Tata Steel Europe with the German giant Thyssenkrupp AG. In October 2017, he sold Tata Teleservices to Airtel. By the end of 2017, the group had stabilized. The controversy surrounding the removal of Cyrus Mistry had died down and the Tata group was ready for a new innings.

It was a fresh start under the chairmanship of another leader, the first non-Parsi to head the group in 150 years. In many ways, the Tata group had shed its old skin for a new avatar.

An Interview with Ratan Tata

I had always wanted to have a chat with anyone with the Tata surname. I was keen to understand what made them stand apart—what made them do what they did one generation after another.

One usually sees the spirit of enterprise in a family die within three generations. The first generation struggles by starting from scratch. It is an enterprise they start at home or on a small scale, which the next generation then amplifies and transforms into a proper business. More often than not, the third generation, born with the proverbial silver spoon, soon manages to destroy all the brand equity and trust built over two generations, the business starts making losses, and all is lost by the time the fourth generation takes over. This has been the case with many business houses. Barring a few exceptions, such as the Tatas.

How have the Tatas managed to maintain their values and grow their businesses one generation after another? An uncommon trait among the Tatas is that despite being born in a business family, none of the members give much importance to personal wealth and daily cash flows. Most industrialists and businessmen who focus on cash alone do not grow beyond a point. How are the Tatas different? Someone had once said that the only city in India in its true sense is Mumbai; the rest are just overgrown villages. At the risk of hyperbole, we can say

236

the same about the Tatas—they are India's original industrialist family. The others are overgrown traders.

Growing up, I had a few close relatives who had worked with the Tatas. I had heard a lot from them about JRD and stalwarts from the Tata companies like Darbari Seth. Listening to anecdotes about them made me more keen to meet someone from the family.

When I started working as a business journalist, I got the chance to observe some of India's leading businessmen and witnessed the arrogance they had developed over time. But that wasn't the case with the Tatas. I was once surprised to see JRD get a standing ovation when he entered an auditorium where a journalists' conference was taking place. He felt like the lovable patriarch of a family. He was old yet charming, with a spring in his step. He did not seem bored. In fact, he sported a kind of knowing and mischievous smile on his face. He seemed content and carried not an iota of arrogance or pride.

We are generally used to hearing people of that age spout advice and talk of how energetic and active they were in their younger days. But JRD did nothing of that kind. At that time, there was an industrialist who was in the news for wanting to grow as fast as possible. JRD was asked a question: 'Would the new industrialist be responsible for stopping the Tata juggernaut? Would the Tatas be left behind? What is your view?' JRD had answered, 'Business cycles are temporary, class is permanent!'

His response increased my eagerness to meet him. But he passed away and I never got the opportunity. I was able to observe Ratan Tata's tenure quite closely, thanks to my job in a financial daily. Like JRD, Ratan Tata did not spend time in social circles. He had no special friends in the media. I read a lot about the Tata group over the years, and so I was thrilled when I got the opportunity to interview Ratan Tata for this book in 2013.

He breathes and lives the Tata values. There is an elegantly detached air about him. It becomes more pronounced and endearing when he talks about himself and the Tata group businesses. There is a sense of maturity when he looks at past events. He is neither emotional nor cold in his responses.

When I met him, he had just retired from the group. He was not working out of Bombay House, though no one would have objected had he wished to. He moved away to ensure that Cyrus Mistry, his successor, would be at ease. He was in his new office in a narrow and crowded lane in Mumbai's Fort area. He could have easily chosen an office in a more upmarket building, but had chosen not to.

Our meeting was scheduled for 3 p.m. I got a message at 2.55 p.m. that the previous meeting would end in another five minutes. Tall and imposing, Ratan Tata arrived at 3 p.m. sharp. He was seventy-five but had none of the visible health problems of a man that age. He took off his suit, loosened his tie, sat down, and our informal conversation began.

GK: JRD had once told his sister that he had been able to achieve whatever he did thanks to the Tata surname. When you took over, did the same thought occur to you? How much of a role do the Tata values play in what you do?

RT: The 'Tata-ness' is the biggest responsibility I carried on my shoulders. I had to live up to its values. It was something I was always aware of. The name carries certain values and it was my duty to ensure that we protect them. These values were something I was born with. I had grown up seeing how the employees—and domestic helpers too—were treated by the Tata family members. I did not have to do anything differently. It was quite natural for me.

GK: When Jamsetji decided to get into business, he had a grand vision for himself. He did what no one had done before. Creating an artificial lake high up in the hills and getting the water down for generating electricity was a first-of-its-kind exercise in the world. Jasmetji did that. JRD was the creator of Air India. He rapidly expanded the Tata empire. What vision did you have when you took over the Tata group? Were there any specific dreams you were chasing to fulfil?

RT: Like JRD, I too loved planes and am enamoured by them. I love cars too. Not just driving in them but the technology behind it. I had a dream that we must create India's first fully indigenously built car. The Indica was thus born. My dream was also to create the cheapest car. The Nano was the result of such a vision. But we did not stop at creating the cheapest and fully indigenous cars. The prestigious Jaguar brand is part of the Tata stable now. Jaguar Land Rover is now part of our group. I did not do anything new in the area of airlines or steel but we made a mark in the automobile field. Looking back, it has been a satisfying journey. I created something new and it gives me immense satisfaction.

GK: There is something unique about the Tata group. Indians feel that it is their own. Not many would know that more than 60 per cent of the group's revenues are from outside India, yet it has a special place in the hearts of Indians. Why do you think this is so?

RT: (Quiet and contemplative) Such a feeling or emotion is not because of the Tata name. The group has been associated with all things new. It has been part of the change which India has undergone over a century. The group has earned this trust and love thanks to generations of efforts put in by its people. The group is not a royal family where the firstborn would become the head. Each successor has ensured that he earns the respect with his work. It requires one to put in a lot of hard work. And the hard work is rewarding and beautiful. It gives tremendous satisfaction. It has never happened that just because you are a Tata, you would develop these values. One has had to work for it.

GK: How did each generation manage that? Even today, the youth of the country aspire to work for the Tatas. Why is it so?

RT: Well … I suppose the values which we talk of are visible to them in action. The way we interact with the customers and employees attracts them, I suppose. I hope each successive generation in the Tata family will ensure that the values are carried forward.

GK: When you took charge, there were stalwarts running different businesses. They were emperors in their own right. Did you think, or do you think now, that JRD was a little too democratic? Did the Tata group have to pay the price for his being too nice to others?

RT: I don't think so. JRD was a lovable person and that trait of his reflected in the Tata group too. JRD used to say, 'The doors to my office are always open—be it an ordinary janitor or the director of a company.' Anyone could approach him and talk to him. JRD used to say, 'The janitor has the same rights as the director. He too is an employee.' It happened so often that JRD would stop his car at a bus stop and ask the employee waiting for a bus there to hop in! The employee would many times not know that the person offering the ride was JRD. He would later realize on seeing his photo in a newspaper! JRD's genial nature was an important part of his personality.

GK: Did that ever cause an obstruction in the growth of the group?

RT: Never! There was no question about it. JRD's behaviour was natural to him.

GK: Don't you feel his good-natured behaviour was detrimental to growth? During the permit and and licence raj, did JRD's overly democratic approach not hamper the group's growth?

RT: Not at all! JRD was not overly democratic. In fact, there is nothing like overly democratic. Either you are democratic or you are not. You are thinking of his strength as his weakness. He was firm in his views and would not get swayed by others. But his behaviour was genial and friendly. If he saw a man stumble and fall in the streets, he would rush to help him. He would not bother to ask who he was. That was a value he carried in life. It is unfair to say that his democratic approach caused problems for the group.

GK: I remember Mr Soonawala saying it would have helped if JRD had been a stricter person.

RT: People used to say JRD used to give them a long rope. But that was his style. His philosophy of life. He used to trust people. He used to take everyone at face value until he or she betrayed him.

GK: In retrospect, do you believe he took far too long to decide his successor? After all, you have been with the group since 1962.

RT: I had not joined the group to take over as chairman. I never believed he saw me as his successor and treated me so for those many years. I think the decision was taken at the right time. In retrospect, I do feel that had the decision been taken earlier, I would have had more energy to do things. But JRD was fully in charge and had the same zeal and energy as in his earlier days. He had a towering personality. When I was made Chairman, I was terrified. My god! How would I match up to him? I was worried that he would be in Bombay House instructing me, advising me. But from the day JRD retired, he never interfered. I never felt he was looking over my shoulders. He never poked his nose in any of my decisions. He remained a mentor. It is his greatness.

GK: JRD was so loving in nature. Everyone loved his presence. Yet, when you were made the chairman, there was bitterness felt by some.

RT: I am not 100 per cent sure, but I do believe he had indirectly promised a few people that they would be made chairman. He had strong likes and dislikes. He had considered a few people as suitable for the post. But, over the years, he grew disillusioned with them. Then he would think of someone else. Finally, he selected me. It was good in a way. Had I been the apple of his eye from day one, I may have met the same fate as others. (Laughs out loud)

GK: Did he not consider Nusli Wadia too as a potential successor?

RT: Nusli was like a son to him. JRD did not have children and he used to shower his love on him like a father. He did believe that Nusli could be an able successor but, for some reasons not known to me, that did not happen and some disconnect grew between the two.

GK: Do you think our lack of trust in our own competencies has set the country back a few decades? Otherwise, we could have had a fully indigenous car and seen a domestic airline do well back in the 1960s. Don't you think the governments then could have acted better?

RT: (Sighs deeply and answers carefully) Looking back, I do feel that our country could have been different. But we have taken all that very philosophically. There is no bitterness, let me assure you.

GK: No bitterness? Wouldn't the Tata-Singapore Airlines joint venture have taken off much earlier?

RT: No, there is no bitterness. Yes, had it happened, it would have been great—to have the airlines take off much earlier. JRD created Air India. But it was later nationalized. JRD used to believe that he could launch another airline with the help of the government. The deal with Singapore Airlines was one such proposal which was objected to by one person.

GK: Pramod Mahajan? Or was it C.M. Ibrahim, Aviation Minister in the I.K. Gujral government?

RT: Neither. (Mentions an industrialist in the aviation sector he doesn't want to name.) It was he who was behind Pramod Mahajan's objection.

GK: Does that hurt you—to realize that these men are so selfish that they are willing to put the country's development at stake for some personal gains?

RT: I don't recall JRD feeling bitter. Yes, he did feel bad. But he would never allow his thoughts to affect his love for the nation. He sometimes used to get fed up. I was with him in those days. He would feel that a proposal would get rejected by the government. He used to feel disappointed. But never bitter.

GK: You were with JRD when Air India and New India Assurance were nationalized. George Fernandes tried to nationalize TISCO too. Did JRD ever feel that the government had let him down?

RT: He did feel that he was being pulled back but he never felt let down. He surely used to feel bad about his proposals being rejected, but he used to wish the government would give up its permit and licence raj mentality and think of the progress of the nation. He used to rue the fact that the government was not willing to look at it that way. He used to object to the way the government functioned but he never allowed himself to get bitter about it. He took it all in his stride. He was very philosophical about it.

GK: That is his greatness. Things changed when Rajiv Gandhi took over as PM. You were ascending to the top of the Tata group around the same time. How was your experience with him, against the backdrop of the relationship between JRD and Indira Gandhi?

RT: I did not work with him much. I don't have much experience of Indira as well. Rajiv was young and looking to change the country. He did try a lot in the first eighteen months of coming to power. But he was later mired in politics. He used to always ask how we could do something, rather than trying to find out why we could not do it. But politics got the better of him.

GK: You had to take some tough decisions after taking over: Russi Mody, Ajit Kerkar, the Tata Finance controversy...

RT: I had to take some tough calls. Tata Steel was in trouble and TELCO too was not faring well. We had to deal with Rajan Nair. Those were tough days. But these things taught me a lot. It prepared me for the future.

GK: You had to deal with big personas. These were men who had a name in society. They were stalwarts. You changed all that. You introduced the concept of brand royalty. Those were big challenges.

RT: It was necessary to do all that. To give the group a particular shape. To recreate the Tata brand. There was a lot of criticism then. Many had commented that the Tata companies were going in different directions during JRD's time. There were nearly thirty-five large companies. Tata Chemicals had a vision and a logo of its own, while Tata Steel represented something else. The group's image was not being represented by any one company. It was not consistent. My contribution has been to create a single identity which is reflected across the group. We started charging for the brand usage. We did not force any company but made it clear that if they used the Tata name, they needed to pay for it. We made an agreement with all companies based on which they had to follow certain rules, values and ways of working. If they were using the Tata name, they were bound to follow them.

GK: Did it help? The Tatas did not have much shareholding in Tata Sons at that time.

RT: We increased the shareholding. We started demanding royalty only after we had 26 per cent holding in Tata Sons. Else, the companies would not have listened to us.

GK: Was it easy? There were big guns like Darbari Seth, Russi Mody and others who had minds of their own.

RT: There was initial objection. Not that it was easy to implement our policies. But once the companies started seeing the benefits, it was easy.

GK: Did the stalwarts not feel that you were challenging their supremacy?

GK: Of course, they did. But they had no choice. Those businesses which were not using the Tata brand—the Taj, for example—we did not force them to use the Tata name. We did not try to change the name of Titan watches. But when the companies realized the value of using the Tata name and being associated with the group, they themselves came forward to join.

GK: Numbers show that the group reached new heights during your tenure. What is the learning you feel most proud of?

RT: I remember my days with NELCO. It was in huge losses and struggling when I was asked to look into it. We had cash flow issues and were worried about not being able to pay the workers' salaries. I had to borrow money from banks to be able to tide over the crisis. I learnt a lot then.

GK: How relevant or sufficient was the experience to run a group like the Tatas?

RT: Had that not been enough, I would have had to make more mistakes to learn! (Laughs) I learnt a lot about handling labour issues. I used to interact a lot with the workers' unions.

GK: You were never interested in politics. Naval Tata fought a Lok Sabha seat but you never advised him on that. You never discouraged him either. Or did you?

RT: I asked him not to. Many in the family too did so. He was keen, unlike me who was never enamoured by politics. He lost. He was then keen to be nominated to the Rajya Sabha.

GK: Was it because of the fact that your rival group's K.K. Birla was a member of the Rajya Sabha?

RT: I am not sure. I was in touch with Balasaheb Thackeray then. One of his partymen, Dattaji Salvi, was the trade union leader at NELCO. He was creating a lot of problems for us. I used to meet Balasaheb to complain about Dattaji. He would listen at times, but not always. Later, there was a funny incident when we launched the Tata Estate. Balasaheb bought the car. The central locking system had some issues and the car would get locked at times on its own. Balasaheb joked with me saying I was keen to get him locked inside. (Laughs loudly) He returned the car later.

GK: Now, at this stage in life, do you get a feeling that you were born in the right family but not in the right country?

RT: Never! I have never felt that way. In fact, I feel lucky to have been born here. It was coincidental that the opening up of the economy and liberalization took place at the same time when I took over. Maybe, had liberalization not taken place, I may have gone back to the US. I have been lucky. Many sectors opened up for investments. We were able to do what we were not allowed to for decades. JRD had struggled so much! I was able to reap the benefits of it!

GK: I ask this question to you as an Indian. Accumulating wealth has never been given much importance in India. John D. Rockefeller and

Jamsetji were born in the same year. But Jamsetji was never able to make the kind of progress Rockefeller did. Had the Tata group been in the US or Europe, do you think it would have progressed much more remarkably?

RT: It is unfortunate that we do not give importance to wealth creation. It is a tragedy. I agree that the group would have progressed a lot more had it been in the US or Europe. But we would not have been able to make a difference the way we did in India. Jamsetji had a vision of building the nation. It was about building India. Had we been in the US, we would have been one of the many contributing to nation building.

GK: Do you think changes are taking place here? In the way people look at industry?

RT: I definitely feel so. Everyone wants growth but with it come jealousy and pettiness. We try to pull the other person down, but I feel that the youth of today are different. It is heartening that the Tata group is part of the change. We do believe that wealth creation is an important part of it.

—⁓—

The interview was over. Ratan Tata spent a little time at home, conferred with the veterinary doctor regarding his dog's health, and then left for Singapore. The next day's newspapers carried the most important news of the day. The Tata group and Singapore Airlines were coming together to form an airline company. Interestingly, we had spoken about the airline business in our meeting. But he never mentioned the imminent joint venture which was announced the next day.

It was another indication of a man who does not let on what he does—he who does not lord over his own empire!

Bibliography

In writing this book, I drew material from newspaper reports and a few books. Some of my sources are listed here:

- Bhat, Harish. *Tata Log: Eight Modern Stories from a Timeless Institution*. New Delhi: Penguin Books, 2014.
- *J.R.D. Tata: Letters and Keynote*. New Delhi: Rupa & Co., 2004.
- Lala, R.M. *Beyond the Last Blue Mountain: A Life of J.R.D. Tata*. New Delhi: Penguin Books, 2000.
- Lala, R.M. *For the Love of India: The Life and Times of Jamsetji Tata*. New Delhi: Penguin Books, 2006.
- Lala, R.M. *The Creation of Wealth*. New Delhi: IBH Publishers Pvt Ltd, 1992.
- Lala, R.M. *The Joy of Achievement: Conversations with J.R.D. Tata*. New Delhi: Penguin Books, 2000.
- Piramal, Gita. *Business Legends*. New Delhi: Penguin Books, 2010.
- Piramal, Gita. *Business Maharajas*. New Delhi: Penguin Books, 2000.
- Radjou, Navi; Prabhu, Jaydeep; and Ahuja, Simone. *Jugaad Innovation: A Frugal and Flexible Approach to Innovation for the 21st Century*. San Francisco: Wiley, 2012.
- Ramadorai, S. *The TCS Story and Beyond*. New Delhi: Penguin Books, 2013.

- Sabavala, S.A.; Lala, R.M.; and Vakil, Supriya. *Keynote J.R.D. Tata*. Pune: Mehta Publishing House, 1989.
- Witzel, Morgen. *Tata: Evolution of a Corporate Brand*. New Delhi: Penguin Books, 2010.
- Websites of Tata companies.

Index

Acknowledgements

I would like to express my gratitude to:
- Ratan Tata
- Raj Thackeray
- R. Venkataramanan (Venkat), former Vice President, Chairman's office, Tata Sons, now Managing Trustee, Tata Trusts
- Mukund Rajan, former brand custodian of the Tata group
- Tata Central Archives
- The PR machinery of the Tata group

About the Author and Translator

Girish Kuber is the Editor of *Loksatta* and writes frequently in the *Indian Express*. He is also the author of six books in Marathi. He lives in Mumbai.

Vikrant Pande is President of Northern Arc Foundation, Capital. He has translated several books from Marathi to English, including *Raja Ravi Varma* and *Shivaji: The Great Maratha* by Ranjit Desai, *Shahenshah: The Life of Aurangzeb* by N.S. Inamdar, *Karmachari* by V.P. Kale and *Shala* by Milind Bokil. He is a graduate of IIM Bangalore and has worked in the corporate sector for more than twenty-five years.